W9-BTS-011

ANGEL ON MY
SHOULDER

ANGEL ON MY
SHOULDER

AN AUTOBIOGRAPHY

NATALIE COLE

WRITTEN WITH DIGBY DIEHL

WHEELER
PUBLISHING, INC.
ROCKLAND, MA

★ AN AMERICAN COMPANY ★

Published in Large Print by arrangement with Warner Books, Inc. in the United States and Canada.

Wheeler Large Print Book Series.

Set in 16 pt Plantin.

Library of Congress Cataloging-in-Publication Data

Cole, Natalie, 1950–.
    Angel on my shoulder: an autobiography / by Natalie Cole written with Digby Diehl.
        p. (large print) cm.(Wheeler large print book series)
    ISBN 1-56895-991-5 (hardcover)
    1. Cole, Natalie, 1950–. 2. Singers—United States—Biography.
    3. Large type books.
    I. Title. II. Series
[ML420.C636 A3 2000]
782.42164/092 B 21   CIP

ACKNOWLEDGMENTS

"To whom much is given, much is required..."
(Luke, Chapter 12, Verse 48)

I had always promised myself that if I ever had the nerve to write a book, it would stay under lock and key until the day I died and went on to glory. By then I wouldn't have to answer any questions, and I could thumb my nose at the world while playing my golden harp up in heaven all day. Alas, the joke is on me, and God has decided to keep me right here to squirm and suffer through it all along with you, dear reader. I must admit that writing my autobiography was an awfully humbling experience.

So I guess I should do the right thing and give credit where credit is due. To the scores of individuals who have prodded, cajoled, and comforted me through this record of my life I owe my deepest thanks, love, and gratitude. They are as follows:

To my father, without whom I would probably have no story to tell.

To my mother, who has had more influence on me than she may even realize.

To Nansey Neiman-Legette, who started this whole thing about eight years ago and would not let me rest because she actually thought

I had something of value to share, even back then...

To my editor, Caryn Karmatz Rudy, who gave me wonderful guidance and sage advice. I am also grateful to Jamie Raab, editor-in-chief at Warner Books, for continuing to believe in this project; and to Mel Berger, my agent at William Morris, for his tenacity and persistence. My appreciation, as well, to Heather Kilpatrick in the Warner Books legal department, to Molly Chehak, assistant to Caryn, and to copy editor Fred Chase.

I cannot say enough about my collaborator and writing partner extraordinaire, Digby Diehl. We sat for many weeks, talking, laughing, and crying, and in the midst of it all, we have become good friends—and it's a good thing, because the man knows *way* too much about me! Sincere thanks also to his wife, Kay, who, thank goodness, has a better eye for grammar and spelling than Digby does, and who worked with us on almost every phase of this book.

I am most grateful to my manager of eighteen years, Dan Cleary, who I think is even more excited about this project than I am. I thank him for his faith in me, his perseverance, and his love; we still make a great team. I also must thank Angela Bradley in Dan's office for putting together endless numbers of photos, and for having to listen to my rantings and ravings five days a week! She is a saint.

Thanks, too, to my son, Robert, who was more than happy to give his spin on what a wacky Mom he has—and he did me proud. And to my sisters/angels: Carole Cole, Timolin Augustus, and Casey Cole Ray, who have been more supportive and loving of me than I deserve. Carole, especially, gave 150 percent to help restore my memory bank and reacquaint me with numerous events. I am truly blessed to have them in my life.

To the other members of the Cole clan, Eddie Cole and family, Freddy Cole and family, Mr. and Mrs. Ike Cole, Mr. and Mrs. James King, all my cousins, nieces, and nephews: You are all a part of this book in one way or another, and I cherish the memories and moments we continue to share. Thank you, as well, to my Aunt Charlotte, who can certainly write her *own* book about this family one of these days!

A lot of thanks and gratitude goes to one particular cousin, Pamela Harris, who remembered things that, frankly, I wished she had forgotten, but also for the time she took to recall events with loving care and detail, as painful or as joyous as they might be.

Many thanks and love also to Anne Yancy and her family, who continue to love me unconditionally.

I wish to thank my personal assistant, Benita Hill Johnson, who held me up throughout this long arduous process and will need a new set of knee pads from praying for me so very hard. I could not have gotten through this without her, and God could not have blessed me with a better friend.

Speaking of friends, I have to say thank you to a few women, upon whose friendship and support I have depended for many years. Although they may not have contributed directly to the writing of this book, they have each added so much to my life that every little bit has helped. So here's to my girls, Connie, Sylvia, Judi B., Tammy E., Linda C., Cecille and Carol P., Patricia J., Lizzie-Boo, Nance, Lynn, and Sonia... Big hug and kisses to Vincent Kandis and his family; also to Philippe Le Boeuf, a dear friend and a gentle man. Both continue to play a very important role in my life, and I am grateful for the privilege to be a part of theirs.

There were several people with archives on my career who were generous in opening their files and helped me put people, places, and things in the right order. My thanks to Jennifer Allen, my publicist at PMK; Tommy Steele, Frank Bowen, and Maggie Sikkens at Capitol Records; and to my supportive fan Keisha Pitts-Bullard for sharing her clippings with me. Thanks to Jeffrey Jones at Dick Clark Productions for getting me a copy of my 1978 television special, and to Gary Tellalian at Ken Ehrlich Productions for providing transcripts of interviews done in connection with the Lifetime Television segment on my life. I am equally indebted to Kevin E. Taylor, a longtime friend and fan, for his incredible file of clippings that he has faithfully collected over the years, but more than that, for his tireless efforts to track down some "fugitive facts" from my past. I am additionally grateful for his invaluable and meticulous assistance in preparing the discography.

A number of individuals went above and beyond in their research endeavors to unearth pieces of information that most thought were long gone: My sincere gratitude goes out to Nancy Webster-Thurlback, who researched my days at Northfield, Hazelden, and the *Unforgettable* project, and who also found the long-buried story of the drug bust in Toronto. My thanks, also, to Sidney Kirkpatrick, who dove into the early music years in Chicago and into the details of Las Vegas; and to Elaine Fandell, who found documentation of the tale of "Flukie" and his colorful demise.

My hat is off to four individuals who had to listen endlessly to my voice (and I wasn't even singing a note!): Sandy Taylor, Nan Breckenridge, Nancy Webster-Thurlbeck, and Julie Wheelock. They transcribed the hundreds of hours of interview tapes on which this book is based, and they did so at a speed that was positively aerobic.

Thank you to Ralph Goldman, who played a very crucial part in my life; also Larkin Arnold; Steve Cooper; my attorneys, Jay Cooper, Carl Grumer, and Bill Hulse; Seth Riggs, my vocal coach; and Kyle Lapesarde for taking the time to share their perspectives on portions of my life.

A special thank-you to Chuck Jackson and Bradley Walker. And to those individuals whose names I may have forgotten, forgive me, please!

There are a few more angels who I need to thank, and although they are no longer here with me, they still perch on my shoulder at various times as I travel life's journey. They are: Marvin Jerome Yancy, Janice Williams, and Evelyn Cole.

Last but most importantly, I thank God, the Creator of *all* angels (seen and unseen), who took all my weaknesses and turned them into something he could use for *His* glory. Truly, He is The Potter, and we are the clay.

I hope, dear reader, that you will discover the threads that weave their way through this story: humor, joy, and peace. What a pleasant surprise to discover when it is all said and done, this is what I have left. I happily pass it on to you....

This book is dedicated to my son,
Robert Adam Yancy.
Reach for the moon,
and you just might catch a star.
I love you.

Introduction

DAUGHTER OF
NAT KING COLE DIES
IN VEGAS HILTON INFERNO

That was the banner headline from tomorrow's paper that I composed for myself as smoke poured under the door to my hotel suite. It was so thick that it was getting hard to breathe, but as bad as it was in the room, it was worse out in the hallway—a lot worse. The corridor was nothing but a billowing black cloud. I couldn't see a thing, but I could hear the windows blowing out on the floors nearby, and the sound of breaking glass was getting nearer all the time. Going out the window of my room wasn't going to work—I was on the twenty-fourth floor. I was trapped in the room with my bodyguard.

"It looks bad—real bad. This is it." The terrified look in his eyes told me that the time had finally come to make my peace with God. The rehearsals were over. The curtain was about to drop on the life of the daughter of Nat King Cole, aka Natalie Cole.

I knew what I had to do to prepare to die.

"Okay," I told him, reaching for the kit that held my cocaine and my freebasing para-phernalia, "but if I'm going to go, I'm not going straight."

Looking back on the roller-coaster ride of my thirty-one years, I couldn't help but marvel that this headline could have been written several times before. Only the means of my demise would have been different. There could have been:

DAUGHTER OF
NAT KING COLE,
HIGH ON LSD,
LEAPS FROM 20TH FLOOR
DORM WINDOW

---

when I was in college.
Not too much later I barely missed:

DAUGHTER OF
NAT KING COLE
ODS ON HEROIN
IN TENEMENT DRUG
DEN BATHROOM

---

just as my singing career was getting started. Each time, someone had intervened when I otherwise should have been dead. Make that Someone with a capital "S." There was always a hand there that just kept plucking me out of situations when I should have perished. My survival was so miraculous that there was no one else who could have done it but the Lord.

The day I thought I was going to die started out pretty ordinary. It was February 10, 1981, and Bill Cosby and I had just finished our headline engagement in the Hilton main showroom the night before. Uncle Bill, as I called him, left town right away, but rather than returning home to Los Angeles, I decided to stay on in Vegas for an extra day. I wanted to just chill out before Dad's brother, my Uncle Freddy, opened in one of the clubs downtown. Besides, it was something of a family reunion. Freddy's sister, my Aunt Bay, and her daughter, cousin Janice, as well as cousin Eddie had rooms down the hall from me. Thank God I'd already put Robbie, my four-year-old son, and his nanny on the plane home.

I was looking forward to my first time off in more than a month, and for the moment it was just me and my bodyguard in the room. I didn't usually have a bodyguard, but since my divorce the previous year and the burglary at my house a few months earlier, my manager thought it was a good idea to have someone on hand to look out for me. Nate Bowman had been an NBA player with the New York Knicks. He was six foot ten, and weighed over 250 pounds. With him at my side, no one would dare mess with me.

He had ordered us dinner from a local soul

food restaurant. The food had arrived late, at about 8:45, and the guy who brought it up to our room was the first to tip us off to the danger that lay ahead. "Man, there sure is a lot of smoke," he said.

Nate stepped out the door of the suite to see for himself and came back in concerned. "It's nothing," I told him, grabbing a barbecued rib. "The alarms and the sprinklers haven't even gone off."

The delivery guy was all excited to meet Natalie Cole, but at the same time he was nervous, because there was smoke in the elevator and in the hallway. He wanted to hang out and talk, but he also wanted to get the hell out of there.

It wasn't long before we heard a bunch of shuffling in the hall as people left their rooms. I was still la-di-dah about it. Despite all the commotion, I was trying to enjoy my dinner, and I wasn't about to be part of any cattle stampede to the elevators.

I had no intention of hiking down the twenty-four flights of stairs to the lobby, either. I figured that if it was bad enough to evacuate, I'd get a phone call from the hotel management. Meanwhile, the furrow in Nate's brow got deeper and deeper. "Shouldn't we be getting out of here?" he asked repeatedly. Finally I picked up the phone and called downstairs, if only to get him off my case. "Yes, there is a fire," said the unruffled voice on the other end of the line, "but it's under control and there's nothing to be concerned about. Just stay in your room, Miss Cole. If it gets serious, we will send someone to evacuate you."

That sounded reasonable enough to me. By this time I could hear the clanging of the exit doors opening and closing, and the echoing of many footsteps in the stairwell. Still no alarm bells, still no sprinklers, but the elevators had shut down—as they're supposed to do in a fire—and the only way down was on foot. I still wasn't worried about Nate and me, but I wanted to make sure that the rest of my family was okay.

I called my cousin Eddie in the adjoining room. No answer. I thought that was strange, because he had been there only a few minutes before. I knocked on his door, and then went inside through the connecting door. He was gone.

He had skedaddled so fast he all but left an Eddie-shaped hole in the wall, like in the cartoons. I couldn't believe that he'd up and gone without at least talking to me. But he had. I grabbed Eddie's phone and called cousin Janice and Aunt Bay. I still wasn't concerned for myself, but Bay was sixty and Janice at an even five feet weighed at least as much as Nate did. Both of them would need a little head start to hoof it down to the lobby. "Go on downstairs now," I told them. "Just a precaution. You're probably making this trip for nothing."

I called the front desk a few more times, and got the same cooing reassurance that all was under control. I finished eating and told Nate that I was going to take a shower. About

5

twenty minutes later, I stepped out of the bathroom and Nate said once more, "I think we need to get out of here."

This time I believed him. I put on my robe, got my purse, and opened the door. The smoke in the hall had become really thick. I knew there were Exit signs out there somewhere, but I couldn't see them. This was no Girl Scout bonfire—the smoke looked and smelled awful, as if someone had bombed an oil refinery. I wasn't about to step out into that. Except for the sound of breaking glass, there was also this eerie silence, like Nate and I were the only two people left on the entire floor. I quickly closed the door and got back on the phone to the front desk. The fact that I could still get through was reassuring, but I didn't like the idea that they'd forgotten us. "Now that you've evacuated everybody else," I said with a slight edge in my voice, "when are you going to come and get us?" The girl on the other end of the line didn't seem all that concerned. She told us to be patient and that someone would be there to get us very soon.

I'd no sooner hung up than the smoke started coming in under the door. I looked out the window. There were fire trucks every-where, and a great throng of people was milling on the sidewalk below. Everyone in the crowd seemed to be looking right back up at me.

I picked up the phone one more time. "What the hell is taking so long? We can't see a damned thing in the hall. You kept telling us to stay in the room. We did that. Now we're stuck here and everyone else has split!" As I slammed the receiver down, Nate began to panic.

"Maybe we could tie all the bedsheets together and go out the window."

The man was no longer thinking clearly. "We're twenty-four stories up and we've got maybe seven stories' worth of sheets. Do the math," I said. "No way we're going down the side of the building. But grab the sheets and blankets—towels, too—I've got another idea."

We stripped the beds, dumped all the linens into the bathtub, and turned on the water. Then we got in the shower and wet ourselves down. As we emerged, the sprinklers and fire alarms finally went off in the hallway outside.

By this time the smoke was literally pouring in under the door. Somewhere in the back of my mind, I remembered that in case of fire, the best air was closest to the floor. We started setting out all the wet stuff on the carpet, and Nate and I both got down there horizontal. Immediately thereafter, I had cause to regret having gotten in the shower with him, even though we'd both been fully clothed. "Natalie, I love you," he began as he caressed me. "I've been in love with you since I started working for you. It looks bad—real bad. This is it. We ought to make love here and now, because it's the last chance we're going to get."

Testosterone—it, too, should be a controlled substance. "I'm flattered by the offer, but no thanks," I said. "If we're gonna die and it comes to a choice between having sex and getting high, I'd rather get high. If I'm going to go, I'm not going straight."

I fished my freebase kit out of my purse—the pipe, the coke, and the rest of the goodies—everything I'd need. We got down on the sopping-wet bedsheets, ready to roll up in them if it came to that. Nate sat on the floor next to me with a look of pure disbelief. Even though I had never lit up in front of him, he knew I did drugs, but he was both amazed and disappointed to learn that in a two-way contest with cocaine, he came in second. I began setting up to start cooking—for a kid who flunked chemistry, I was a great cocaine cook. It was an utterly ridiculous scene. My horny bodyguard was sitting on the floor next to the bed, wanting to fly united into the hereafter. I was down there under the coffee table, about to smoke myself into kingdom come.

At this point I fully expected to die, and I began to look at my situation with a little broader perspective. As the smoke got thicker, it occurred to me that this had to be some kind of trial by fire, like in the Bible. And it also occurred to me that I was failing the test. You know how they always say that when you're about to go, your life passes before your eyes? I started thinking about all those times before in my life when I had tested God. Fool that I was, I was about to do it again.

As I prepared to light up, I made a bargain

in my mind with the Lord. I said, "Now Lord, if you let me take a hit off this pipe, then that means I'm finished. I'm going to get high, and then I'm going to die. I could be wrong, but Lord, I don't think that you mean for me to go this way. If you intend to save me one more time, don't let me take a hit. You're either going to save me, or I'm going to get so high I'm not even going to feel the flames."

I was putting the pipe to my lips when the door was blown off its hinges. Through the smoke appeared two archangels, with wings on their backs and silvery faces—it was one of those God moments. The twin angel Gabriels then strode into the room. Honey, I was so amazed I dropped my pipe, and it took me a moment to realize that my angels were firemen in full regalia, with oxygen masks and tanks on their backs.

The firemen pulled us to our feet and led us out into the hallway. Everything was black— the floors, the walls, the ceilings. The smoke was mostly gone, but it was like walking through a forest strewn with dead leaves. Everything on the floor crackled.

As the firemen led us to the stairwell going up to the roof, I broke away and headed down the crispy corridor. I wasn't worried about Eddie, but I had to know if Janice and Aunt Bay had made it out. When I went into their room, everything was charred. The bed was partially burned up, and the TV had melted. I thanked God that I saw no bodies.

The firemen were pulling me away just as

I spotted Janice's Bible on the nightstand. It looked like she'd put it down only a minute or two before. It was in near perfect shape, just a little singed around the edges. I picked it up and allowed myself to be escorted to the roof. There they loaded Nate and me into the helicopter, and within a few moments we were climbing into the air over the lights of Las Vegas, headed for Sunrise Hospital. The doctors and nurses of the ER were waiting for us when we arrived. I was still clutching Janice's Bible as I was wheeled in on a gurney, thinking that it was a miracle that both of us, the Bible and me, were still here.

Right up until this day I don't know how it was that the fireball that swept up the elevator shafts and down the hallway missed our room. Eight people lost their lives in that fire, including one man on our floor, and another who had died jumping out a window. Two hundred and fifty-three others were seriously injured. Nate and I were virtually the last two people to be evacuated.

Physicians examined both of us, and took X rays. Nate suffered from smoke inhalation, and the damage to his lungs was quite severe. His lungs never fully healed, and a few years after the fire he died from respiratory problems. Although Aunt Bay came through the fire in good shape, Janice suffered from smoke inhalation from the walk down to the ground floor. A few years later, she, too, died from a lung condition.

Me? I was fine. I had no smoke damage to

my lungs, none at all. As they wheeled me back from X ray, the doctors were standing there shaking their heads, saying, "I don't know how you did this."

I know how I did this, and I didn't do it alone. Nate had really bad smoke inhalation from that experience; I had none, and we were in the same room the whole time. That's not some physiological thing. That ain't nothin' but God. I feel as if an angel intervened to save my life that night, just as had happened many times before, and has been the case many times since. I couldn't help but believe then, as I do now, that God put me on earth for some particular reason, and He is not done with me yet.

I think it was a miracle that I lived to tell this story. Looking back on my life, it seems that surely God had something in mind for me.

I was born into a life of extremes and I have led a life of extremes. I was born with both the blessing and the burden of my family legacy, which have given me both some of the greatest advantages and some of the greatest disadvantages a person might hope for.

The one quality God has given me that has perhaps contributed the most to the extremes I have lived is impulsiveness. This impulsiveness has allowed me to step out on a limb, time and time again. It led me to a love of roller coasters in my childhood, and it fueled my courage to pursue a singing career despite my mother's disapproval and the huge shoes my father left to fill. Somehow, I went out there and I did it. It enhanced an adventurousness

11

that made me willing to try just about every
kind of music and musical style—jazz, rock,
rhythm and blues, opera, and even the beautiful music my father made famous. It has
allowed me to grow and grow and grow—in
every way—despite the fact that I have led my
life in public view, right from the day I was born.
But growth is not always easy—it can be so very,
very painful—and it involves making mistakes. In my case—I made many mistakes
and many *big* mistakes.

Impulsiveness has also been my curse. It has
made me foolish—sometimes very foolish. If
the upside of impulsiveness is spontaneity, the
downside is recklessness. My impulsiveness
includes the strange and dangerous desire to
taste every kind of experience on earth. Just
like a baby who wants to put everything in its
mouth or stick its finger in every hole—I
wanted to try everything—good, bad, and
indifferent. Looking back, it seems that I
dove head first into every black hole I encoun-
tered, and before I knew it I was stuck and
having to claw my way out. I saw my boyfriend
shooting heroin, and of course I had to try it—
right then and there. A fellow addict showed
me how to print up bogus checks—I had to try
that, too. Nothing, it seems, was too high or
too low for me to try on for size.

The curious thing is that no matter how low
I have fallen, or how high I have flown—I
always have felt that God was there for me and
that I could talk to Him. Although I may
have stretched things to the limit, I've always

felt that God forgave me—over and over again—that His angels have been present in my life both in bad times and good. And I've always hoped that one day I would redeem His faith in me.

I can only speculate that God gave me the advantages, gifts, and opportunities for a reason. To some degree or other, I do live in the public eye. When I've soared to the top, the press was there to trumpet my accomplishments to the world. And often, when I hit bottom, the press was there, too. I've always admired the courage of people like Betty Ford and Kitty Dukakis, who were able to dust themselves off and take advantage of the public position they held to bring issues such as breast cancer and drug abuse to the fore. I am hoping that I, too, can make good use of my public position to help others claw their way out of pits that they have fallen into, as I have done.

My life has been a series of miracles. There is so much that I have learned—and through the grace of God I have lived to tell the tale. It is my hope that the story that I tell here will offer hope, help, and insight to anyone who needs it. I believe that this might be some of what God and His angels have been, literally, saving me for.

CHAPTER 1

A Childhood
Filled with Music

Singers are often asked about their musical influences, and for someone with a famous musician for a father, this question is one of the most common. But when people ask me if my father sang for me as a child, they seem disappointed by the truth: He never sang us romantic ballads like "Mona Lisa." He sang gibberish songs that gave us kids a bad case of the giggles, and crazy rhyme-and-sound songs, like the ones I learned later at summer camp. These all had the kind of completely silly lyrics that children have loved forever. There was one about an elephant that jumped so high, high, high over the sky, sky, sky, and another one that started "Miss Sue, Miss Sue, somebody's in your cellar." He did sing one little nonsense I-love-you song that he'd recorded, called "Kee Mo Ky Mo" (which was the flip side of "Sweet Lorraine"). Before I was born, he actually did an entire album, *King Cole for Kids* (1948), that was nothing but children's songs.

I cherish these memories, and I love the fact that when he was home, he was just being Dad. He wasn't performing. I think that because he was so serious with his career, when he was with us, he just wanted to play. That's part of the blessing and the burden I inherited as a birthright. The blessing was that when he was home, he really spent what has become known as quality time with us. The flip side of that was that he was gone for weeks, sometimes months, at a time. When you make your living as a singer, you have to go where the gigs are.

I don't remember him once singing seriously at home with just the family, but it was always a special treat when he'd bring home acetates of new recordings he had just worked on in the studio at Capitol that day. (Capitol Records headquarters is on Vine Street in Hollywood, in a building that looks like a stack of LPs. To this day it is known as "The House That Nat Built.") Dad would play them in the library on his beautiful custom-made Seeburg Selectomatic sound system. This was a very froufrou home jukebox, ultra-high-tech for its day, the first of its kind. Once you selected what you wanted to hear, it played it automatically. It was all in gold, with a big glass you could see through. We were never allowed near it, but after dinner, Mom and her sister, my Aunt Charlotte, and some friends would join him to sit around and discuss the new songs he brought home. When I got invited to listen, I felt very grown-up.

Dad's music was great, but then there were so many great sounds that came into our ears when I was a child, so much wonderful music. There was always music playing at our house in one room or another. Every afternoon, my mother would go into the library and select something to listen to. It might be Sarah Vaughan, or Nancy Wilson, or the Jackie Gleason Orchestra, or Billie Holiday. My parents wanted us to have this cacophony of musical styles—jazz, classical, Broadway, rock, opera, pop, you name it. And we would catch every note of it. Early on I was madly in love with Elvis Presley. Dad wasn't into it at all, at least not for himself as a performer. He used to say, "Mr. Cole does not rock 'n' roll." But Baba, my Aunt Charlotte, knew how much I loved Elvis (and his music), and took me to one of his shows at the Palladium. After that I slept with the souvenir booklet from the concert under my pillow. I really feel so fortunate that my mom and dad didn't censor our musical experience, because it has had a strong influence on my life and career.

Dad would bring home all kinds of music for us in his eclectic manner. He made a point of driving to a small record store in the poorest, blackest part of South Central Los Angeles, where he could purchase records by Moms Mabley, Redd Foxx, blues singers, and other performers who were only available on "race records" that were not sold in the regular record stores.

Capitol often gave him copies of their latest

releases—sometimes in the candid hope that
he would like a song and record it himself. That
was one place where we really lucked out—
Capitol was also the Beatles' label, and I was
thrilled when Dad came home from work
with the one album every teenage girl coveted:
Meet the Beatles. I was a head-over-heels Beatles fan. (Back then every teenage girl had a
favorite Beatle. Mine was John.)

So I was the first on my block to have the
Beatles album, and, honey, it was one helluva
block. We lived at 401 South Muirfield Road
in Hancock Park, one of the most exclusive
neighborhoods of Los Angeles. This was
where the Shells of Shell Oil lived, the Chan-
dlers (who owned the *Los Angeles Times*), the
Van de Kamps, the family that owned the
Von's supermarket chain, and Governor Pat
Brown and his family. It was also where the
Los Angeles chapter of the John Birch Society
held its meetings.

How exclusive? So exclusive that the neighbors tried mightily to exclude my parents when
they first bought the house in 1948. It was a
mansion by anyone's definition of the word—
all brick, twelve rooms, three fireplaces, very
East Coast-looking and just what my mother
wanted, but there was one teensy problem. It
seems that there was a restrictive covenant that
went with the title to every house in Hancock
Park, limiting ownership in the neighborhood
to white folks who celebrated Christmas.
Negroes, Jews, people of "ethnic persuasions,"
and other "undesirables" were barred.

When the Hancock Park Property Owners Association heard that my parents had bought it, they called a meeting. The neighbors graciously invited my father to attend, but only to inform him why he couldn't live there. They actually told my dad that they didn't want any undesirables moving in. "Neither do I," he responded in the oft-repeated family story, "and if I see any, I'll be sure to let you know."

After a great deal of legal maneuvering and a letter from my mother to Eleanor Roosevelt about the unfairness of it all, and despite a couple of shots fired through the front windows and a sign hammered into the lawn that read "Nigger Heaven," my parents moved in. Well, there goes the neighborhood.

All this was before I was born. By the time I arrived, the neighborhood had adjusted to us, more or less, but we were still the only black people for miles around. I was born Natalie Maria Cole at 6:07 P.M. on February 6, 1950, at what was then called Cedars of Lebanon Hospital. I weighed in at seven pounds eleven ounces. I was my parents' firstborn child, but I have an older sister, Carole, also known as Cookie, and that takes some explaining.

My mother, Maria, had two sisters, Carol and Charlotte. Carol married and had a daughter, but died of tuberculosis in May of 1949. Since her husband had died the year before, her four-year-old daughter, Cookie, was an orphan. My parents adopted her and brought her home to Hancock Park right about the time my mother realized she was pregnant with me. Carole got the nickname "Cookie" from my father's favorite comic strip, *Blondie*—Cookie was Dagwood's daughter. After I was born, my mother's other sister, my Aunt Charlotte, also came to Los Angeles and was instrumental in raising us. Cookie and I called her Baba. We all loved the comics and we referred to Mom and Baba as black versions of Betty and Veronica from *Archie*.

A singer and poet, Baba was the free spirit on my mother's side of the family. Since Mom traveled so much with Dad, Baba was like a mom to us when we were growing up. She didn't have to be a disciplinarian, she could just be the favorite auntie, and that's what she was. Baba also handled the family business affairs and correspondence, made Dad's appointments, and kept his calendar. She had her own home and didn't live with us when they were touring—we had nannies and maids for that—but Cookie and I saw her every day. Most important of all, Baba was a great cook and we loved to hang out in the kitchen with her.

Mom and Dad took Cookie into their hearts as well as their home, and the two of us were truly raised as sisters. We were pals, but we were different in many ways. She was the little lady, and I was the tomboy. For much of my childhood, we had Mom and Dad to ourselves.

Even though they nicknamed me Sweetie, I wasn't altogether an easy kid. I didn't consider myself a particularly rebellious child, but I think if you asked my mom, she would probably choose her words very carefully and say that I was very *independent*. Independent and sassy and my own person: That's me. Early on, if you compared my behavior with my sister's, I was the one who would challenge my mother, and that was something you just didn't do. Especially in the era that we were brought up in, you just didn't do that. But I made friends easily, I was a sociable person, a pretty good kid, and I did well in school. She really didn't have a lot of discipline problems with me.

Not that I didn't have other problems. Ever since I was born, I've been allergic to almost everything. My allergist once told me I should live in a bubble. I was allergic to milk when I was born, and had to be fed on soy and goat's milk. Even so, I was a fat, happy baby. I was so fat that I didn't walk until I was nearly one and a half years of age. After that there was a conga line of substances that left me scratching, sneezing, and wheezing. I was allergic to chocolate, and I was allergic to acids like orange juice or anything citrus. I was allergic to wool; I was allergic to mohair; and I was super-allergic to weeds and pollens. I still am to this day.

I was allergic to the boxer dogs that my father loved dearly. I really don't remember the day when the renowned CBS newsman Edward R. Murrow "visited" us for his television show, *Person to Person*, but the boxers were just puppies, and they were on TV with

21

us. What most people don't know is that although Murrow seems to be having a con-versation with us, we were in Hancock Park, and he was in a studio in New York. He couldn't see us and we couldn't see him. I do have a photograph of the four of us—me, Cookie, and Mom and Dad—with the four adorable little boxer puppies in our laps. On the tape, Mr. Murrow asked me which of them I wanted to keep, and I gave the three-year-old's predictable response: "*All* of them!"

I was also allergic to our cat. One day, a cat just showed up on our doorstep. He was a good-looking black and white alley cat, and we named him Handsome. He and I were insep-arable, despite the fact that I was severely allergic to him. I just kept popping my asthma pills and tried to ignore my wheezing. Hand-some slept with me and ate with me and did everything except take baths with me for about six months. Then, one day, the front door was open and he just sauntered out, more or less the same way he had arrived. My mother called him, and she said that he stopped in the driveway and looked back at her as if to say, "Ta-ta. It's been lovely. Thank you very much. See you later." And we never saw him again.

I had a happy childhood, in the sense of crea-ture comforts—Cookie and I were indulged not just with cats and dogs, but with pretty clothes, ice skating lessons, horseback riding lessons, piano lessons, and all the trappings befitting a cultured household. This came from my mother's side of the family, specifically from my Great-Aunt Lala.

Great-Aunt Lala was Dr. Charlotte Hawkins Brown, and she was *somebody*. The granddaughter of slaves, Lala is a significant figure in black American history. She was born in Henderson, North Carolina, in 1883, moved to Cambridge, Massachusetts, as a child, and was educated at the Salem State Normal School. Returning to North Carolina as a teacher, in 1902 she founded the Palmer Memorial Institute, one of the first prep schools for African-Americans, in Sedalia, North Carolina. (The school was named for her friend and patron Alice Freeman Palmer, the first woman president of Wellesley College.)

By the time she died in 1961, Charlotte Hawkins Brown was a nationally recognized educator, lecturer, and religious leader. She was a friend and colleague of Eleanor Roosevelt, Langston Hughes, W. E. B. DuBois, and Booker T. Washington. Mom and Baba attended Palmer and stayed with Aunt Lala at her home, which she called Canary Cottage. When the Hancock Park neighbors didn't want my family to move in, my mother didn't just take it into her head to write to Eleanor Roosevelt out of the blue—when she was a girl, Mrs. Roosevelt had been a familiar visitor to Aunt Lala's home.

Great-Aunt Lala was also the author of a book on etiquette, *The Correct Thing*, and she was a powerful influence on my mother's thinking about manners, proper dress, social status, education, and general behavior. *Proper* is the operative word here. Under Lala's tutelage, Mom was trained to be a lady, to be comfortable in sophisticated social surroundings. She knew how to sip tea, and how to set a table. She had excellent posture and dressed in quiet good taste. Her English was (and is) impeccable—no bad grammar, no oozy Southern drawl, no vulgarity. By the time she was finished at Palmer, whatever rough edges my mother might have had were all sanded off. She had better manners than anyone else in Hancock Park—hell, she had better manners than 99 percent of the folks on the planet. You might think of Lala as the quintessential Henry Higgins, and like Eliza Doolittle, my elegant mother would have passed for a duchess at any snooty patootie society ball, even though her father had been a mailman.

I really looked up to her. She was very much a lady, and I loved getting into her dressing room and being surrounded by all her perfumes and makeup. She always smelled good and she was bigger than life to me, which is ironic, because when I think of my dad I don't think of him the same way. She was very organized, and she was very formal, yet she loved to host parties, and she didn't mind too much if we were around. She didn't cook, but we had great meals. My mom gave me all the femininity and all the prissiness that I have, and her wonderful taste and class, most of which she herself learned at Lala's knee.

Lala was big on culture, and young ladies were supposed to develop their talents in the arts. It seems to me that I always had a big box of pastels, but I liked it better than I was good—couldn't draw worth a lick. I was always buying new chalks and a big canvas and going at it, even though I was never really good at it. Reading was another matter. As soon as I learned how to read, I devoured books like a lunatic.

We had a set of the Childcraft books in our library when I was a child, and I loved browsing in them. My favorites were the poetry volumes. There were some wonderful, sweet poems in those Childcraft books, and I recall the feeling of how innocent and refreshing they were. I would read those poems hour after hour. I even wrote my own poetry sometimes. At some point Dad gave me my first tape recorder—it was one of those beige reel-to-reel Wollensaks that weighed a ton, even though it was no bigger than a toaster. I'd read the Childcraft poems or my own poetry into the tape recorder. I don't think that I ever used more than one reel of tape. I just kept erasing and re-recording. It never occurred to me to change it.

Sometimes I would put music to the words. I'd find my favorite poems in the Childcraft books, and then I would make up little melodies to go along with them. This is when I started driving my mother crazy, because I'd recycle the same melody over and over for every poem. The hardest part was singing and

CHAPTER 2

The Black Kennedys

The first time I sang "in public" was on a Capitol recording called "I'm Good Will, Your Christmas Spirit." I was six. A woman named Beth Norman had written a Christmas story and a song. She was going to read the story, and she asked Dad if I wanted to sing it. (Of course, she also got him to pose with playing at the same time, so I would end up with maybe four chords and all my songs would sound the same. For a grown-up with sophisticated musical taste, it must have been like fingernails on a blackboard, and one day she snapped, "Can't you come up with any-thing else!" I was not discouraged—I loved to sit at that piano and take those little poems and try to make a melody—even if it was always the same. That's where a little bit of the desire was planted in me to write songs. I don't know whether it was the music or the stories, but the process was interesting to me. I would sing into the microphone and listen to the playback. It was a big giggle for me, but I certainly wasn't dreaming of a career as a singer.

me for the record jacket, even though he didn't sing on the record.) My job was to be the voice of the angel, a little singing voice that would tie the narrative together with brief solos in between sections of the story. I remember being very focused and disciplined. I took it very seriously, and tried to be very dramatic. The recording sounds cute and funny, however, because I was missing my two front teeth, so I was Good Will, the Chrithmath Thpirit. One of the magazines reported that I got my first royalty check from this gig—a grand total of $46.10. There is a picture of me at that age with my dad that I still use in my show when I sing "Unforgettable," smiling my toothless smile. Damn, I was cute!

By this time I'd already been on *Art Linkletter's House Party*. I have no independent memory of it, only what people have told me, but supposedly I said something about having to go to the bathroom. (They're still doing potty humor on TV—we never seem to grow out of it.) That was his specialty, of course, getting kids to blurt out double entendres or to inadvertently divulge family secrets. There was a little boy who said, "My dad told me not to tell Mommy about his girlfriend!" They actually aired that show. This was all grist for a series of best-sellers Linkletter put together called *Kids Say the Darnedest Things*.

I thought I had a terrible voice when I was a child. I was embarrassed by the tinny reproductions of my voice on the tape recordings, but I loved to make them. Now, Cookie and

I had sung with my dad on a song called "Ain't She Sweet." There's a version of that still around somewhere, and it's hysterical. We've got a big band behind us, and at the end the band is really cookin', and you can hear our little voices singing, "and I ask you very con-fi-den-shal-lee, ain't t sheeee sweeeet." No two ways about it—I was a ham! You can really hear my voice—I was loud, honey, just soooo loud. I was hamming it up all over the place. It's funny, but when I look back and listen or see myself, I was not shy. I really wasn't. I was a natural, but I never thought to do anything with it until much later.

Even though I loved to perform and sang throughout my childhood, singing was not something I dreamed of doing as a grown-up. First I wanted to be an airline stewardess. Didn't we all? I just liked those little uniforms and the idea of seeing the world. After that, I had wanted to be a doctor, a dream that came in several different flavors—surgeon, pediatrician, psychologist—and lasted until I got into college. Being a singer was never in the running.

To me the point of singing was to get atten-tion, especially Dad's attention. Cookie and I worked up rather elaborate little shows for my parents whenever my dad was home. Sometimes we would show off for company, but often enough we didn't even need an audience. We would just put on a show for our-selves. My sister impressed me with her ability to mimic at an early age. One year, Cookie entered a talent show dressed up as a man. She did an act as jazz pianist Ahmad Jamal. She borrowed Dad's jacket, his shoes, and his hat, and she pretended to play his hit song "Poinciana." She got all the moves right and sounded great. It was my first time seeing anyone do that, and I was amazed. It is not surprising that as an adult she became an accomplished actress.

Cookie loved Broadway, and Broadway show tunes. She is one of the reasons I am so enthusiastic about Broadway musicals to this day. She had records of all the shows, and I would sit in her room and listen to them or act them out. We went several times to New York when we were young—my parents kept an apartment there—what the bicoastals would call a pied-à-terre. It was on West 66th Street, just two bedrooms, but I thought it was great. Whenever we went, Mom and Dad took us to Broadway musicals, and we came back with our heads full of the most wonderful music you could ever imagine. Our godparents took us to shows as well, and my mother really encouraged that. I still don't think I have seen many better musicals than the ones I saw as a child. I saw *Damn Yankees, Li'l Abner, My Fair Lady, The Sound of Music, Gypsy, The King and I, South Pacific, Oklahoma!, Peter Pan,* and my absolute, all-time favorite, *West Side Story.* As I got a little older, I especially loved *Bye Bye Birdie.*

Dad recorded an album of songs from *My Fair Lady* (1964) and lots of show tunes on other albums. He did "The Surrey with the Fringe on Top," but on the whole he probably sang more tunes from Hollywood than from Broadway. He never did anything onstage from the Broadway shows he took me to see as a child, but once I started singing, I sure did. Broadway was really a major musical influence on me. As a young girl I'd heard some of the greatest music from the American repertoire, and I knew them all by heart. I could have sung them backwards, forwards, left and right, and without missing a beat. I mean, I *studied them*.

From every musical there's a song that just touched me—sometimes more than one. "I Won't Grow Up" from *Peter Pan* still delights me. Mary Martin, the Broadway star who had been so brilliant in *South Pacific* as nurse Nellie Forbush, was amazing as Peter in that show. She lit up the whole theater—I was certainly lit up. And like every other child who saw it, I walked out of there a believer in fairies. I love that sweet song Daisy Mae sings in *Li'l Abner* called "Namely You." From *My Fair Lady*, there's "On the Street Where You Live," and "I've Grown Accustomed to Her Face." I can't pick any one song from *West Side Story*. From "Gee, Officer Krupke!" to "Maria" to "I Feel Pretty," every song from that show is a favorite. Each song just wore me out—I remember listening to the album until I was exhausted. I was really into lyrics, even as a child. I listened carefully and tried to understand, because I wanted to sing along.

The first time I was ever onstage with my father, I definitely did not sing. It was the summer of 1957 when he was performing at the Cal-Neva Lodge in Lake Tahoe. He was onstage, performing, and I just wandered out from behind the curtain, a little seven-year-old in pigtails, looking lost. I must have been trying to mimic him or sing with him (there's the ham in me again), because I remember that the audience was screaming with laughter and he didn't understand why until he turned around, and there I was. He laughed, too, but he made sure that in the future I was not running around backstage unsupervised when he was performing.

As I became older, I was always in the audience rather than backstage. I wanted to sit and watch. I just enjoyed watching him perform, you know? He was funny and he was fun, and I got a big kick out of sitting there and watching the people react to that person who was my dad onstage. I remember when I started performing, one of the things that I wanted most of all was to be able to make the room so quiet and rapt with attention that you could hear a pin drop, because that's what my dad was able to do. When that finally happened for me, I was so happy that I cried. That meant they really wanted to listen to me.

The first time I ever saw my father perform was at the Hollywood Bowl. At that time, there was a reflecting pool right in front of the stage, and from where I was sitting, I was afraid he would fall in. Even at the age of seven, I could not fail to be impressed by two things. First, he loved what he did and was very good at it. Second, he had an electrifying effect on the audience. That is where my basic knowledge of performing comes from. I think my dad encouraged me by example, rather than encouraging me by words.

Because of my father's example, I guess it was inevitable that I'd learn to play the piano. This was when I was driving my mother crazy at home, plunking away at our piano and composing the same song over and over with a variety of Childcraft lyrics. She thought maybe I was trying to say something, so she found a woman named Peg Thompson who was willing to come to the house to give me lessons. Eventually I started going to her apartment in Malibu for them, and I liked that because she lived right on the water. She was a strange woman, a tiny little lady with transparent skin and white, white hair. Despite being a heavy smoker with a voice like a sailor, she was fragile. She had the skinniest legs I think I've ever seen on a human being—little spindly bird legs. I don't know how she walked.

I enjoyed taking piano with Peg, but she was a better teacher than I was a pupil. Before piano I had tried the cello. I liked it fine, but my mother didn't care for it. She thought it was unladylike, because you had to sit there with your legs open. And ladylike was important (hello, Great-Aunt Lala!)—we couldn't wear pants outside the house. I didn't own a pair of jeans until I was about thirteen—me—the tomboy.

The piano was a suitable musical instrument for a well-brought-up young lady, and I took piano lessons for four or five years. I did not inherit my father's gift as a pianist, but even so I am sorry that I did not continue. Peg taught me mostly classical, plus a little jazz, but she could tell I really didn't have a knack for it. Somehow, she got me to sing a little, which was strange because she was supposed to be teaching me piano and she didn't sing herself (not with all that gravel in her voice). Anyway, she put together a group of her students and taught us a few jazz and pop tunes. Dennis Dragon, Carmen Dragon's son, was the drummer and Skip Riddle, Nelson Riddle's son, was a piano player. We played for our parents at our house, and I think we played together on a couple of other occasions, but it wasn't anything more than a recital group. There are some cute pictures of me at age twelve, singing with this group. The only song I can remember is "Cielito Lindo," but I know that we had a bigger repertoire than that.

Of course, my childhood wasn't all music. I loved being outdoors, and I made myself very familiar in our neighborhood. I was a Girl Scout and I went door-to-door, selling cookies. The times had changed enough so that the neighbors who had been so hostile when the Coles moved in had finally come around some. To them, I was Little Miss Sweetie. Of course, a lot of times I was ringing doorbells, I wasn't selling no cookies: I had the best time ringing doorbells and disappearing. I was a bit of a prankster.

33

I was also a daredevil. There was this hill in our neighborhood that I would go down on my roller skates. I would be terrified every time, but I'd do it anyway, which maybe says a lot about me. Perhaps that's where I got my guts from, because after that I was into roller coasters, loop-de-loops, upside downs, and all that other kind of stuff. Yep, I love roller coasters. I'm into screaming and laughing. My first roller coaster ride was on the old wooden one that used to be at the wonderful old P.O.P. amusement park on the Pacific Ocean Pier (which was torn down long ago) in Santa Monica. Over the years, I've tried to hit every roller coaster in the country. At one time I was a member of the American Roller Coaster Association. They have a monthly newsletter that they send to you about the newest, biggest roller coasters.

Aunt Lala had ingrained in my mother the importance of education. Thank goodness, I was a pretty good student as a child. Both Cookie and I went to Third Street School during our early years, which is the neigh- borhood public grammar school in Hancock Park. After that, my sister went to John Bur- roughs Junior High School in Hancock Park, and moved on to Los Angeles High—which she liked way too much. L.A. High was a true melting pot of races, nationalities, and social classes. My sister was classically pretty, and by this time she had a hot little body. I think that she was having way too much fun at L.A. High, because my mother said, "You're outta here," and bang! She was over at girls-only Immaculate Heart, where she learned to wear a uniform and be very prim and proper. (Mom wanted to send her to the nearby private Marlborough School for Girls, but at that time they had an all-white policy.) I was still laughing at Carole's Catholic school "punishment" when Mom plunked me down in Cathedral Chapel, a strict Catholic grammar school where I attended grades six through eight. Gotcha!

Dad had nothing to do with these decisions. He wasn't home enough to really have a say in these matters, and he would have done almost anything to make my mother happy. Besides, it would not have occurred to him to intervene in something that was so obviously within her area of expertise.

Dad was born Nathaniel Adams Coles on St. Patrick's Day, March 17, 1919, in Alabama. (He dropped the "s" from the end of his last name when he got into the music business.) Having grown up in my father's shadow as "the daughter of Nat King Cole," it's strange to think that today there are many who don't really know who he was. Having started out as a jazz singer and pianist in the 1940s, he was one of the first black artists in popular music to appeal to white audiences. That popularity meant that he was in great demand as a concert performer, and spent a great deal of time on the road. By the 1950s and early 1960s as I was growing up, my father had become one of the most popular singers of his day, and his songs regularly hit the *Billboard* Top 10. "Mona Lisa," "Unforgettable," and "Nature Boy" were some of his biggest hits.

Dad's upbringing couldn't have been more different from my mother's. There were no "somebodies" in his family. His father, Edward, was a poor Baptist preacher who moved the family to Chicago in the 1920s. His mother, Perlina, was a preacher's wife. Dad had three brothers—Eddie, Freddy, and Ike—and two sisters—Evelyn and Eddie Mae. The family never had a lot of money, even after they moved north, and they were not "cultured." They were very devout—Dad's parents didn't want him to be a secular musician at all. They wanted him to stay in church and play the organ. My Uncle Freddy told me that when they refused to get him a piano, Dad painted the eighty-eight black and white keys of a piano keyboard on the windowsill to practice.

For someone who grew up like Dad, from a social standpoint, my mother was a great catch. She was a beautiful light-skinned woman of elegance and refinement, and he was a dark-skinned man without a lot of education who could sing and play the piano. Despite his wealth and fame, Dad was the one who had married above his station—and my mother's family never let him forget it.

With the notable exception of Baba, my mother's sister, her family generally disapproved of him. It was bad enough that he was too black. (In those days, there was a great deal of intaracism—prejudice by blacks against blacks—and dark was considered socially inferior to pale. My mother called it "a matter of breeding.") Worse still, he was married when he met my mother. Worst of all, he was an entertainer, which they considered an unseemly profession. When my parents were newlyweds, Great-Aunt Lala, horrified that her Episcopalian niece had married a Baptist, recently divorced lounge singer, did the "correct thing" and arranged a wedding reception for the newlyweds at the Canary Cottage in Sedalia—but she herself refused to grace the party with her presence. The wedding itself was big-time: The Reverend Adam Clayton Powell married them on Easter Sunday, March 28, 1948, at his famed Abyssinian Baptist Church at 138th Street and Lenox Avenue in Harlem. The church was packed and several thousand people stood on the sidewalk for a glimpse of the couple. After a honeymoon in Acapulco, well, the honeymoon was over. The mutual distaste between the two sides of the family created a lot of tension in my parents' marriage, and made life awkward for us kids as well. Mom made it pretty clear that she didn't have much in common with Dad's relatives, except Dad.

My father was a populist. He loved movies and took us frequently. I'm not sure if it was my first movie, but one I remember very vividly as a child is the Walt Disney animated classic *Fantasia*. It scared me and fascinated me. I was overwhelmed by the combination of powerful imaginative images and deeply emotional music. Dad never tired of seeing *It's a Mad Mad Mad Mad World*, and we laughed ourselves silly together several times. During one viewing, Dad laughed so hard that he literally fell out of his seat. No wonder: This crazy story about a race to find some hidden money co-starred Spencer Tracy, Edie Adams, Milton Berle, Sid Caesar, Buddy Hackett, Mickey Rooney, Ethel Merman, Phil Silvers, Peter Falk, Buster Keaton, Dick Shawn, Jimmy Durante, Andy Devine, Terry-Thomas, and Jonathan Winters. What a cast for comedy!

Our family watched a lot of television, too. In 1956, my father made history with *The Nat King Cole Show*. He is sometimes incorrectly described as the first black performer to star in his own prime-time network TV show. But he would be quick to point out that both Hazel Scott and Billy Daniels had preceded him. I don't think we kids ever thought about there being anything historical about his program. For us, it was just great to see Dad and some of his friends that we had grown up with, such as Mel Tormé, Ella Fitzgerald, and Tony Bennett. It was a good thing, however, that *The Nat King Cole Show* wasn't competing with *I Love Lucy*, because my sister and I were loyal viewers of both. We also loved *Amos 'n' Andy* and *The Jackie Gleason Show*, and I was in love with Edd "Kookie" Byrnes on *77 Sunset Strip*. We never missed *Alfred Hitchcock Presents*, and we watched a lot of scary movies on Saturday afternoons, which was my favorite time to see them. I was glued to the tube, frozen with terror by Frankenstein, Dracula, the Wolf Man, and all those other crazy old black and white horror flick monsters.

TV watching aside, there was always a lot going on at our house, and it would have been easy enough to spend my whole childhood watching the world come to me. I was eight years old the first time I went away to summer camp, and I was devastated. I couldn't figure out what I'd done wrong to make Mom and Dad want to get rid of me like that. Cookie and I were being "sent away"—shipped off for eight weeks to some place in Michigan with a bunch of kids I didn't know. The camp was Camp Martin Johnson near Irons, Michigan, about five or six hours out of Chicago. It was a beautiful camp on about five hundred acres of land on Big Bass Lake. Here I was, a California city kid, a little on the spoiled side, standing around outside the YMCA in Hyde Park, eyeing all these other kids who were about to get on a bus with me and go out to God knows where.

Sure enough, two weeks into this terrible punishment, I was on the telephone begging my parents to let me out: "Please come get me! I can't take this! Please, I want to come home." Mom and Dad just kept reassuring me: "You'll be fine, darling. Just relax. You'll be fine." Six weeks later, I didn't want to leave. It turned out to be one of the most wonderful experiences of my childhood, and I made many friends that I came back to see for the next three summers.

The camp program was full of activities. I became an expert canoe paddler, and I got so good at it that I eventually developed a genuine six-pack—washboard abs. Who knew how cool that was then? I was a skinny kid at that point, but the exercise at camp made me strong. I rode horses during the summer, and by this time it had become a real passion for me. When I went to camp, I was already riding and I was pretty good. Back home Cookie and I took riding lessons at a place called Pickwick Stables in Burbank, right by the Los Angeles River and the network of trails that led into Griffith Park. We'd be out there maybe twice a week—I learned to ride when I was nine or ten years old. I associate those lessons with chocolate, since I wasn't allowed to eat candy bars because I was allergic. I'd sneak myself a Snickers bar from the vending machine as a reward after my lesson. It was not a pleasure without consequences—I figured I'd indulge now and scratch later. Little did I know that I was allergic to both the chocolate *and* the horses!

At camp, though, I discovered my favorite horses: palominos. The camp owned two of these beautiful animals—one was named Dan, and the other was Big Boy. They were both large, with big haunches and long golden manes. I fell off a few times because I'd always pick the biggest horses. As usual, I had no fear. Camp also meant lots of swimming, arts and crafts, riflery, archery, and even a kid's version of surviving in the woods. We really learned how to *do* stuff. It was pretty rustic, especially for some of us urban princesses who were accustomed to cooks and nannies and housekeepers. I learned outdoor skills, but I also learned a lot about being self-sufficient at camp—how to make beds and wash dishes and clean the floors, things my family paid other people to do back home. The outhouses were down the dirt path, so in addition I also learned a few practical lessons—like not to be drinking too many glasses of water at night.

My fellow campers were an unusual mix of wealthy white kids and ghetto kids from the South Side of Chicago, and I'm sure they gave scholarships to the kids who came from poorer areas. I don't know how or why they managed the camp that way, but this was nothing like my experience at home, where everyone was privileged, and I remember being powerfully impressed that everyone was able to live side by side, having a great time. I went back to Camp Martin Johnson the following three summers, and developed a pattern of staying in Chicago for about a week before and after camp with a friend of my mother's named Okie Lawson. Okie and her husband, Bill, lived on 79th and St. Lawrence in Chicago. She was black and she was not by any means wealthy, but she and my mother were dear friends. I called her my Aunt Okie, even though we were not related. She'd play bid whist card games at night and have her friends over, so I saw a whole other side of life with this woman.

There were block parties and rent parties where everybody danced to lots of terrific music: We were on the brink of the Motown era. No one ever locked their doors. I wasn't raised in an environment like that, so this was an eye-opener for me. Plus, there were a whole lot of black people, not a common sight at home.

I remember lying out on Aunt Okie's porch at night. I could hear music up and down the block, and I loved what I heard—"Shop Around" by the Miracles (later renamed Smokey Robinson and the Miracles); "Too Many Fish in the Sea" by the Marvelettes; "Tonight's the Night" and "Will You Love Me Tomorrow" by the Shirelles; "For Your Precious Love" by the Impressions; "I'll Have to Let Him Go" and then, later, "Dancing in the Streets" and "Nowhere to Run" by Martha Reeves and the Vandellas, and on and on. It was a graduate seminar in R&B. Looking back on it now, I suspect that the camp and my stay in Chicago with Okie was one way my parents were gently introducing me to the "real world," and if Chicago was the real world, I thought it was great.

I was a little older in 1963, when instead of going to camp, I went to Gillette, Wyoming, with another girlfriend of mine, Judi Basolo, whose father owned a cattle ranch. His name was Bud Basolo and he and his wife, Georgia, were good friends of my mom and dad. Bud was a rancher who came up with the idea of breeding bison with beef cattle to produce a heartier meat-producing animal dubbed the beefalo. The government gave him 66,000 acres of grazing land to experiment with the beefalo. I remember flying into Casper, Wyoming, and then driving to their ranch in Gillette.

On the Basolo ranch, there were plenty of horses, and I was still horse-crazy. I was out riding so long every day in the hot sun that my hair turned red. I not only rode; I loved to hang around the corrals and talk to the horses. Every evening, just as the sun was setting, I would go out to see them. They were pretty fresh—not all of them had been broken in for riding yet and they were still a little frisky. I would sit on the top of that corral fence at sunset, and one day I began to sing to them. I remember being amazed that they calmed down, came over, and paid attention while I sang. There was a particular horse with a beautiful white star on his forehead that I wanted to befriend. For the first couple of nights, he was the only horse that wouldn't come over to hear me sing. Finally, I won him over. After that, I was convinced I had this singing rapport with horses.

I was still singing, but those horses and my family were the only audience I ever thought I'd have. Carole (sometimes we called her Carole, sometimes Cookie) and I would sing with Dad from time to time, but only because it was cute. Early in 1960, we went with Dad to the NBC studios to rehearse a song we were going to sing with him on a TV show. Dad sat down at the piano, and we perched on top of it to sing, but in the middle of our song, Ralph Edwards walked in and announced to our completely stunned father: "Nat King Cole, This Is Your Life!"

I was surprised myself. I hadn't been told what was going to happen because the *This Is Your Life* production people were afraid that a nine-year-old couldn't keep a secret (and they might have been right). The concept of this show was that each week someone, usually a celebrity, would be surprised and presented with his or her life history, complete with appearances by friends and family members the person may not have seen in a long time. I didn't understand this, so, ever the ham, I kept singing as Ralph Edwards was trying to ambush Dad. When I finally stopped singing, Ralph Edwards introduced a lot of people from Dad's past, including Oscar Moore and Wesley Prince from his first trio; Uncle Eddie and Aunt Evelyn; Mom; and finally Dad's father, the Reverend Edward Coles. When I look at the tape today, I can see that my father is wishing that he could be somewhere else—anywhere else. But we definitely surprised him—on national television.

By this time, Carole and I were old enough to accompany Dad on some of his more interesting trips, and two in particular stand out in my mind. My first trip to Mexico City was on Dad's *Cole Español* album tour in 1959. I was nine, and it was a very beautiful trip. People loved my father in Mexico and loved his music. While we were there, my father took us to see murals by Orozco, Siqueiros, and Diego Rivera. It was also another step in my gentle immersion into "real" life—this was the first time I saw how poor people lived. (I'd met the Chicago ghetto kids at camp, but I'd never seen their houses.) I was brought up in a very lovely home in a beautiful neighborhood, and couldn't imagine what it felt like to not have all the things that I had. I did take that for granted. My sister and my nanny were with us, but I don't think Mom was there. She would not have wanted us to be exposed to that kind of environment, but Dad did, and he won out because Mom was home taking care of my new brother, Kelly.

I was no longer the baby of the family. My dad had always wanted a son, and when I was born they thought that I was gonna be him. When that didn't work out the way they planned, they eventually adopted a baby boy in July of 1959. They named him Nathaniel Kelly Cole, but everyone just called him Kelly. I remember going to the Children's Home Society the day we brought him home. At that point he was a little under six months old (his birthday is February 8, just two days after mine), and he was just precious.

In April of 1960, *Ebony,* the publication that is considered the "black *Life* magazine," did a cover story ostensibly written by my dad (but aided greatly by a staff reporter) entitled "Why We Adopted Kelly." When they were considering adoption, Dad had made a big point with the orphanage of wanting a kid with an athletic bent, someone who loved sports. It was not something he would have understood in those very sexist times (Donna Reed and Harriet Nelson were the female role models of the day), but until Kelly came along, I tried very hard to be the boy in the family, and pretty much succeeded. Dad liked sports cars. He liked the fights, he liked baseball, and I liked everything my dad liked. Even if I didn't like it, I *still* liked it— like eating sardine sandwiches—because that was my way of getting involved in whatever he was doing when he was home, so we could spend time together.

The spread in *Ebony* on Kelly's adoption was not atypical. Throughout my childhood, and even before that, there was always a fascination with the Cole family in the black press. Pictures of my parents' honeymoon were all over the magazines, and after that there were spreads from time to time showing the glamorous, affluent Cole family in their Hancock Park mansion with their servants. Stepping back and looking at it from a historical point of view, we were the black Kennedys. Like the Kennedys, when we traveled as a family, we did so in grand style. Undoubtedly, the most important trip I took as a child was in May of 1960, when my father went to England to sing for Queen Elizabeth. Carole and

I got sprung from school so we could go. We stayed at the Savoy Hotel in this big, fabulous suite. I had never been to London before, so everything was very new and strange—and high. The beds were high, the toilets were high, the chairs were high. But it also seemed cold even though it was May, and the people were very white, I mean, pasty white. Of course, we seemed to be the only black people in the whole city. I couldn't understand a word they said, and I hated the food.

I was too young to go to the performance at Victoria Palace, where Dad sang for the Queen, along with Liberace and Sammy Davis, Jr., but that wasn't particularly unusual. Most of the time when we went with Dad on tour, we didn't go to the concert. We traveled with Dad because it was the easiest way to spend time with him. He didn't need us there cheering for him in the audience, but he liked to know that we were waiting for him when he got back.

In London, Dad took Carole and me to see the sights. Naturally, we saw the changing of the guard at Buckingham Palace and Trafalgar Square and Piccadilly Circus. However, my favorite was Madame Tussaud's Wax Museum, and I could have stayed there all day. I just reveled in all the creepy stuff because of my love of horror movies. Of course, my favorite part was the torture chamber. I was excited by the details of how they would torture or lock away criminals in different parts of history. At Madame Tussaud's you could see them chop people's heads off, or hang them—it was just wonderfully gruesome and gory. From London, the family went on to Monte Carlo, where Dad sang for Princess Grace. (Quincy Jones was in the band on that tour!)

Because it was London, Carole and I got special dispensation to travel, but most of the time Dad went on the road, we had to stay in school. No matter how much we wanted to travel, our education always took top priority. I'm really grateful to my mother for instilling that in me, and I hope I've been able to pass on a little bit of that to my son. My mother gave me a lot of solid values, and even though I lost a lot of that footing for a period of time, I came back to what she taught me. I truly believe, if you give children the basics, somehow, somewhere, if you pray hard enough, they will return to those values, and they'll end up being really close to the people that you raised them to be. But you've gotta give it to them, and you've gotta give it to them early. Otherwise it doesn't take hold.

CHAPTER 3

The Magic of Christmas

The fact that my parents traveled constantly meant that the importance of the holidays as family time was magnified. And of all the holidays, Christmas was the most important. We began planning months ahead and our house, which was already pretty impressive, was turned into a winter wonderland every year.

We had a lavish outdoor display that featured a life-size Santa Claus with sleigh and all his reindeer. There were choirboys and big candles on the sides, and Christmas music was played constantly through outdoor speakers. It sounds pretty over-the-top, but in Los Angeles, we had to make up for the lack of snow. With the backdrop of our English Tudor house and the fir trees that were part of the regular landscaping, it really looked very Christmasy, particularly in the evenings.

For as long as I can remember, decorating the Christmas tree was the specialty of Sparky Tavares, my father's valet, confidant, and traveling companion. A huge tree was always placed in our high-ceiling foyer to greet guests, and it was covered with spectacular ornaments that my mother had collected from all over the world. I remember watching diminutive Sparky up on a tall ladder, reaching out precariously to make sure that each little gem was perfectly placed.

Like most kids, Carole and I would be awake at dawn on Christmas morning, sitting on the stairs, sneaking peeks at the presents, and waiting for our parents to put on their robes and slippers. When they finally emerged, there would be an orgy of unwrapping, happy screaming, and unbridled conspicuous consumption under the tree. The favorite present I remember best was a life-size Eloise doll. The doll had elastic straps on her shoes, so you could put her on your own feet and dance with her—which I did. I also loved styling her hair. As a child, I was really obsessed with hair. I spent far more time on Eloise's hair than she did herself—the real Eloise pretty much let that go. Eloise was the heroine of a series of charming books by Kay Thompson. She was the impish little girl who lived with her nanny, her dog, and her turtle in an elegant suite at the Plaza Hotel in New York. Her primary delight in life was raising hell with the staff, roller-skating in the hallways, pushing all the buttons in the elevator, and in general making a pest of herself. Like me that Christmas morning, Eloise was six.

After we'd torn open everything in sight, we were joined by Aunt Baba; Nana, our nurse; Ida, our cook; and others for breakfast. I'm not sure why, but we always seemed to have a big traditional Jewish breakfast on Christmas. I had two sets of godparents: David Daniels, the doctor who delivered me and was my pediatrician all through childhood, and his wife, Hannah; and Sam and Mona Weiss, friends of my parents' from the music business. Carole's godparents were Jackie and Ada Gale, a music publisher and his wife that my parents became very friendly with. All three of these couples are Jewish, and they would often join us on Christmas morning. We'd sit down to a mountain of fresh bagels, lox and cream cheese, whitefish, and scrambled eggs, before we went upstairs to try to fit into our Christmas dresses.

Christmas dinner at our house was a true Hollywood production. It was also a wonderful combination of my mother's stylish sense of elegant entertaining and my father's bigger-than-life sense of generosity. Our oversized dining room had a table with a seemingly endless number of leaves—it seated twelve easily. At Christmas, that table all but begged for mercy under the weight of an amazing assortment of foods. There was too much of everything. Next to the salmon, turkey, pâté de foie gras, platters of cheeses, gleaming bowls of salads, steaming heaps of vegetables, and an array of traditional Christmas cookies and apple pies, were chitlins, yams, collard greens, fried chicken, perfect barbecued ribs, and lots of other Southern black dishes—all served side by side in the same silver serving dishes. Mom knew how much my dad enjoyed Southern cooking, and she presented soul food in the same way she presented traditional Christmas fare. That dinner was a telling statement about my family, about our eclectic tastes, and the variety of our friends.

Amidst this lavish display, the centerpiece was a real shocker: a whole roast pig, complete with a big head with an apple in its mouth and a little curly tail. Most people couldn't believe their eyes. They had never seen anything like that before. There it was, sitting on an elegant china platter, surrounded by polished silver cutlery and serving utensils. Whooooeee! As a kid, I was delighted. That thing was bigger than me!

Invitations to the Cole family Christmas parties were much sought after in Hollywood—or so I am told. In any given year, the guest list would include Louis Armstrong, Peggy Lee, Frank Sinatra, Ella Fitzgerald, Lena Horne, Danny Thomas, Nancy Wilson, Mel Tormé, Pearl Bailey, and Sammy Davis Jr. As children, we were simply introduced to Auntie Ella or Uncle Frank. That was how my parents let us know they were close friends, but we had no idea of the magnitude of the personalities around us. There's a picture of me during a recording session of Dad's at Capitol Records where I'm standing between my father and Louis Armstrong, with Ella Fitzgerald seated in the background. The look on my face is entirely so-what.

I was surrounded by music legends, but I didn't know enough to be awed—they were just grown-up friends of Dad's who were around at Christmas and whenever my father was home. These were nice people who were warm and fun-loving folks—people who loved to drink, loved to party. When they'd gather round the piano, they really let their hair down, and I could tell that they loved what they did. In our house they were very uninhibited and not the least caught up in who they were.

During the holidays, we were allowed to invite children of our own ages to our house; the kids' party took place out in the garage that my parents had converted into a fabulous entertainment center. On an added second story, there was a children's playroom, complete with its own soda fountain and an elaborate maze of Lionel train tracks. Downstairs, there was a more sophisticated room for the adults, with gorgeous wood paneling that my mom had gotten from Marion Davies's old mansion. We loved playing there with our friends. But all too soon after New Year's, Carole and I would see the trunks and the bags come out, and we knew that Mom and Dad were going on the road again. Deep inside I think I identified on some level with Eloise. The reason she lived this privileged life at the Plaza was that her mother was always off galavanting somewhere, sending presents as a substitute for her presence.

It was a given that my mother traveled with Dad as often as she could, and it was a pattern that had been established right from the start. I was just over a month old when she left Cookie and me in Hancock Park and took off on tour with Dad. Nana and Ida were already in residence; Baba arrived that fall when Mom went with Dad to Europe. They didn't return to Los Angeles until almost Christmastime. It may have preserved their marriage, but it was painful for us kids.

This was the burdensome part of being "the daughter of Nat King Cole." Although it made me sad when they left, I tried to keep a happy face. As children, we understood intuitively that we were not allowed to make a scene or act depressed, because doing that would only upset our parents and would not change the dates for the tour. There was an unspoken but deeply instilled trouper tradition in our family, one that has helped me in my own career and hurt me in other ways. We all understood that no matter what problems or conflicts were swirling around us, we were in show business: The show must go on. We learned to make emotional adjustments for the pain we felt, and some of that deferred pain came back to haunt me later in life.

Since my mother traveled with Dad, it meant that we were home a lot with people other than our parents taking care of us. It was one of those things that I didn't realize was unusual until I got older. Not that I was despondent about this at the time—I surely had a happy childhood. I had my dolls, my games, and my tape recorder, and I enjoyed playing alone. I can still remember walking around our backyard, having the best time creating little scenes with my dolls. They were my performers and they were my audience, if you will.

They were also my companions. When I was young, I spent a lot of time playing by myself.

Early in 1961, my mother made an astonishing announcement. At the age of thirty-eight, she was once again pregnant. I was sitting on the floor in her bedroom with Cookie when she gave us the news. I didn't take it well; in short, I was appalled. Eeew, gross! I was just starting to get used to the idea—Mom sure was cute when she was pregnant—when the news got worse (at least from an eleven-year-old point of view). We were all at dinner, and I should have known something was up because we were eating—just the family—in the formal dining room. Dad was home for dinner (which already made it a special occasion) and over dessert Mom announced that she'd been to the obstetrician. Everything was fine, but she wasn't just pregnant, she was double pregnant. She was expecting twins. My father pushed his chair back, said not a word, and walked out of the dining room. I can imagine that he fainted not long after.

Casey and Timolin were born on the twenty-sixth of September, and when they brought those baby girls home, I was in heaven. They were just so darling. I had two real-life dolls to play with. Cookie was older, still at home but really beginning to live her own life, which let me be the big sister. I loved changing diapers, despite the fact that I was afraid of that big ole diaper pin—it used to scare the mess out of me. I was amazed to discover that babies really do smell good—clean babies,

that is. The smell of babies' butts—there's
nothing like that. I looked forward to seeing
them after school, and at first this wasn't
easy, honey. When they came home from the
hospital, we had a German nurse taking care
of them, and holy moly, this woman wouldn't
let us get near 'em. You had to go into the
nursery with a mask on. Everything was
sterile—she was a Nazi when it came to
hygiene. Her name was Karoline Eberspacher,
and she had a very thick Chermann ahkseht.
She came into our family very stern, but the
twins knocked her down quick. In very short
order, all that toughness melted, and she
joined the rest of us in loving them to death.
Meanwhile, Kelly was a toddler and into
everything, and Cookie's teenage hormones
were in full bloom. In the midst of all this
domestic upheaval, my dad was struggling
to bring a musical to Broadway. I believe he
was inspired to do that from having seen
Sammy Davis, Jr. in *Mr. Wonderful* and *Golden
Boy*. It was called, at various times, *Wild Is Love*,
I'm with You, *The Wandering Man*, and, at one
point, *The Merry Young World of Nat King
Cole*. It was basically a revue with Barbara
McNair, with an orchestra and a chorus line
providing the support for Dad as he sang a series
of his hits. By the summer of 1961, he had
revamped the show extensively and wanted to
give it some out-of-town tryouts in Southern
California. I went to him with my brash
eleven-year-old confidence and told him that
I wanted to be in the show with him. He was

probably pretty skeptical about the idea, but he agreed to let me audition for him and some of his production people. I sang "A Tisket, A Tasket," which, of course, I had learned from the Ella Fitzgerald recording.

Either he took pity on my youthful ambition or he thought I had some talent, or both. Whatever motivated him, he let me sing a song with him from *Gigi* that Maurice Chevalier sings with Louis Jourdan, "It's a Bore." It was a cute song to do with a little girl. He sang about all the wonderful things in life and I just shrugged and retorted, "It's a bore," just as a kid would.

My mother was concerned that I was just too young to be onstage, but I was determined to be in this show with my dad, and it was very exciting. I only performed a couple of times in the show, first at the Greek Theater in Los Angeles, and later in Riverside, California. I still remember how nervous I was that first night at the Greek. It was one thing going onstage and performing in front of thousands of people for the first time. (The ham in me didn't have much problem with that.) Going onstage with your father was quite another. I was so anxious that I thought I was going to throw up and pee at the same time—I just could not get it together.

I was absolutely beside myself with fear. I was sitting onstage on a stool in my cute little sailor's outfit—knee socks, white gloves, little sailor cap, all navy blue and white—the curtain was just about to go up, and I just had to talk to my dad. The problem was that the song just didn't work if I couldn't keep a poker face, and at that point, I wasn't at all sure I could pull it off. I said, "Dad, I can't do this. I'm gonna laugh, I just know I'm gonna laugh. When I get nervous, I start laughing. I can't help myself."

And he said, "Sweetie, you're not gonna laugh. If you laugh, I'm gonna whip your butt."

Showtime! Needless to say, I didn't laugh. In fact, my first review in *Down Beat* magazine noted: "The most appealing bit in the first half was 'It's a Bore,' which Papa Cole shared with his daughter, 11-year-old Natalie. The child came across with poise and aplomb in singing and spoken lines and with every mark of a professional." I think my dad was proud of me, because on the last night that I was performing in the show with him, he let me stay up late and take a bow with him at the end of the show. There is a photograph of me and Dad singing "It's a Bore" in that show that I use in the *Unforgettable* section of my own show.

At the time, 401 South Muirfield Road may have been the only Democratic household in Hancock Park, and we certainly were happy when Kennedy defeated Nixon in 1960. Dad had sung at the Democratic National Convention in Los Angeles when JFK was nominated, and was honored to be asked to sing at his inauguration in January of 1961. They were friends.

In November of '61, Dad performed at a

Democratic fund-raiser at the Hollywood Palladium. He excused himself early, however, in order to escort Carole at the Links Cotillion debutante ball at the Beverly Hilton. Toward the end of the evening, JFK made an unscheduled appearance at the Hilton, Secret Service entourage in tow—basically he crashed Cookie's coming-out party. He shook hands with every deb that night. Kennedy's arrival naturally created a sensation, and there were photos all over the black press in the days that followed.

I missed all the excitement and had to stay home because I was too young, so I heard about it all secondhand. Of course, I wasn't the only kid cooling her heels in the house that night. Little Kelly was there, as were the twins, who were just two months old.

Dad maintained his relationship with JFK pretty much to the end. He was performing in Washington in August of 1963, and the President pulled him aside to ask him what he thought about the upcoming Martin Luther King march—the one that culminated in the "I have a dream" speech. I don't know what his answer was, but I can only assume that Dad would have told the President that he supported King in his efforts. Dad supposedly came home from the trip to the White House with five autographed pens and some PT-109 tie clips.

The first time I ever saw my father cry was when John Kennedy died. Dad was at home watching TV when the news broke that

Kennedy had been shot in Dallas. Then came the news that he was dead. I walked in from school and there Dad was, crying. He was a friend as well as an admirer of John Kennedy's, and I believe that affection was returned.

The two men had a lot in common besides politics. One was the love of a good time. Another was surely the unrelenting pressure of living your life in a goldfish bowl. The Kennedys were not the only white family to face that difficulty, but the Coles were certainly one of the first black families to confront that problem. Perhaps because we were the first to have to deal with it, my parents did the best they could to prepare me for what I was stepping into.

When I was small, the economic and social blessings of my heritage were right in front of me every day. God knows it wasn't much of a burden being "the-daughter-of Nat King Cole"—except that that was the sum total of who I was. As I got a little older, that burden got heavier. I started asking myself, "Other than being the daughter of Nat King Cole, who else am I? Who was 'Sweetie' or 'Natalie,' other than my father's child?" I found the answer disturbing—I didn't have an identity, at least I didn't feel as though I had an identity. I was "the-daughter-of," and whatever I had, it seemed to be because of him.

Strangely, when you have grown up in the public eye, people often feel as though they know you, but at the same time you feel that you don't know yourself. As an adult, many people who loved my father's music felt that this gave them a special intimacy with me. Even in school, everyone knew who my father was, and I often felt as though I was just some representative of his, an extension of him. In the back of my mind, I always felt as though I never knew who my friends were, who my *real* friends were. I didn't know whether they liked me for me, or because of who my dad was. Since I wasn't sure who I was either, that was an ongoing agony.

Approaching life with this burden made me very insecure, and I went out of my way to get people's attention. I became a people-pleaser. Whatever it took to be popular, to fit in, I did. I wanted so much to be accepted by these confident, happy white kids I saw at school every day. For a long time I told myself that I didn't really care why they were accepting me. That was my downfall. A lot of the things that went wrong in my life happened to me because I just didn't have the confidence to say, "That's not good for me. I shouldn't do that. Those people aren't really the kind of people I should be around."

That's where the angels came in—over and over and over. I made so many wrong choices looking for myself. I should have been dead many times over. I've been a frequent caller on God's 911 hotline, but He has always answered, and for that, I am eternally thankful. It has been a quest, a continuing journey in search of this person I know is out there—or rather, in here.

CHAPTER 4

My Father's Death

The last time I saw my father relaxed and happy, as I knew and loved him all my childhood, was September of 1964, when he took me to register for my freshman year at the Northfield School for Girls. As he had done many times before, he sat beside me in the limo, smoking nonstop. This time he might have talked about the impending World Series between the New York Yankees and the St. Louis Cardinals, or about the boxing wunderkind named Cassius Clay who had just beaten Sonny Liston, or about his touring

---

I can see that I am still not at the end of that journey of self-knowledge, and I will not reach the end of my search until I come to the end of the confusing, fascinating, painful, joyous, complex process called life, and I meet my Maker. What I do know is that Natalie Cole has had to go through everything that she's had to go through to be the woman that she is today. I've come a long way, and I believe that one of the reasons God created me is so that I can tell you what I have learned so far.

show, *Sights and Sounds*, that was opening in Tahoe, or about getting ready to film *Cat Ballou* in Hollywood. I honestly do not remember the specifics. I do know that Diana Ross and the Supremes crooned "Baby Love" on the radio, the fall colors of the Massachusetts scenery flew by, and I was happy to have Dad all to myself. He never once mentioned the excruciating pain he was already suffering in his back.

When we arrived at Northfield for registration, his presence nearly caused a riot. No one had expected Nat King Cole to show up at this small prep school, and there was no security to prevent hundreds of girls from crushing in to shake his hand or get a closer look. Dad was just as cool as always, and I was grinning ear to ear with pride. Yes indeed, "the-daughter-of" was a good thing to be that day, a very good thing, indeed. As always, he good-naturedly signed autographs and talked to the girls who would be my schoolmates. Then he took me into the administration building where the headmaster, Edmund S. Meany Jr., greeted him privately. Dad helped me to get settled, and then with a hug and a kiss and a "Bye, Sweetie. See you at Christmas," he was gone.

What was a young black girl from Los Angeles doing at a prep school in a small Massachusetts town? The answer has a little to do with my mother's passion for education, and even more to do with Great-Aunt Lala. When Lala founded the Palmer Memorial

Institute in Sedalia, North Carolina, she based it on many of the same principles as the Northfield Seminary for Young Ladies. Northfield had been founded in 1879 by educator and religious leader Dwight L. Moody. Lala's niece and namesake, Charlotte Hawkins—my Aunt Baba—was a Northfield graduate, class of 1938. (Following in the family tradition, both my twin sisters, Casey and Timolin, are Northfield graduates, too, class of 1979.)

When I approached the end of the eighth grade at Cathedral Chapel, I was given a choice about where to go to high school—sort of—but I suspect in the end that it was really a put-up job. My mother dutifully took me to see a couple of other schools, including the Bishop's School in La Jolla, and even Lala's own Palmer Institute, but I suspect that her heart was already set on Northfield. Bishop's was okay, but I remember wanting to go out of California. Even though Lala had passed away, Palmer was still prestigious and Mother knew the headmaster, but despite the family history (or perhaps because of it), I didn't want to go there. Thus it came to pass that Aunt Lala's passion for education, which had been thoroughly instilled in Mom, was visited upon me as enrollment in the Northfield School for Girls.

The school had a long tradition and connections as a feeder school to colleges such as Smith and Wellesley. It had fashioned itself to be very traditional, very Ivy League—a girl's prep school that was comparable to what Exeter was for boys. I'm sure my mother had it in the back of her mind that when I graduated, I'd just make that short trip down the highway from my prestigious girls prep school to a prestigious girls college.

Although my dad gave me a great start by establishing my celebrity status at Northfield, the beginning of my first year there was a bumpy ride. I felt much more lonely than I had when I went to Michigan and Chicago in the summers. Cookie had gone with me then; now I was flying solo. There weren't many black girls at Northfield, and there were no black teachers, but I didn't think that was a big deal at the time. We moved in rarefied company back in Los Angeles, and often as not we were the only black anything wherever we went.

That was very much by design. My mother really tried to keep us more in a certain kind of situation with a certain class of people—"well bred," as they used to be called. I'm sure that learning how to be comfortable in that kind of environment eventually paid off by opening up doors for me that would have otherwise been nailed shut, but as a kid I just wanted to meet and greet all kinds of people—I was all over the map.

I certainly wasn't going to meet any but the well bred at Northfield. The girls were from what is called "old money," a concept that was entirely alien to me. I grew to appreciate it later, but at first the New England concepts of history and tradition were difficult for a California girl to absorb. Back east I discovered that there was a completely different perspective on how old was old. "Old" at Northfield was the *Mayflower*; "old" in Los Angeles was anything still left standing from before the Eisenhower administration.

It was clear that as "the-daughter-of," I was supposed to hold my own in the company of "old money," and I had a strong commitment to making my parents proud of me, so I buckled down and worked hard. But even so, I had a rough time academically—classes here were much harder than what I'd been used to at Cathedral Chapel. The school dated from the nineteenth century, and I was positive that some of the professors did as well. Honey, we're talking *decrepit*. I struggled. I took one class that I thought would be a cinch—music appreciation—that was taught by a guy who was half blind. He had the thickest glasses I had ever seen. Not only did he look like Mr. Magoo, he was boring, too. It was about the only time in my life that I hated music.

As the leaves fell and Thanksgiving came and went, the weather got cold and nasty. I wasn't used to that. I was a tad homesick. "Bye, Sweetie. See you at Christmas..." I fastened on Dad's last words to me and started counting the days to the holidays, and a classic Cole family "Chestnuts-roasting-on-an-open-fire" Christmas—with the big tree, and all the food and the presents and all the friends and family, young and old.

When I arrived home, I found that Christmas

was going to be very different this year. In fact, Christmas would never be the same. When I saw Dad, there was no mistaking his singular voice, but otherwise I might not have recognized him. He'd lost a lot of weight and looked ancient and skeletal. I was numb with fear when I realized that this person in front of me was but a shadow of my father. He was sitting in the bedroom in a rocking chair that he liked, but he wasn't able to get up. His hair was white and all but gone, his skin was dark gray and papery. He was foggy and somewhat out of it, because he was so doped up with Demerol to kill the pain. My father had lung cancer, the poisoned legacy of a lifetime of smoking. I don't remember whether he spoke or we hugged or what happened. Nobody said so, but I knew in my heart that he was dying.

I was pretty foggy with my own pain. My mother hadn't prepared me for this development, probably because she was having trouble herself coming to grips with what was happening to him. She had never even mentioned to me that he was sick, but then, a lot of the details of his illness had been kept hidden—even from her.

While I was away at school, I had what amounted to a transcontinental moat between me and all the trouble at home. The only thing I was aware of was that Dad had been spending a lot of time on the road (nothing new there), and that Mom had been spending more time in Hancock Park with Kelly and the twins. My mother had just come back to New York from Paris when she got the phone call from Baba telling her that Dad was in St. John's. That was the seventh of December. I don't remember the rest of that Christmas. Our house, which always rang with music day and night, was silent. I was torn between wanting to run back to school because it was so painful for me to be home, and not wanting to leave at all. Eventually I returned to school in a daze.

Nobody told me he was dying. To the contrary, back at Northfield I kept getting optimistic reports about his progress. On January 25 they operated to remove the cancerous left lung, and the next day I received a rather dispassionate telegram saying that the surgery was "successful."...Successful...which actually meant that they had successfully removed his lung and he didn't die from the operation. I don't think I heard anything more until the fifteenth of February. Somebody came into my first-period biology lab and said that I was wanted back at my dormitory. I hated biology, and on most days I would have welcomed any excuse to get out of that wretched lab with its smell of formaldehyde, but this particular time it didn't feel right.

When I walked back to the dorm, our housemother was waiting for me. She was the sweetest little lady and I had developed a close relationship with her. Her name was Miss Trask, and she had to be eighty years old. She had no business being a housemother. She should have been out in the garden enjoying the sunshine and not trying to deal with a bunch of crazy girls like us. As soon as I walked in and saw her face, I knew something was wrong. Really seriously wrong. Her eyes were a bright cornflower blue, and they were brimming with tears.

She talked in a whisper all the time, but at first she couldn't say a word. She didn't have to. I knew. It's horrible for anyone to break this kind of news to a child, worse yet for a person who is not family. It was a difficult, painful situation.

It's always very bizarre when you try to think back on events like this. In some ways you remember everything; in other ways it seems like it happened to somebody else. The dormitory I lived in was actually a beautiful old house. The room where I met Miss Trask was our living room, which had big windows and white lace curtains, and sunshine was pouring in, making it glow. You expect a day like that to be a rainy, dreary, foggy, dark day. But it wasn't. It was a crisp, clear February day. The air was just a little nippy, and the sun was shining.

What's astonishing is that I didn't cry. I just went to my room and started packing. Headmaster Meany and his wife were lovely people who drove me to Bradley Field in Hartford/Springfield and put me on a plane for Los Angeles.

It was to be a memorable flight for all the wrong reasons. The guy sitting next to me was a talking alcoholic who drank his way from coast to coast. For five hours he was ear-banging me from the bottom of his champagne glass. I don't remember a word that he said, but in a way he kept me from focusing on what was going on inside me. I just kept looking at him. And all this time, I didn't shed a tear.

We landed at about six o'clock that evening. Cookie met me at the airport and took me home. The whole thing was surreal—I was floating through a world I knew so well, but everything was different. First of all, we went to the front door, which is something I never did. You don't go through the front door of your own house; you go through the side, or the back. As we came through the entryway, my mother answered the door. My mother never answered the front door. Someone else always did that. She was wearing black, and before this I don't think I had ever seen my mother wear black. I had held it in all the way from Massachusetts, but when I saw my mother standing there in black, I broke down. I don't know how long I cried.

The next day Cookie and I went to the Angelus Funeral Home to view the body. They showed us to this rather large viewing room. It wasn't cozy at all, but quite austere and chilly. There were only two chairs in the room, one on either side of the coffin. Dad was lying in there with the lid open, and after we tiptoed in and looked at him for the last time, we sat down. The two of us were just looking at each other, trying to absorb all that had happened, when we heard a remarkable sound. Dad had a funny habit of often seeming distracted when you spoke with him. You never knew if he was listening, because he might not respond until maybe five minutes later. You could make a statement such as, "Dad, I got an A plus on my spelling quiz today," or "I saw this really cool car today." If he was reading the paper or looking at the television, you knew that he wouldn't respond immediately. He heard you, but he didn't hear you. Five minutes later, he'd look at you and go "Huh?"

Just, "Huh?" That was it. It was a grunting sound that Dad and Dad alone made, and it used to drive us crazy, but that was just his way. It was always a little late, like he was on tape delay.

While Cookie and I were sitting in this cold, empty room, both of us swear we heard Dad say "Huh?" at the same time. We'd been talking back and forth a little, but there was a moment of quiet, and from somewhere in the area where that coffin was, there was definitely a sound that was unmistakably Dad's familiar "Huh?"

Every time my sister and I think about it, we just crack up with giggles, because it seems so wonderful and so silly. I'm certainly glad Cookie was there with me, because otherwise I would have doubted my sanity. Maybe it was a sound projected from outside the room. Maybe the coffin shifted a little bit on the table. Or maybe God just said, "Let's give these little girls something to carry with them in their lives, something that is just for them."

Well, we went running out of the room yelling, "Daddy spoke! He said something!" We weren't such little kids: my sister was twenty and I was fifteen, but under circumstances like that, you're not exactly yourself. Which is why the adults discounted us. To this day, we both swear we heard it, and I'll die saying I heard it. That's exactly what I think God would want us to remember, and I think Dad would want us to remember. In that moment, in the midst of all that darkness, there was a little moment of lightness, and it was so much like him.

The funeral a few days later is another blur in my memory. What I do remember is that it was held at the beautiful St. James Episcopal Church that we all attended on Wilshire at St. Andrews Place. As we arrived, I remember seeing thousands of people waiting outside the church and lining the sidewalks along Wilshire Boulevard. More than four hundred friends and colleagues were inside St. James. I barely recall seeing anyone, but I was told that the mourners included Steve Allen, Count Basie, Jack Benny, Governor Pat Brown, George Burns, Billy Daniels, Sammy Davis, Jr., Sy Devore, Jimmy Durante, Jack Entratter, Leonard Feather, Gordon Jenkins, Robert Kennedy, Peter Lawford, Johnny Mathis, Billy May, Ricardo Montalban, Nelson Riddle, Frank Sinatra, Danny Thomas, and many other wonderful people.

Because my father had been so ravaged by the painful ordeal of his death, my mother requested that the casket be sealed. Throughout the services, we carried on bravely. Cookie held Kelly's hand, and my brother went through it all stoically, even if he didn't really comprehend what was going on. The resemblance to John-John at JFK's funeral only fifteen months earlier was all too painfully apparent.

At the funeral, the casket had a beautiful blanket of roses over it. I took one and kept that rose in my Bible for as long as I possibly could. It was there for years until it just disintegrated. Even after the petals were gone, the smell stayed for a long time.

The funeral was the worst day of all our lives. The family carried itself with grace and dignity—which was after all the "correct thing" in these circumstances. We kept it together on the outside—barely—but we were all torn up on the inside. Our friends, our family, our relatives—I mean everybody. It was just such a heart-wrenching event that everybody was devastated.

Since that day, my family has never been the same.

My father is buried in Forest Lawn Cemetery, but I haven't been back to the grave. I haven't had any desire to visit that part of my life again. Because I carry him here in my heart, I don't have to go to a physical place. I adored my father. He had a sweetness and a gentleness that most men either lack or are afraid to show. He wore his fame comfortably—

it didn't impress or change him. My father gave me a joyous, secure childhood, a rich legacy of music, and a powerful, supportive love that has lighted my way through even the darkest moments of my life. But the fact that I never got to say goodbye, never got to tell him one last time how much I loved him, ate at me for years to come.

CHAPTER 5

Acting Out

I don't want to go back. I don't want to go back. Please don't send me back there."

I remember lying on the bed in my mother's bedroom and pleading with her about not returning to Northfield School for Girls. I could see my family falling apart, and I felt suddenly alone and unprotected without Dad. A part of my life was over and had been buried right along with my father.

I don't think any of us realized just what a cornerstone my father was until he was gone. My mother was so devastated that she just couldn't step into that void. Some matriarchal widows can pull the family together and say, "Okay, this is what Nat would have wanted and this is what we're going to do." Mom, for whatever reason, wasn't able to do that. Her life, her whole world, had revolved around my father. Since I'd been at boarding school, I knew nothing of Gunilla Hutton, the woman Dad had been having an affair with, but my mother certainly did, and it must have made dealing with the aftermath of his death even more difficult for her.

"I don't want to go back."

Mom told me, "You have to go back. I'll be fine." Which was a lie, of course. My mother was shattered. I don't believe that she has been able to fully absorb the loss of my father; consequently, she has never healed.

Somehow it was easier for each of us (Mom, Cookie, and me) to fend for ourselves emotionally. The center of our world had fallen out; the person who had been our glue was gone. We each had different pains to deal with, and none of us knew how to heal ourselves, or help heal those around us. That kind of damage may take a lifetime to repair—or it never happens at all. Our family just fragmented into little pieces.

So we retreated into our corners. Cookie was already on her own, Mom stayed in Los Angeles with Kelly and the twins, and I went back to Northfield and proceeded to get into various levels of trouble.

I didn't have a lot of people that I could talk to about how I felt at that time. The years between twelve and fifteen are crucial for a girl, no matter what the circumstances. But when you lose your father in those tender years, without any stable, nurturing relationship with your mom, you feel lost. In some ways, it's as if you're still a small child, but all alone. I never really got to make the transition from little girl to young woman.

The people at Northfield were sympathetic, which is not the same as supportive. They weren't really equipped to help me deal with my situation. My mother was on the wrong side of the continent. My sister and I had talked a little bit during the confusion and chaos of the funeral and its aftermath, but we didn't have much time. At school, I had friends, of course, but I never felt comfortable talking to them about what was happening to me and my family after my father's death.

There was, however, one girl, Kristen Pickett, with whom I shared my feelings. She and I became good friends, which apparently caused the administration at Northfield great concern because she was gay. Of course, in 1965, there was a terrible stigma attached to homosexuality. My friendship with Kristen became the subject of whispers and scuttlebutt around the campus. The school warned my mother that I was being seen around campus with this lesbian, and, of course, she called to admonish me about the shame and disgrace of a gay lifestyle. I don't remember whether or not she actually asked me if I was sleeping with Kristen. However, she went on at length and left me no doubt about her feelings on the subject. The truth is that we had a really close relationship that was not sexual. Kristen was a kind of hippie with a casual attitude, but she was extremely smart. I went with her one day to meet her family, who lived in Pittsfield, Massachusetts. Her father was a very intelligent man—that's where she got her brains—but I came away feeling that there wasn't a lot of nurturing in that household, and I think that's one of the reasons we bonded. Intuitively, we were aware that we didn't get a lot of that as we were growing up. She was kind of a misunderstood kid, and, at that time, I was feeling misunderstood, too, so we gravitated to each other.

Eventually, and not surprisingly, they kicked Kristen out of the school. Not for being gay—they couldn't do that. They had to come up with something else, but the real reason was that she had started a relationship with another girl at the school—a beautiful girl a little younger than me. And it was just not acceptable at that time for kids to have an openly gay relationship.

Northfield wasn't the most pleasant experience for me, because I associate it with being kept away from my father when he was dying. But it was a challenging academic environment. I learned discipline and independence. I was away from home for the first time; my father died; I was trying to get decent grades; I was in an all girls school; there ain't too many black folks there.... There were just too many hurdles.

But there was also a big part of me that wanted

77

to prove to my mom that I could do this. I wanted to show her that I was capable of being a good student and a good daughter. And I did show her, for a while, but after my second year at Northfield ended, I had not been back home in Los Angeles for more than a few weeks when I got into much bigger trouble than just having a gay friend. I was shopping at Bullock's Wilshire one afternoon with my girlfriend, Jan Collins, whose dad, John Collins, had been my father's guitar player for many years. In that era, Bullock's was the biggest, fanciest department store in Los Angeles, our version of Saks Fifth Avenue. It was a six-story Art Deco monument to shopping. On that afternoon, I decided to try on a bathing suit and not take it off. I walked out without paying for it.

I knew that what I was doing was wrong. I certainly had the money to pay for that suit. Yet at the moment, I felt a thrill, a strange kind of satisfaction as I walked out of the store with the stolen bathing suit. That thrill passed quickly when a security officer asked us to step back into the store, please.

I have thought a lot about what would have caused me to shoplift at the age of fifteen. Several psychologists were sure that it was a reaction to my father's death. There's no doubt that I was almost mad at my father for dying. I missed him terribly, and there was so much I wished I had been able to do with him and say to him. I think that "mad" just covers up how sad someone really is, and those feelings were very much in my heart at that time.

But the shoplifting was more acting out at my mother than a reaction to my father's death. Mother and I were at a crucial point in our relationship. Either we were going to get closer or we were going to get further apart. Certainly we weren't going to stay the same. And, as seemed to be the case of many relationships in my family, things just got further apart.

My mother really clung to her younger children at that time—Kelly and the twins. Kelly was six; Casey and Timolin were three, and the twins, of course, were the last things my dad left her. She had thought that she wasn't going to get pregnant ever again, and she really didn't want to get pregnant ever again. But there she was, with the twins—sometimes life just happens. She became very close with the girls, and their early lives were very different from mine. The way they were raised was very different from the way Carole and I were brought up. Kelly, my adopted brother, was in between the two sets of girls, but certainly, being the only man-child in the family, he carried a lot of privileges in my mother's eyes.

The shoplifting was my way of rebelling, a way to get my mother's attention. It was also kind of a dare thing, too. I always had money in my pocket and there was no reason at all for me to steal, but if you are a spoiled kid, as I definitely was, you have a little bit of a chip on your shoulder—you want to see if you can get away with it. In my brief shoplifting career,

I had boosted a few pens, pencils, and sunglasses and gotten some cheap thrills. The bathing suit was taking it to a higher level. Of course, I was not conscious of such motivations at the time. It was only many years later that I could put my behavior in some kind of perspective.

When the security officer walked up, my poor friend Jan had no idea what was happening. She was a good Catholic girl and I guess I was starting to behave like a heathen. Nonetheless, we remained good friends. In fact, she was one of the few black friends I had growing up. When she realized what I had done, she was mortified. When the people at Bullock's found out who I was, *they* were mortified. The head of security alternated between chastising and sympathizing as he accompanied me downtown to the Los Angeles police department.

The police put a good scare into me and took me down to Juvenile Hall, but I was never formally arrested. At "Juvie," I was met by my father's attorney, Leo Branton, who was also Kelly's godfather. Cookie and I grew up with his kids and shared many holidays and happy memories. Anyway, he came to take me home. Regarding the shoplifting incident, he was very understanding—or maybe he just knew what was waiting for me at home.

I think we drove around for a little bit so my mother could calm down. I don't know how much that helped, since there was surely hell to pay when I got there. Even the outside of the house looked angry, and inside, Maria Cole was breathing fire. If I had been trying—consciously or unconsciously—to get my mother's attention, I succeeded. She was furious. She could not stop railing at me. I had disgraced the family, marked myself for a life of troublemaking, and—worst of all—I had somehow damaged the memory of my father. I think my relationship with my mother changed drastically at that point. Immediately, she sent me off to a psychiatrist. She then decided that I had to get a job. I guess she thought I needed to do something with my time and not spend it in stores where I would be tempted to shoplift.

I spent the rest of the summer working as a switchboard operator and receptionist at a sanitarium. It was actually more of a retirement home. The owner was a friend of my mother's, so she gave me a job. I was making $1.10 an hour. That's where I learned the old work ethic. I was a dynamo at that switchboard, and I was proud of earning my own money. Although it started out as a punishment for getting into trouble, my job turned out to be a good thing.

My mother also decided that I should come back to Los Angeles to finish high school after my sophomore year at Northfield, which was fine by me. Once Kristen was gone, I knew that I never wanted to go back. That September she enrolled me at the Buckley School in Sherman Oaks, one of most prestigious prep schools in the Los Angeles area.

Hallelujah! I was out of the nunnery!

Undoubtedly, she did this because she wanted to keep a watchful eye on my activities, but I didn't care; I was happy to be home with the twins, and my brother, Kelly. I loved being back in my own room and being the big sister. After Mom got over being upset about the shoplifting, she and I were okay. She was helpful in allowing me to be a little more independent. She really wanted me to be more autonomous, because my mom was not the momsy kind of Girl Scout-PTA person who's going to be involved in everything her children do. That's just not who she was. She encouraged independence to some degree, but also wanted to exercise control over the house. I think her attitude was kind of a good thing for me at the time.

I was now sixteen, and I learned to drive and soon began to take our Chevrolet Impala to school. I vividly remember my first accident. I was leaving the Buckley parking lot after classes one day when I stepped on the gas and realized too late that I was in reverse. I smashed into the car behind me, which was a GTO driven by a girl who was a friend of mine. Neither of us was hurt and the GTO was hardly scratched, but the Chevy was a mess. I was petrified at the thought of facing my mom. I ran in the house in tears and blurted out, "Mom, I just had a big, fat accident!" It was one of those times when you know your mom is just going to kill you. Instead, she was very cool. She was concerned about whether I had been hurt and she told me not to worry about the car. I was *really* relieved.

At Buckley, there were few other blacks, but

it was coed and I certainly wasn't the only daughter of someone famous. Walt Disney's grandchildren, Phyllis Diller's son Perry, Dick Van Dyke's sons—we had a lot of common ground. For the first time, I felt as though I really fit in and I liked it. I was a cheerleader, I had a lot of friends, and I was dating one of the hottest guys in the area, a handsome young black man named Eric from Loyola High.

In truth, I knew virtually nothing about sex, and was a virgin when I met Eric. I had sort of skipped sex education. My mother didn't tell me anything about sex, about periods, about breasts, about nothing. When she first learned I was using Tampax (before Eric), she freaked out, because in those days, if you used a tampon, that meant you weren't a virgin. I learned everything from Cookie, because no one else talked to me about that kind of stuff. I remember being seventeen and giving myself my first douche. I got the equipment from my sister. It was this old-fashioned bag with a hose that you were supposed to hang in the bathtub—I mean, it looked like an octopus. But I learned all of those feminine things from my big sister, not from my mom.

Eric was my first serious, steady boyfriend and my first sexual experience. After dating for a while, we were both very anxious to "do it." On the fateful day, Eric picked me up from school in his white Mustang with the black convertible top. He always kept some Jack Daniel's in the glove compartment, and I think we had a little nip for courage. His parents were not home, so we went to his house and up to his room and got into it after a little awkwardness. Things were going along quite romantically when an unmistakable, unforgettable voice began to sing on the radio. It was my father.

Eric and I both freaked. It was as though my dad was there, knocking on the door. I don't even remember the song, but it was definitely him, and we both felt his presence. It was an eerie moment, but I am happy to say that Eric and I got over it and resumed our activities to different musical accompaniment. I am also happy to say that it was a wonderful experience and I'm grateful to Eric that it was.

My relationship with Eric helped me to have an extremely positive outlook on sex in general. In addition to being gentle, considerate, and fun, he was also a good student and an inspiration for lots of study sessions. Sometimes we would stay up all night studying for tests—and maybe a little hanky-panky. We occasionally took a Dexedrine to study. Uppers like Dex are not a high—it just keeps your ass awake so you can read all that stuff.

But this was 1967—junior year—and the entire universe was getting high. In 1967, smoking a joint was not considered a big deal by anyone under the age of thirty, and I was very curious about the experience. Exclusive, conservative, preppy Buckley was also where

I discovered marijuana. One night, about seven or eight of us were all packed into a car that was supposed to seat five, and somebody passed around a joint. I was hanging out with some real rich, snooty kids and I was just so glad to be a part of the in crowd that I went along with whatever was happening.

Whew, Lord! Did I get high! I remember that I got the giggles after my first toke, and shortly thereafter everybody in the car found everything going on around us scream-out-loud hysterically funny.

We all got the blind stoney munchies, and went to a diner. I loved how good the food tasted—just about everything I put in my mouth tasted wonderful. By the time we had to get home or catch hell from our parents, I was too high to read the road signs. They all looked like hieroglyphics to me. Nobody could remember how to take me home. We wandered around the streets of Hancock Park, lost and laughing, until I saw a sign that seemed awfully familiar. I stared at it, trying to figure out where I was. We were sitting in front of my house, but I was too loaded to know it. It seemed like harmless fun, but, for me, this was the beginning of a long journey into drug use.

So I finally got home—on time, thank goodness—but I knew enough not to go see my mother. Usually, before I went to bed, I would go into the den or to her bedroom and kiss her good night. I didn't dare go in there that night. I just took my little butt right to bed.

The next morning she asked, "What's wrong with your eyes?"

It wasn't just lack of sleep; they were still red from smoking dope. I said, "I think I'm getting a cold," and quickly looked away. When I think about it now, I wonder if my mom was really as dumb as I wanted to think she was.

When I graduated from Buckley, my mother announced that Father had left a little money for me, and I used mine to buy a little navy blue Volkswagen and a nose job. My nose... When I was a teenager, I always thought it was too broad and flat. So I found a plastic surgeon, Dr. Max Pegram, who agreed to make my nose smaller and more narrow, but he almost backed out when he discovered that I was "the-daughter-of." In the end, he chose to do less than what I'd wanted. He told me it was my destiny to look like my father. Gee, thanks, Doc.

With my nose in bandages, I decided to get a summer job where no one could see me looking hideous. No one sees telephone operators, right? I went to work again at a switchboard. It was one of my more interesting jobs. I answered the phones during lunchtime for several doctors' offices in Beverly Hills. I answered the phones for the Department of Mental Health, and my supervisor was a six-foot-four transvestite who had a personality somewhere between Auntie Mame and Minnie Pearl.

When we sat down to decide about where

I should go to college, my mom and I chose the University of Massachusetts at Amherst together. There was never any question that I was going to go to college—somewhere. Education was always number one in our house, absolutely number one. My father had dropped out of high school at Thanksgiving time of his sophomore year. My mother was lucky—after she got her diploma, she went to secretarial school. In those days, college wasn't what young black people did. It was a privilege, not a given.

My mother wanted her children to have a good education. For a time I thought about going to Howard, but she didn't want me going to a black college. I had a girlfriend there who told me, "Yeah girl, we're partying!" So she dinged that right away. She made no secret of her desire for me to attend a college in New England—preferably one of the sister colleges of the Ivy League. You see, Mom was born in Harvard Square in Cambridge, Massachusetts, and has always loved the East. Eventually my mother's Ivy League dream was fulfilled, in a way. My sister Timolin was one of the first ten women accepted into Amherst College. She graduated with honors from there, as did her twin, Casey, from Brown University in Providence, Rhode Island.

Although my memories of Northfield are mixed, I grew to enjoy the New England atmosphere while I was there, and Amherst is certainly one of the most beautiful areas in New England. My mother knew that after

Northfield I couldn't deal with another all girls school. So UMass, as part of the Five College Consortium—with Amherst, Hampshire, Mount Holyoke, and Smith—was a good compromise in her mind. Besides, as I regularly reminded her, it had an excellent premed program, and Mom was delighted by my aspirations to go into medicine. I wanted to become a doctor because I had the youthful idealistic dream that I could find a cure for the awful thing that killed Dad. That was before I discovered that I was really bad at chemistry.

CHAPTER 6

Becoming Black

UMass was a rather progressive, even a bit confrontational, institution, located in a gorgeous woodsy setting near the small historic town of Amherst. I'm not sure my mother was quite ready for the discoveries I was about to make there in the next few years. We were the first university to protest against the Vietnam War, and I was proud of that. It was a pretty big deal when we shut down the school, and having the teachers on our side was something I can never forget. When you and your professors stand side by side and speak out together, it's a terrific feeling.

UMass was truly the first "melting pot" environment that I experienced. In 1968, it was already beginning to be one of the more diversified student bodies in the Northeast—although that wasn't saying much. But I was part of that whole generation that was raised to ask questions—I was taught to be curious, to ask why, to have my own opinion. When I was growing up, it was always okay to challenge stuff—to not be satisfied with the way things are just because that's the way they've always been. And UMass encouraged that kind of independent thinking.

When I showed up, I was a mildly hippie-ish Californian. I was always a good dresser, always sharp. I got that from my mother, who had that Eastern good taste. I was wearing this buckskin fringe suede jacket that I wish I still had, and I was decked out in these little boots and little Afro puffs. I just thought I was the cutest thing. I was making a fashion statement, but it wasn't saying I was black. At that point I don't think I knew what black really was.

As I was walking back to my dorm one morning, a tall, dark-skinned young man approached me wearing traditional African attire and sandals. The contrast between how he was dressed and how I was dressed could not have been more pronounced. He introduced himself as Abdullah Something-or-Other, swept his eyes over me from head to toe with disdain, and pronounced, "Sister, you need to get yourself together, and you need to learn about your blackness." He was all in my face about how I wasn't black enough—I couldn't believe the way he talked to me. I was indignant.

Part of me wanted to shout, "Don't you know who I am?" but that was exactly the problem— he knew *precisely* who I was: "the-daughter-of." He was actually from Boston, but when I saw him in all his radiant blackness with his deep, resonant Afro-accented voice, you sure could have fooled me. At that moment, he had the commanding demeanor of an African tribal leader. I was intrigued and intimidated.

His tone softened. "We want to welcome you, my black sister, my beautiful black sister," he said. Now, I was intrigued and intimidated— and charmed. Abdullah handed me a stack of books and pamphlets, and proceeded to give me a recruitment rap for the Black Students Union. He told me there was going to be a meeting that night in the basement of one of the campus buildings. "You need to come down and meet your black brothers and sisters and get acquainted," he urged. "We know who you are, and you should know us." He left hanging in the air the not-too-subtle suggestion that perhaps because I was "the-daughter-of," I thought I was too good for other black folks— and after he departed, he left me standing there with my mouth open.

Up until that time, there just hadn't been

a lot of focus on my blackness. Dad was truly color-blind. He was an egalitarian. That was one of his strongest beliefs: Color did not matter. As a kid, I didn't really have any kind of a black experience as far as having a lot of black friends or even tracing any of my roots. I'm ashamed to say that my knowledge of my family tree was and is rather scant. For some reason, I don't remember getting a lot of history about either side of my family lineage from my parents.

When I was about twelve, I was a member of the Holiday Club, a club for black girls. Its members were the daughters of the black elite of Los Angeles—my dad was the only parent who was an entertainer. The other girls' fathers were doctors, lawyers, professionals, so it was a snooty club—but it was fun for kids, too. I'm sure that our mothers meant well: They were determined to turn us into proper ladies by having luncheons, teas, cotillions, and such. We met about once a month, and I did make a few lasting friendships in that group—these are lovely women that I've stayed in touch with—we still crack up together. There were about a dozen members, and that was about as many black friends my own age as I was around at any given time. Other than that, I didn't have many black friends. How could I? There were maybe six black girls at Northfield; it was the same thing at Buckley. Cookie used to joke that we pretty much integrated any school we went to the moment we stepped on campus.

It didn't seem much different when I got to UMass. There were approximately two hundred black kids in the entire student body of eighteen thousand. As I walked into the black students' meeting that night, I was feeling more than a little apprehensive. I had no idea what to expect. The meeting was already in progress when I arrived, and everyone turned to look at me as I walked in. I felt very out of place, and the room was packed—it seemed as though the entire black population of UMass was in that basement. Hell, they probably were. An articulate young guy who looked a little like Huey Newton was addressing the crowd, and as I stumbled around in the dim light of the audience trying to find a vacant chair, he stopped in mid-sentence to acknowledge me in a warm, genuine manner: "Welcome, sister." I felt four hundred eyeballs upon me and tried to make myself smaller as I nodded and sat down.

The speaker talked about his ideas for a Black Studies program and the need for more black faculty members. He said that the black student population at UMass had to act together to work for changes on the campus—and to support the impoverished black communities nearby. This guy was not talking revolution or rabble-rousing. Well, maybe a little. But primarily he was making good sense. Most black students at UMass were from the ghettos in Roxbury and Springfield, and voices around me were murmuring in assent: "You tell it," and, "Amen, brother." By the end of the meeting, I knew that this was a group of people with whom I felt at home.

Thus began one of the most important periods in my life. I became very conscious of my blackness, from a pride point of view, during my time at UMass. I had an opportunity to visit Africa many years later, and when we touched down on the continent—in Johannesburg—a very strange and wonderful feeling came over me. It's an affirmation of your roots, of who you are.

I guess you could say I've had a curious relationship with my roots. As I've mentioned, I have two sets of godparents—both of whom are Jewish. In Hancock Park we lived like a wealthy white family would live—which is to say like all of our neighbors. Before I got to UMass, I had never, to my knowledge, consciously experienced any racism that I recognized. In hindsight, maybe I didn't want to. There probably was some, but it went right by me. I went to all white schools pretty much all my life, and I never had a problem getting along with whites. At home, my mother hired blacks to raise us and feed us and drive us.

As a kid, I was always friendly with "the help" at our house. They were down-to-earth, country-raised black folks—they had those roots, as did my father's family. I loved my father's relatives, what little I saw of them. Actually, when I did see them, I would really gravitate to them. As I got older, I ended up having a very, very strong bond with my dad's sister, my Aunt Evelyn, who we called Aunt Bay. Because she was grounded spiritually, she never lost her roots, and there was a homeyness, a warmth and strength that came from within her. It's that thing you notice when you walk into someone's house and they've managed to bring their culture with them—they are proud of it. You feel it as soon as you walk in—they haven't lost it, abandoned it, or left it behind.

You might say I grew up in something akin to cultural schizophrenia—I could step away from that privileged Anglo world back into a black world at home, where there were relationships with the people who were still steeped in traditional black culture. I went from a totally all white atmosphere to this totally black experience that existed right in the middle of it. And it was seamless—I could go from one extreme to the other, from zero to a hundred, in a matter of moments.

When we were children, Carole and I got our hair done by this black lady we called Aunt Effie. She had a little salon in the basement of her house that you entered through a storm door in the back. There was also a man who did our hair sometimes. He was the first gay man that I ever met, but who knew about being gay then? I was like eight or nine years old. He and his lover were very good friends of my mother. His lover was my mom's interior decorator, and helped her put that house together. We called them Uncle Edward and Uncle Frank. They were sweet and loving people and made my early experience with homosexuality very positive.

I didn't realize how unique my upbringing had been till I got to college. Privilege had buffered me from the grittier aspects of black life in the United States, but once I started hanging out with other black students at UMass, my cultural education really began. These were people who lived in real neighborhoods. They lived near a store, where people behind the counter knew you and would run a tab for you. Where we went shopping near Hancock Park, everyone kind of knew each other, but I couldn't walk in and say, "I'll pay you next week when I see you."

I began to make friends with many of the kids at the meeting, and they welcomed me warmly into their homes. I was amazed at other people's houses. First of all, they were small—that's the first thing you notice if you were raised in a big house like I was. Small, maybe not as clean, because they don't have people to do that, and Mama works all day. Lots of kids, lots of people living there. And then there were the smells—food, lots of food smells always. Walking into these houses, you're always smelling food, as if the people who lived there didn't do anything but eat. But that was their enjoyment, that was their pleasure. They always had a TV and they always had food. I know this sounds as though I was a totally spoiled princess and pretty naive, but you have to understand that this was my experience. I can't apologize for it—it was what it was.

95

At UMass, my black friends would eat that Southern food all day long. I was amazed— it's not that we didn't eat Southern food in our house, especially during the holidays, but it was traditional or ceremonial—at Christmas, chitlins were in the same league as fruitcake or sweet potato pie. I didn't realize till much later that my mother was sneaky when I was growing up. She's New England-bred, but she would eat chitlins secretly on the side— and not out of a silver dish, either. I had no idea—she was always so highbrow, and I thought that she would never even touch something like that. (For those of you who don't know what chitlins are, don't miss out.)

A memorable highlight of my freshman year was meeting Dr. J., aka Julius Erving, bas- ketball player extraordinaire. We were in English 101 together, which was taught by John Healy, who was a good, but demanding, teacher and Julius was having a tough time in the class. Frankly, English was one of my better subjects—thank you for all those years of essay writing, Northfield—and I helped him. We hung out together and studied and were pals.

Julius may have struggled in English class, but on the basketball court, he had already earned his doctorate. The way he played was a thing of beauty, even when he was a college freshman. He used to jump and spin and fly and slam-dunk, with moves that were mind- boggling. No one in Massachusetts—or any- where else, for that matter—had ever seen an athlete perform like that before. He put the UMass Redmen basketball team on the map in a hurry.

I can't pretend that I wasn't in awe of him, and one night he took notice of me. We were over at his apartment studying English when, impulsively, we tossed Shakespeare aside and got down to an in-depth study of human physiology. What can I say? Julius had as many amazing moves in bed as he had on the basketball court. I was pretty inexperienced, but he knew more than enough for both of us. It was definitely a night to remember. You know that old cliché of "having the stamina of a stallion"? Well, honey, it is not just a cliché when you experience it. Julius was a lover extraordinaire, too, and we didn't stop until we heard the bells ringing for morning classes. It was a one-night tryst, but it was a loooong night—six hours' worth. It was great, but I couldn't walk the next day, and I had the worst case of bedroom hair you've ever seen.

Strangely enough, Julius and I went back to being pals after that amazing night and never slept together again. The next year, Julius was drafted to play pro basketball with the Virginia Squires of the old ABA, and he rocketed into basketball history. I don't even know whether Dr. J. remembers our wonderful night together, but I'll never forget it.

The next year at UMass I met a boy named Jimmy, who became my steady boyfriend. He was a delightful guy with a great disposition, kind of quiet and very smart, but his lifestyle was totally different from what I'd grown up with. He was from the projects in Springfield—his mother worked for the Post Office—and he was very cool. He wasn't slick—and believe me, I've met some of those—he was smooth, which is very different. He had a big Afro, and wore dashikis and little granny glasses.

He and I were this hot little item. He had wonderful hands and he was a great lover. He made me feel good, and he helped me to overcome some of the emotional baggage I carried about sex. As a child, I had been fondled several times by a male family member—someone we all loved and trusted—and had been exposed to his adult sexual desires. As most molested children do, I had kept this secret in my heart and never spoke about it until Cookie revealed that he had touched her in inappropriate ways, too. Thank God for the honesty and support of my sister. But those early confusions faded away in the pleasure of Jimmy's love. Jimmy was a sweet, sweet man, and he wanted to marry me, but we were such opposites, and I wasn't ready to marry anybody.

Jimmy loved being black, and I learned a lot about being black from being with him. I guess you could say that I went from being a little white girl in black skin to being a serious black sister. I thought I was a revolutionary. I grew this Afro that went out for days. My mother almost had a heart attack; she didn't know what to do with me. She thought I was going to turn into Angela Davis.

I worked briefly with the Black Panthers with their breakfast program for children, and with the Head Start early education program for economically deprived children. The fact that there was no Black Studies program at UMass was still an issue, and the black student body banded together and marched on the administration building to demand more black enrollment, more Black Studies courses, and more black teachers. Eventually we did end up with some excellent black professors. It took a while, but we got it done.

I was very proud to be a part of that university and that academic institution. The only thing that we were competing about in school was just to be smart. It wasn't about even being black as much as I felt I wanted to compete academically and athletically. And I had that opportunity. I really did. I was given every opportunity to do the best that I could. I wasn't the smartest kid in the class, but I wasn't the dumbest, and I never felt that I couldn't achieve and be good at something. And I think a lot of that encouragement came from my teachers, black and white alike.

The social side was good, too. I was a partying fool—Jimmy and I loved to par-tay. We smoked marijuana and drank Harvey Wall-bangers—orange juice, vodka, and Galliano liqueur—which were all the rage at the time. I wasn't really into the fraternity and sorority scene, although Jimmy belonged to Alpha Sigma Something-or-Other. However, the frat scene was big at UMass, and when I was a sophomore, I was encouraged to run for Carnival Queen. Winter Carnival is still a huge event at UMass—all the fraternities do ice sculptures and floats, a little like the Rose Parade, and the queen presides over the parade. A good girlfriend of mine, who was white, won, but I was first runner-up—not bad—so I was on the float with her, the first black girl ever to place in the Carnival Queen competition. I was very proud of that—especially since I never thought that I was particularly pretty. For our carnival concert that night, Bill Cosby was our MC. That's how we met. He started telling me how he knew my dad, and we've remained friends ever since. I call him Uncle Bill.

I also began to sing—but just a little. A friend of mine named Eddie Peterson had a group that he was singing with. I don't know what ever happened to Eddie, but he had a silky smooth voice like Johnny Mathis. On this particular weekend, he got strep throat, and he asked me if I would rehearse with his band. It was all very casual, because they knew I was Eddie's friend, and I had come to see him a few times when they were working. The guys in the band went into one of the rec rooms in the Student Union and closed the door. After they set up, we just started messing around. The Student Union was this big complex—the bookstore was there; the cafeteria was there; and there were always lots of people milling around. People passing by stuck their heads into the room where we were playing. By then everyone knew I could kind of sing, but no one knew I could *really* sing—I'm not sure I did either. That afternoon I belted out everything from "On a Clear Day You Can See Forever" to "Proud Mary." I was having a great time. The next thing I knew, the room had filled up with people sitting on the floor, listening to us jam.

Afterward all my friends gathered around me and said, "Girl, you oughtta sing—you really are good!" It was the first time anyone had ever suggested that I was cut out for a career in music, and the very thought of it scared the pants off me. I was worried about what my mother would think if she found out I'd been singing.

I had majored in child psychology, and thought I was serious about it. As happy as I was at UMass, I transferred to USC for the beginning of my junior year, fully intending to graduate from there. My dreams of entering the field of medicine had evolved into psychology—I was great in English and history, but not so good in the sciences (chemistry was the pits, and I hated dissecting those frogs!), which you had to excel in to go to med school.

There were no frogs to dissect in child psychology, and I really enjoyed the subject. The human mind is something that I'm both puzzled by and entranced with—why people do the things they do and how they think, what makes them tick. I wanted to get into child psychology because I wanted to get to people before they became adults. I wanted to work with kids between the ages of six and fifteen, and my idea was for music to be a part of the therapy. I was especially interested in working with under-privileged kids to help shape and expand their minds.

The grand plan was to major in psychology, go to grad school, go to the University of Heidelberg (I had a minor in German), get my master's or doctorate and open a clinic. I had all this worked out: USC had a very fine psychology department, and I figured it would be a lot easier for me to get into their grad school if I did some time there.

And once I got there, doing time was exactly what it felt like. USC was boring. I did meet O.J. Simpson there, and that's how we became friends. We ran into each other out in front of the library, in fact he practically ran me over. He was the new football hero on campus and I was quite impressed. We've been friends ever since, and some years later I visited him and his first wife, Margaret, in Buffalo, where he played for the Buffalo Bills.

While I was at USC, I decided to get a part-time job, which was nothing new for me. By this time I was twenty-one years old and pretty much independent. I had my own apartment on Oxford Avenue in downtown Los Angeles and a crazy roommate named Millie, and my little navy blue Volkswagen. For some reason, I was always the one in the family who was the go-getter, the one who didn't mind working. Beginning with that job my mother made me take at the sanitarium, I was always doing something. I'd been a switchboard operator, a camp counselor, a receptionist in a doctor's office, a waitress, a file clerk, a salesgirl. I developed a solid work ethic. I knew what it was to work, and I liked it.

While job hunting, I experienced a not-so-funny incident when I went down to the Angelus Funeral Home in Los Angeles to apply for work. My family knew the owners and the father of one of my girlfriends worked there as a mortician. I pulled into the parking lot but when I went inside, a lady said something to me that was very strange: "We just brought your Uncle Eddie in." Uncle Eddie was my father's oldest brother. They probably assumed that I was there as a representative of the family—to check out the body—because they ushered me into the back and showed him to me. That was bad. They had him propped up against what looked like a barber chair, stiff as a board. He was leaning kind of like a cardboard cutout against the chair.

I was traumatized and ran out. When I got back to my house, I ran upstairs and told my mother what I had discovered. I was pretty shaken up about it, but my mother's reaction was peculiar. Obviously she had already received the news while I was out, and appeared irritated and rather dispassionate. I remember wondering, "What the heck is wrong with her? Why isn't she upset about this?" The truth was that my mom was not that close to Uncle Eddie and wasn't nearly as upset about his death as she was mad at the people at the mortuary for showing him to me. I went to Uncle Eddie's funeral several days later. She did not.

Another reason I worked was because I couldn't just go and say, "Mom, can I have a couple hundred bucks to blow?" I was really into sunglasses at the time, and still to this day I always have a couple dozen pairs of sunglasses. Other than that I didn't really have to work, because my mom was paying my tuition and expenses. The deal was that she would support me in school if I was willing to do what she asked, which was to complete my education. There was no getting out of that deal, no way. At USC, I'd met a group of singers who wanted me to go with them to Hawaii, but my mother wouldn't budge. It wasn't even like I was *the* singer—this was a group, and I thought it would be a kick to travel with them. "That's not going to happen," she told me firmly. "You are doing well in school and you should finish your education." I was bummed, but she was adamant about getting my bachelor's degree. Part of me knew that she was right, so I got over it. I mean, it wasn't like I was pining to be a singer anyway.

I returned to UMass the summer of 1971, and it would prove to be a turning point in my life. I had already decided that I would live off campus for my senior year and found an apartment not too far from the university. Since the beginning of the fall semester was another couple of months away, I applied for a waitressing job at a restaurant called the Pub in the college town of Amherst. The owner's name was Jerry Jolly. His wife's name was Dolly. I'm not kidding. He gave me an application to fill out and was reading over my shoulder.

"Your name's Natalie Cole?"

"Yeah."

"You're the daughter of Nat King Cole?"

"Yeah."

"Well, don't you sing?"

"Yeah, a little."

"Well, you know," he said, "we're not doing anything with entertainment on the weekends and it's summer and it's kind of slow in here. You got a band? I'll give you a couple extra dollars to bring a band up in here to sing."

"Oh, okay."

Remember my friend Eddie Peterson with a voice like Johnny Mathis? Well, I basically stole his band and brought them to the restaurant. We called ourselves Black Magic. The first night we played was the Fourth of July. It dawned on me that this was the first time I was going to get paid for singing—and all I could think was, "My mother's going to kill me."

CHAPTER 7

Finding My Voice

I had spent the first couple of years in college fairly sober—a little marijuana, the usual college drinking parties and such (kids will be kids)—but when I got back to UMass as a senior, I got into LSD. I shared an off-campus apartment with a girl named Jamie, a pretty young woman with café-au-lait skin and a sultry face and pouty lips. She was very shapely, and she was cool—very cool—and I felt so uncool next to her, except I was the smarter one. Jamie never studied, maybe because she was sure she was going to marry a doctor, but she sure knew how to have fun. She was wild, believe me, she was wild. Together, we were an amazing pair.

Jamie and I noticed funny odors coming from the next-door apartment late at night, and finally asked our neighbor, Marty, what was going on. It turned out that Marty was an enterprising chemistry major who was working his way through college by making LSD and other hallucinogenics on the side. Back then, the news was full of stories about kids who'd taken acid, tripped out, and basically fried their brains, or worse. There had already been a guy who'd jumped out a window on campus; in

1969, Art Linkletter's daughter Diane was an inadvertent suicide in the same way.

Was I worried? Nah. What passed for conventional wisdom among recreational drug users such as Jamie and myself was that this was a quality-control problem. Bad acid made for bad trips or a one-way ticket to the funny farm; the good stuff was groovy. It was also a consumer awareness issue: If you knew your stuff had been made in a lab by a reliable source, it had to be okay. Since Marty had his own rather sophisticated little manufacturing facility, his output was "clean" laboratory acid, which meant it was safe—in our minds.

Marty was a true entrepreneur, offering a wide range of uppers and downers in addition to acid. He made acid, orange sunshine, yellow sunshine, Hawaiian sunshine, stars, windowpane, all the stuff with the hip, catchy names—whatever it was, he made it, and we took it all. He kept it in the freezer, and Jamie and I just went next door and got it. It was the neighborly thing to do. LSD was social—it was always a group thing, never solitary. You didn't do that stuff by yourself.

By early in my senior year, Black Magic had become a fixture at the Pub; people actually came there to hear us play. In very white Amherst in 1972, we were a curiosity as much as anything—four white musicians and a black chick singer—and that alone made us a draw. Basically we were a bar band and we were tearin' it up—I was doing Jimi Hendrix, Janis Joplin,

Grace Slick, Crosby, Stills & Nash, James Taylor, and some Aretha. I was still sporting some of my Afro, and to go onstage I'd wear these boots and hot pants. I was all that and a bag of chips, honey. At least I thought I was. In addition to our gig at the Pub, we also worked at UMass itself, in the lounge attached to a restaurant called Top of the Campus in the Student Union building. There was another club in the basement. I think it was called the Blue Wall. That's where I met Jay Leno for the first time. Jay was doing his comic stuff in the cellar while I was singing up in the crow's nest. Black Magic was pulling in maybe $600 or $800 to play weekends, and we split the money evenly among us. What did I know then?

The first night I went out of control I was actually onstage, singing at the Pub. I took some orange sunshine, or was it yellow sunshine? We were supposed to finish the set an hour before closing time, but by then I was Sunshine Superwoman. I just kept going and going—Owsley's own Energizer Bunny—one song, over and over and over again. Jamie was in the audience cracking up, but everyone else was reaching for the butterfly net. They were looking at me thinking, "She's lost it. She's totally gone and she's not coming back. See ya around, Natalie. It was nice knowing you." I was so zoned out that I just sang myself into a stupor—the guys in the band pretty much had to carry me offstage. After that, I fell into an exhausted heap.

A more reasonable person might have given

up on Marty's magic potions. Un-unh, but not me. I almost became a statistic one night on the twentieth floor of one of the UMass high-rise dorms called Southwest. I was so juiced up that I thought the laws of gravity didn't apply to me. I imagined that if I launched myself out that window, I would actually float gently down to the ground. I believed I could fly— yeah, me and Dumbo with the magic feather.

DAUGHTER OF NAT KING COLE, HIGH ON LSD, LEAPS FROM 20TH FLOOR DORM WINDOW

I was halfway out the window and spreading my wings when some friends of mine who were less wasted than I was hauled me back into the building. It was just God's grace that they grabbed me, because that would have been the end of me, right there. They gave me some blackberry brandy to bring my butt back to kind of seminormal. I don't know why that worked, or even where they found it, but it seemed to bring me out of wherever I was and back to some kind of reality. Nevertheless, I was still high the next morning, thirteen hours later. I was probably the only person walking across the campus to my eight-thirty Psych class whose feet were not touching the ground. And I was not happy about it. I kept praying, "Lord Jesus, please bring me down. If you get me through this, I'll never do it again." He kept His promise. As for me, the "I'll never do it again" only meant that I wouldn't drop acid again too soon. I moved on to do other things like stars and window-panes and mescaline—but I'm getting ahead of myself.

People often ask me why I got into drugs. I think the drugs were just waiting to happen, a culmination of not having resolved things in my life. My father's death was the begin-ning—it wasn't till years later that I was able to understand that I was still grieving for him, and that as "the-daughter-of" I was still walking in his shadow. At this time I was really adrift, a young woman without a dad, and without a good, solid relationship with my mom. I really can't put a lot of blame on her—now that I know a little bit more about the way she was raised, I know that nurturing was just not something she was capable of doing. Her mother died when she was young and she was raised by a stepmother, who, I am told, she didn't like very much. It would appear that her female role model was the formidable Aunt Lala, who spent a great deal more time concerned with what was correct and proper than with giving her emotional support as a child. It's no wonder that as a mother she didn't know how to reach out and help us when any of her children needed it. For some reason, I seemed to be the one who needed that help most often—and didn't get it.

The times were crazy. America was reeling. The period when I was in college was one of the most turbulent in our history. I arrived as a freshman just a couple of months after the assassinations of Martin Luther King and Bobby Kennedy, and mere weeks after the police riot at the Democratic Convention in Chicago. I got my UMass diploma right as a bunch of Cubans were arrested breaking into Democratic National Headquarters at the Watergate Complex. In between were the Black Power salute at the Mexico City Olympics, 400,000 kids in the mud at Woodstock, four dead in Ohio at Kent State, the My Lai Massacre, the trial of the Chicago 7, the Manson murders, the *Pentagon Papers,* and a guy who walked on the moon. It's a lot to wrap your brain around—straight or loaded.

I was still singing with Black Magic at the Pub when I met my first agent, a guy named Dick Booth from Fairfield, Connecticut. I guess word had traveled down the pike that there was this girl in Amherst at the Pub that he should check out, because Dick came there to see me just a short while before I was supposed to graduate. He actually said that classic line, "I'm gonna make you a star." And I thought he was nuts.

Dick had a small agency, but a big heart. I was his find, and by the time I got my degree, he already had jobs lined up for me. We were booked around New England and the Northeast, mostly in Connecticut and Massachusetts. "We" were no longer Black Magic.

When I graduated, I left Black Magic behind and put a new band together. I don't even remember where I got them from, but it really didn't matter. I still wasn't serious about singing as a career—I told myself I'd do this for the summer, just to sock a little money away before going to grad school in the fall.

One of our first engagements was at a restaurant in Greenfield, Massachusetts. As we pulled up to the place, I saw that they had put out a tiny placard that said "Appearing Tonight: Nat King Cole's Daughter." Hello? I mean, not even my own name, just "the-daughter-of." I was furious. I told the manager that if he didn't take down the damned sign, I wasn't going to go on. But the damage was already done—when the room was full, I knew that placard was the reason why. I really hated that, but it continued to happen.

I went into this part of my life with my elbows out. I was very defensive, because it was a way of protecting myself from really being upset. It was a very emotional thing to me—I resented being asked to sing my father's music. I wanted to sing whatever I wanted to sing. I couldn't understand all the comparing. How come they just couldn't appreciate me for what I was trying to do? How come they kept saying that I should sing his songs? I remember snapping at a reporter who told me, "You don't sound anything like your father." He said it like an accusation. "Right," I shot back. "My voice isn't as low as his." I had to learn how to be a little sarcastic with the press because they really got on my nerves.

I didn't know what I'd gotten myself into. I was stepping out there onstage every night on some kind of faith—faith that was not entirely my own. I enjoyed what I was doing, but I didn't fully understand why I was singing, other than that people kept telling me, "You have a talent. You should be a singer." It was coming from everywhere around me—my musicians thought that a life in music would be the most natural thing in the world for me, but I was fighting it. I was tremendously guilt-ridden by the fact that I knew I was supposed to be entering grad school. The last thing I felt capable of doing was filling my father's shoes.

The *first* thing on my mind was figuring out a way to tell my mother that I'd put the master's in psychology and the dream of a clinic on hold. By now the summer was almost over, and I'd struck a new bargain with myself—I'd do this for a year and hit grad school in the fall of '73. I knew she'd be terribly disappointed, but at this point I still thought I was headed for a distinguished career in mental health... eventually.

Even so, the subject was awkward, and I was reluctant to strike up a conversation that would begin, "Mom, I'm not going to graduate school yet. I'm going to run around the world like a crazy person and sing." I avoided the topic for a couple of months until I finally summoned up all my courage and told her what

I'd been doing. I also told her that I wanted to continue, at least for a while.

Just getting the words out of my mouth was difficult. I could tell that she was disappointed, but her response surprised me. "If you're going to do this," she told me quietly, "you can't be with just anybody. We've got to get you with some good people. You need real representation."

At her behest I parted company with Dick Booth, and late in 1972 she took me to New York to talk to the people at Creative Management Agency. (CMA eventually morphed into International Creative Management, and is still a powerhouse in booking talent in the entertainment business.) We had no trouble getting an appointment because CMA had represented my dad. When we arrived, we sailed right into the office of the president, Buddy Howe. He was a lovely, lovely man. He basically watched over me, and connected me with one of his top booking agents named Steve Cooper. Steve and I are still friends to this day, and whenever I see him I just kiss him all over his face—he's terrific.

Steve got me a lot of work. I sang my standard repertoire—songs like "Honky Tonk Women" and "You Are the Sunshine of My Life," but my father's empty shoes kept following me everywhere. People still wanted me to sing his music. I had actually sung "Mona Lisa" once in Connecticut somewhere, but the place started crying, so I tried to avoid it if I could. Some of these joints weren't exactly the

Ritz. I remember playing in a place where there was sawdust on the floor. When I spied the rednecks with big old cowboy hats over in the corner spittin' tobacco, I thought, "What the hell am I doing here?" I knew then that I'd never make it as a country singer. (Then again, never say never. Many years later, I recorded with the great Reba McEntire and *loved* singing country.)

We played the Catskills as a Top 40 band— we could do Top 40, or we could do rock. I had a very versatile band, and that's how I wanted it. By now it was indeed "my" band— we were billed as "Natalie Cole and *Fill-In-Band-Name-Here*." I changed bands like underwear—I guess I was still finding myself musically and always experimenting, so I had to have musicians who could keep up. We went through a whole bunch of names as the personnel changed. While we were still around Amherst, they were the Dissertations. Later, it was Cool Breeze. Whatever we were called, the added attraction was that this was "the-daughter-of"—Nat King Cole's daughter singing pop and R&B, not "Unforgettable."

I must say Steve did a great job for me. By the time I got a record deal it was 1974, only two years after college and I had already played in places such as the Bahamas, Bermuda, and even Madison Square Garden. We were really busy, almost constantly booked, and it wasn't long before Steve told me, "You're working so much that you really need a manager, someone who can guide your career and get you a record deal." He brought me a few people to interview, including Barbra Streisand's then-manager. I turned them down because all they wanted was for me to sing Nat King Cole songs. Then, Steve introduced me to Kevin Hunter, a friend from Montreal.

Kevin followed me around for several weeks before I signed with him. He came to my gigs and we'd talk afterward. He always had really good suggestions. When Kevin first saw me, I was working at a place called the Executive Inn in Buffalo, New York. I was there all the time, right across the street from the airport, doing my Top 40 show. I liked Kevin. He knew a lot about music, and he believed in me. He had a lot of soul—for an Irish guy. When we started talking about my career, I found him to be very smart. The main reason he got the job? He never mentioned my father's name.

These were the dues-paying days. I worked hard and didn't get a lot of money. When I first started with Kevin, we were doing five or six sets a night, forty-five-minute shows, eight to two in the morning. First of all, that's a lot of singing—you really need stamina. Of course, when you are young, you have the advantage of a lot of energy. For the most part, it didn't bother me.

I started in the trenches, and I'd have to say that those early days made me the performer that I am. I never worked a cruise, but I did do nightclubs, dinner lounges, Holiday Inns—

I remember well the bar-lounge in the Holiday Inn in Bridgeport, Connecticut. I played there a number of times. There was another great little spot called the Tap Room in New Canaan. I did the Executive Inn in Buffalo on a regular basis. I also played the Ramada Inn in Binghamton, New York, actually one of my favorite little cities. I was there so much that I probably paid for the wing they added. Almost from the beginning, I sold that place out every time.

Since I chose R&B, not everyone liked us. Mostly these were white clubs that catered to an older crowd. There were lots of places where the clientele was less than enthusiastic. We were just too loud for them. We did the Catskills, which I really hated. Of all the early days, I would say the Catskills were the worst. You knew exactly the kind of audience you were going to get—you saw them the first night, and you knew right away that it wasn't going to get any better. Every last one of them was a dinosaur.

I obstinately stuck with my own music. I was a Top 40 singer with a Top 40 band, and I wasn't gonna sing "Nature Boy" to a bunch of living fossils in leisure suits just because they'd been stuck in a time warp for twenty years. They were snobbish and clueless, and I was stubborn and on the defensive. When it came to being onstage, I was never really timid. When I would get on, something would happen to me and I'd get ballsy—very bossy, very brave. I would just take command. We

117

were booked into a very nice club at the Diplomat Hotel in Hallandale, Florida, right near Fort Lauderdale. While we were performing, this group of people came in, late and loud. I stopped the show dead in the water. After they were seated I read them the riot act— I was twenty-three years old. Kevin was absolutely mortified.

I never was the kind of singer who wanted to perform while people were eating. Some performers don't mind, but I always felt this way: "These people should be paying attention, but instead they're sitting there eating and dishes are clanging. That's rude." I couldn't wait for the day when I would perform for a roomful of people who actually paid to see me, and I would be more than just another course served. That was a goal of mine for a couple of years, because I knew that when my father reached a certain plateau in his career and was working some of the better showrooms like Copacabana, once he went onstage, the waiters would stop serving.

To me that was so very cool. What I wanted for me were things I had seen him achieve in his career, but I never wanted to be like my father. I never wanted to sing like him, sound like him, or do his music. After a while, it became kind of an obsession *not* to do it, to do anything but, just because that's what everybody wanted to hear.

I returned to the Caribbean. We worked in St. Maarten and in the Bahamas. I had four musicians with me. No singers, yet—well, actually, my band sang. It sounds exotic, but we worked hard and the pay was terrible. We were onstage till four o'clock in the morning, six nights a week. On my first trip there, I ended up singing while perched on a stool because I'd rented one of those stupid little motorbikes to go around the island, and didn't make a turn properly. Having ignored the advice "Don't steer—lean into the curve," I fractured my ankle when I fell off the bike, and had to do the rest of the gig seated on that stool. The best thing about it was that I learned how to sing well sitting down. Usually you get your air and energy from standing.

I was doing a few uppers and downers and windowpanes during this period—pushing the envelope, but getting reprieved every time. I had no idea how much I would need God's help in the next part of my life.

CHAPTER 8

Heroin

My college years marked a major passage in my life, as they do for many of us. I felt as though I had discovered my identity as a black woman. I had begun to find my voice as a singer. I had experienced a lot of new ideas, new people, new places, new abilities, and new attitudes within the nurturing cocoon of UMass Amherst. After my success at the Pub, I was a bit of a local celebrity in my own right. Me, Natalie. Not just "the-daughter-of."

I was definitely feeling cocky, sort of super-human—the way you should feel when you are young and the world is your oyster. I was ready to try anything and everything. Unfortunately, I did.

By this time I had a little money and I was living in a beautiful garden apartment in a gated complex in Springfield, Massachusetts, which is right on the interstate on the Massachusetts-Connecticut border. I'd moved there when I was still with Dick Booth, pre-CMA and pre-Kevin Hunter. At that time I was doing a lot of work up and down I-91, which runs right through Springfield, and I got to know that corridor real well.

I had a boyfriend. His name was Ricky and he was as cute as could be, but he was kind of a bad boy. He should have been wearing a neon sign that read **_Trouble_**. And the truth is I have some bad in me, too. Hence going from neat-looking conservative guys to guys who are more than just rough around the edges was no big deal for me. And anyway I've always been a sucker for a great smile. He was fine and he was sexy, and he was just oozing with this little macho thing he had going. We hooked up and I ended up getting hooked on heroin.

One day I was supposed to meet him at a

friend's house. I pulled up in front of the house and knocked. The door was unlocked, so I walked in. I called out, but nobody answered. I went upstairs, above the second story to a top floor like an attic. There was my boyfriend, with his friends. They were all shooting up.

I went over and sat near the window on this beautiful sunny day. Then I asked to try it, right then and there. Even though I was shocked to find them doing that, I was still trying on some level to make people like me, to be one of the gang. I also thought hard drugs was LSD, and acid was fun. I'd already done that, so you couldn't tell me nothin'. I was so stupid, I didn't even *know* I was stupid.

Rick gave me a little mound to snort. Now, almost everyone who snorts heroin for the first time gets violently ill. They get nauseated and throw up. But not me, nosirree. For better or worse, I am blessed with a garbage can constitution. And—no surprise here—I liked it. I was like Mikey in the old cereal commercial. The only reaction I had was to get totally high. That was my introduction into the world of heroin.

I was working a lot with the band all the time now. In May of 1973, I was one of the last acts to work at the old Copacabana, where my father had had so much success early in his career. Unlike Dad, however, I wasn't the headliner. I was the opener for a group called the Cornelius Brothers and Sister Rose. At the Copa I got to meet Jules Podell, a man with a big cigar and high friends in low places. He was cool with me, very cool, but he didn't give me a lot of credit for being able to stand alongside my father's shoes—let alone fill them.

A heroin high is like being deliciously sleepy, feeling warm and flushed, with not a care in the world. I loved the feeling and wanted to go to the next level, from snorting to skin-popping. Skin-popping is like getting a tetanus booster at the doctor's office—in medical terms it's intramuscular, not intravenous. I was slowly getting addicted, and I learned how to administer the shots myself. I went from skin-popping once a day, to twice a day, to four times a day, but I had no trouble performing. So why not up the ante some more? I wanted to try the real deal. I wanted to learn how to shoot up.

Within a month or so, Rick showed me how to do it. The procedure is like giving blood at the doctor's office, except that stuff is going in, not coming out. The crazy part is that I have small veins, and they are known as "rollers." For someone like me, a blood transfusion, should it become necessary, could be a critical process. So how crazy was I?

I've got one vein in my left hand that I basically killed. I'm a leftie, so working with my right hand and shooting up into my left hand became a real test of my manual dexterity. It was the only vein that worked, and it worked well for a while, until it just didn't work anymore—I wore it out. I could tie my wrist with almost anything—a belt, a scarf, a string. I could even do it without tying off. I remember a couple of times I was looking for veins in my ankle. I was a very creative junkie.

Eventually I got hooked. I hid my addiction as best I could from my mother. This was not as difficult as it would seem. Although my proper, image-conscious mother would have been all over me for my drug use, her attention was diverted by the new life she was struggling to build for herself. By this time my mother had been remarried for a few years. Her new husband was a screenwriter named Gary Devore. When my mom got serious about Gary, she was nervous about how we would all deal with it. He was white, pretty cool, and Jewish. He was fifteen years younger than she was at the time and very different from her previous husband, my dad.

I was grown, so I wasn't looking for a father figure. Well, that's not exactly true. I was still looking, but in all the wrong places. (My mom and Gary were long divorced when he came to a tragic end. Driving back to Los Angeles in 1997 during a rainstorm, he disappeared. He was missing for more than a year before his Ford Explorer was found partly submerged in a flood control channel. His wife at the time tried to cast suspicion on our family in regards to his disappearance. But that's another story.)

When she remarried, Mom sold the family estate in Hancock Park, and they all moved to Tyringham, in the artsy part of western Massachusetts. The twins really grew up there.

Tyringham was Norman Rockwell territory. It's not far from Stockbridge, best known to many baby boomers as the location of Alice's Restaurant, made famous by Arlo Guthrie.

My relationship with my gangster boyfriend Rick ended after a physical altercation between the two of us. When Rick slammed me up against the closet door, that was it. I don't even remember the reason, but it wasn't important. I was very thin, and he was pretty strong, but junkie or no junkie, I wasn't having any of that. I threw him out with his suitcase and his two Dobermans.

A couple of weeks after I got rid of him, I got evicted, too. By this time, I was so addicted that all of the rent money was starting to go to my habit. I got behind in the rent, and when I came home from a trip, the front door was padlocked. I pretty much lost everything and had to move into a small one-room efficiency apartment, with a Murphy bed that came out of the wall. It was clean, but it was one room, for Pete's sake. I guess the best part is that I was working a lot and wasn't there very much.

I was going down fast into my addiction. I had become quite friendly with a guy nicknamed Tiny Tim and his wife who lived in Springfield. They lived in the projects and I visited them frequently. One night I was over at Tim's, and the word was that he had gone to Mexico to bring back some brown heroin. At that time, brown was the crème de la crème of heroin—better than white, purer than white, and deadlier. I shot some of it. I was in the bathroom, and before I knew it, I had collapsed under the sink. As I was going unconscious I remember visualizing what the obituary headline would read:

**DAUGHTER OF
NAT KING COLE
ODS ON HEROIN
IN TENEMENT DRUG
DEN BATHROOM**

By the grace of God that didn't happen. Tim and his wife intervened by injecting me with salt and water. They saved my life. They may have been unlikely angels, but they were angels just the same.

Tiny Tim was just one of a collection of new pals—I no longer saw any of my old friends from UMass. Another was a hooker named Peaches, who had been a heroin addict for years. She was known all over Springfield, and Lord only knows why she took a liking to me, of all people. Sometimes we would shoot up together. Peaches was tall and thin and not terribly pretty, and could talk you out of your warmest clothes on the coldest night of winter. She was not the most attractive prostitute I'd ever seen, but as a lady of the night she was successful enough to support her habit and pay her rent. And if business was slow, she also had another line of work.

Peaches was an expert booster—she was the kind of woman who could walk out of the A&P with an Easter ham wedged between her thighs. Hell, this woman could take a piano and no one would notice. Most of her thievery, however, didn't require such heavy lifting. Like Fagin with the Artful Dodger and Oliver Twist, Peaches had a little gang of light-fingered bandits who specialized in stealing welfare checks out of people's mail-boxes. In a place like Springfield, everyone knew when the government payments were sup-posed to show up—all we had to do was wait for the mailman to come—and go. Did I say "we"? Yes, that's right, I had been reduced to committing mail theft.

Peaches took it upon herself to instruct me in the fine art of extricating welfare checks out of folks' mailboxes. Welcome to Felony 101, taught by an expert. When I turned out to be useless as a thief, Peaches found me another assignment: counterfeiting and check fraud. I mean, why bother stealing checks when you could just print your own? Two brothers I knew got some check stock imprinted with the names of corporations, and I started making up phony checks in relatively small amounts—$300, $600, $1,000 at the most—chump change, really. They even gave me one of those special typewriters—a Paymaster—that print out the amount in tiny colored dots, like on dividend checks from General Motors. That check writing machine was set up in my apartment—it looked a little like a kiddie slot machine, and I started creating bogus checks. I had my own little start-up cottage industry, right in my own 160-square-foot home. I lived a schizophrenic existence—felon by day, singer by night.

It was as if I'd turned into another person—and for a time, I did. I started calling myself "Lee Cole." Gee, I wonder why I didn't want anybody to know who I was? Honey, I sure wasn't "the-daughter-of" now. I was a long way from that feisty little girl in those "perfect Cole family" shots from my childhood on the cover of *Ebony* magazine. Never mind Unforgettable—try Undesirable. I'd become the kind of person the neighbors in Hancock Park had been worried about.

The most critical thing to keep in mind is that all this was done in desperation to support a drug habit. The lengths I went to—was driven to—were unquestionably suicidal and insane.

Amazingly enough, I was still making it to work. That's the insidious thing about heroin. You can still work. And to a point, you can still do a good job. Then you cross this invisible line and everything starts falling apart. You don't even know you've crossed the border into another country until it's too late. My first truly prestigious gig was a very trendy nightclub called Shepheard's, in the Drake Hotel in Manhattan. Valerie Simpson (of Ashford & Simpson) had a brother who was the soundman up there. Kevin was angling hard to get me a record deal, and this was a place where a singer could really get noticed by people in the business.

I was up there at the microphone on the small stage at Shepheard's, singing Roberta Flack's "Killing Me Softly";

He was strumming my pain with his fingers... Killing me softly with his... [thud]

"Miss Cole, are you all right? ...Miss Cole?"

In my junkie stupor I dimly perceived that someone was talking to me, but he sounded like he was talking to me from a big black hole.

"Miss Cole, you're fired. Please leave the hotel immediately."

Whoever he was, the voice was getting closer. I also felt a piece of cold steel embedded in my forehead. I fell slowly to the floor, semiconscious.

"Miss Cole. Can you hear me? I have called Security to have you removed from the premises."

I had nodded into the microphone—right in the middle of a performance. This was the fourth night of a two-week engagement. Heroin was killing me softly, all right, and Shepheard's fired me on the spot.

Even though I was still living in Massachusetts, a lot of my gigs by now were in New York, and I was traveling I-91 with great frequency between Springfield and Manhattan. One night I was in New York and I needed to get back to Springfield, but the car was out of gas, and I was out of stuff. Stuff...smack, antifreeze, aries, Aunt Hazel, carne, chieva, golden girl, hard candy, horse, number 8, red eagle, wings...the drug world had a thousand names for heroin back in that era. No matter what you called it, I didn't have any.

I was faced with a nasty dilemma. I had to decide if I was going to get gas or dope. I had twenty bucks—with another twenty, I could do both. Cookie by this time was living in New York, trying to make a name for herself in the theater. My sister seemed like the answer to a junkie's prayer. I called her from the gas station, asking her to help me out.

By now she had two sons and was living in a loft in the Village. I'd stayed with her a few times when I didn't want to make the long trip back up to Springfield, but I was so deep into heroin that she was concerned—and rightly so—that I was a bad example for her children. She told me that she was trying to raise her two boys properly, and she needed to set some boundaries. Of course, she was right and I realize that now, but in the shape I was in then, I didn't want to hear about no boundaries. She had kicked me out of her house a few days before, so for a night or two, I slept in my car.

Jonesing and desperate that night in the gas station, I tried to hit her up for twenty bucks, and she told me she didn't have it. I knew she was lying. Twenty friggin' dollars! I was good and pissed, and sick as a dog. I gassed up, got behind the wheel, and started driving. Somehow I got home, but not without throwing up out the car window every couple of miles, all the way up the New England Thruway to Springfield.

Withdrawal from heroin—there's nothin' like it. There's a part of you that just breaks when you come through it. Depending on how full of heroin you are, it takes anywhere from overnight to a couple of days to get it out of your system, and it's horrible. You throw up, you sleep, you sweat, you throw up, you sleep. But awake or asleep, you're delirious, you're cold, and some folks even start hallucinating. It's like a really bad flu, and if you get through it without killing yourself or somebody else, it's no small miracle. It was as if I'd just taken a beating. Something had broken inside me, and I was pretty sure that something was my spirit. It took fourteen hours before it was all over, and I felt as though I had been jumped on by an entire football team.

When I finally came through it, I woke up feeling rotten, but I was "clean." I looked at my reflection in the mirror and scared myself half to death. I didn't have too much time to reflect on my ravaged appearance before there was a knock on my door. When I opened it, there was this big, burly black man standing in the entryway. He showed me his badge, and asked if I'd kindly accompany him down to police headquarters.

His name was Big Al, and he was a detective with the Springfield Police Department. I already knew him by reputation—everyone in the shadow world I was now living in was scared shitless of him. He was a notoriously

tough cop who had zero tolerance for the
Three Ps—Pimps, Pushers, and Prostitutes—
my people! (Oh, I had some seedy friends!)
Despite the fact I was quaking in my boots all
the way downtown, he was actually very
decent to me. That's because it wasn't me he
wanted. He was after the check forgers and the
various drug dealers I had come to know. He
was determined to find them and when he did,
they were gonna do hard time. Al advised
me that if I had any sense left, I would get the
hell away from that town, ASAP.

Big Al didn't arrest me, but he did finger-
print me and sit me down in his office to
have a little chat. Basically he did that to
scare the shit out of me, and his technique
worked real good. Then he got on the phone
with Kevin Hunter and rattled off chapter
and verse from the penal code of all the counts
that could be brought against me. I was a
handy candidate as an accomplice or acces-
sory to charges of burglary, narcotics, grand
theft, and forgery—especially forgery—since
he'd grabbed the Paymaster from my apartment on the way out the door. "Get her the
hell out of Springfield," he said to my manager. "I can't protect her much longer." Big
Al was another one of my unlikely angels.

Kevin knew I was having some problems—
after the disaster at Shepheard's, he had to
know. But he didn't know how far gone I
was. This latest incident clinched it. He told
me in no uncertain terms that he was hauling
my sorry butt out of Springfield. The next day,

131

CHAPTER 9

Harlem

Kevin kept me on a short leash, and for a time, it worked. He installed me in an apartment on the Upper West Side at 93rd and River-side. Steve Cooper kept booking me into clubs, and the clubs were getting better—fewer Holiday Inns, more hip nightclubs—but the requests from the audience to sing Dad's music never went away. I tried like hell to avoid them altogether, but when they really really pressed me, I'd do "Mona Lisa" or "Love." Of course, I was getting requests for all kinds of music. Doing the club scene meant pretty much doing everything, because the audience was always making requests and if you didn't deliver, you weren't invited back. I'd be decked out in this great big Afro wig, and I'd do a rendition of Marvin Gaye's "What's Going On," Laura Nyro's "Stoned Soul Picnic," and a favorite, the Rolling Stones' "Honky Tonk Women." I also sang Crosby, Stills & Nash, James Taylor, Leon Russell, and Taj Mahal. My favorite of all times was, who

I packed everything I owned into my yellow Cougar and left for New York.

else but the Queen of Soul, Aretha Franklin. I sang Janis Joplin, Jimi Hendrix, and Joe Cocker—anything I could wail on. I was definitely a wailer, not a crooner.

I played at the famous Mr. Kelly's on Rush Street in Chicago. My dad had played there, too, and I'm sure my ability to get booked into places like Mr. Kelly's still had a lot to do with him. By now I'd gotten away from only Top 40 and had moved into an even more diverse repertoire that ranged from Broadway to Basie.

I remember doing a string of Aretha Franklin songs one night—songs such as "Dr. Feelgood," "Spanish Harlem," and "Rock Steady"—and feeling pretty good. The audience seemed to like me, and I finished the set thinking it had been a great show.

"Stop doing that Aretha stuff," Kevin told me after the show. "You sound too much like her."

I took that as a compliment. "I can't help it—she's my idol," I said.

It never occurred to me that I shouldn't do her music. Certainly I wasn't in Aretha's category, but I felt where she was coming from, and I was able to finesse a little bit of that and still interpret it in my own way, without outright stealing. Kevin was concerned that this was the time for me to establish my own distinctive sound, which meant that Aretha's stuff was off-limits.

Heroin, too, was off-limits. I managed to stay clean for a few weeks. Maybe I resisted for a couple of months, but eventually I got back into it. From my neighborhood up into Harlem, a person could score by just standing on the sidewalk and waiting for the light to change. For people who've never done drugs, it's hard to understand that there are degrees of addiction; instead of being a hard-core addict, I became an elitist junkie. I could be on heroin, go off for a couple of weeks, and then do it again. (When I finally got into rehab, that made me the envy of the rest of my therapy group—they all wished they'd been able to go off and on the drug of their choice like that. How sick is that? Chalk up another "win" for my garbage can constitution.)

I met a guy named Ronnie who was a pimp and wanted to "help me supplement my income." Ronnie couldn't have been much more than nineteen or twenty when I agreed to work for him. I was hired as the come-on girl, the cutie pie who would pique the attention of potential johns, and what I discovered was how many kinds of men seek out women in this profession. All were middle or upper class—there were no cabbies or bus drivers. I froze my ass off out there in Harlem, USA, in the winter of 1973, as I was acquiring this deep psychological insight. As the lure, I shared space on the street corners with the homeless and other souls fallen from grace. Once I'd made contact and Ronnie had concluded the financial transaction, the real business would happen under the bridge—without me.

The life, the danger, the absolute insidiousness of it all at that particular level is pathetic. We're not talking about being a professional call girl, where you get to put on some pretty clothes, hang out at a bar, and get paid to show well-heeled conventioneers a good time. We're talking about street hookers and what they have to do.

One day I was out there stopping traffic with one of Ronnie's more experienced girls, a veteran named Denise. Ronnie came up to the two of us and said, "Ladies, I have a special assignment. There's $200 in cash and a whole lot of blow if you'll go and do Big John."

Denise was interested in the money; the cocaine was just a fringe benefit. For me the cash wasn't nearly as important as the cocaine, so the two of us struck a bargain. We'd go together—she'd take the cash and "do" Big John; I'd be the chaperone and get the cocaine. The two of us walked into this funky brownstone—it wasn't much warmer inside than it was out of doors—and climbed the stairs.

When we entered the darkened apartment, I felt like I'd walked into a Fellini movie. The first thing I saw was an old man, half asleep, sitting on a chair in the corner. He was wearing a filthy old T-shirt, and he didn't move when he saw us. I don't even know if he was alive, come to think of it. I guess he was supposed to be the one-man audience for this little show.

The next thing I noticed was the biggest bowl of cocaine I'd ever seen in my life. "This is going to work out just fine," I thought to myself.

As my eyes adjusted to the gloom, I saw a tall man lying on the bed. He seemed to be holding a Little League baseball bat on his belly—except that it wasn't any Louisville Slugger. That was his penis, and it was standing at full attention. I mean, it was pointing at the ceiling. I'd never seen anything like that in my life.

At that moment, I can only imagine that I looked a lot like Buckwheat from *Our Gang*— totally freaked out. I know that every hair on my head stood up. I looked at Denise and she looked at me, and our instincts for self-preservation kicked in at that point. We both started backing out the door simultaneously. I never ran backward so fast in my life. No cash. No cocaine. No sale.

That encounter with Big John shocked me out of "the life." The thought of what might have gone down in that brownstone was enough to make me get my head straight and refocus on my career.

Some time later, Jerry Butler was playing at the Latin Casino in Cherry Hill, New Jersey. Together with his close friend Curtis Mayfield, Butler had been a driving force behind the Impressions, and was lead vocal on their hit "For Your Precious Love." Kevin Hunter had asked the club manager if he would put one more girl singer on the show in addition to Jerry's singers. That was fine by him, but he needed to get permission from Butler, who was initially opposed to the idea. Butler changed his mind when he learned that the girl they had in mind was Nat King Cole's daughter, and I went ahead and did the show.

Kevin was excited by the opportunity, because he had heard that record producers Kenny Gamble and Leon Huff were going to catch the show, and he was still working to get me a recording contract. But Gamble and Huff never showed and, ultimately, it was for the best. Back in Chicago, Jerry had a songwriting workshop, and suggested to Kevin that he should get in contact with two members of his group, a couple of guys named Marvin Yancy and Chuck Jackson.

Chuck and Marvin lived in Chicago, but as luck would have it, they were coming to New York shortly. We made an appointment to meet them at Lillian Tang Dance Studios a few weeks later. Unbeknownst to all of us it would be the meeting that would change our lives.

CHAPTER 10

Busted!

When Kevin and I walked into the rehearsal room upstairs at the Lillian Tang Dance Studios, I had no idea what to expect. A young light-skinned black man sat at an old upright piano in the middle of the room—just diddlin', as they say. He was wearing a little sideways applejack cap, like Donny Hathaway, and one of those flamboyant 1970s zoot-suity jackets with the wide lapels—very handsome. He was Marvin Yancy and he had a great energy and enthusiasm about him, and he played that keyboard really well. Oh, yes: He had a great smile, too.

Chuck Jackson was smallish, dark, and handsome, with perfect white teeth and jet black curly hair. He was a real sharp dresser, and I learned that both he and Marvin came from a gospel background. Chuck's gospel con- nection runs in the family—Jesse Jackson is his half-brother.

After introductions were made, things started to happen. Marvin asked me to start singing—"Sing anything," he told me. I don't remember what I sang, but it felt good. I wasn't more than eight bars into the song when I saw Marvin look at Chuck and Chuck look at Marvin and say, *Yessss!* Chuck's eyes were lighting up and Marvin was laughing. I had no idea what was going on but some- thing was happening in that room. Didn't seem like anything earth-shattering to me, but the two of them knew right away that they'd found what they'd been looking for.

Chuck and Marvin had been writing together for a couple of years, and their dream was to write for Aretha Franklin. Except they couldn't seem to get close to her. So they were looking for the *next* Aretha, and that's when I showed up. It's all very ironic, because Kevin had put so much emphasis on my staying away from doing her songs. And here these guys were saying the exact opposite—and I had no, and I mean *no*, gospel experience of any kind.

Marvin and Chuck hadn't much formal training, but they'd had a modestly successful group that they sang in together in Chicago called the Independents. The group had recorded one album, but they were really more interested in writing and producing. The moment I met them, I felt like they knew what they were doing and something good could happen. They had a very original and distinctive sound, and their whole approach, whether it was to music or composition, was just what I needed.

Based on a pending "connection" among the three of us, it was Kevin's plan to put a demo together and try to get a recording contract. Kevin paid for the demo; Chuck and Marvin had contacts with recording studios in Chicago. The plan was that Kevin would shop the demo to the record companies as soon as we were done.

They went back to Chicago and started writing. We put together a four-song demo tape, one song at a time. I was still working on the road, so I'd come into Chicago in between gigs, work with Chuck and Marvin, and go back out again. In a very short time, we became the best of friends.

I was proud of the tape when we were done. Kevin sent copies to major labels such as Columbia, RCA, and Motown. I tried not to be crushed when the answer came back, "Thanks, but no thanks."

Ironically, the biggest interest came from Capitol. A man by the name of Larkin Arnold, who'd started out in the Capitol legal department, had just been brought over to the creative side and named as head of a new R&B division at the label. Because he knew of Chuck and Marvin from their work with the Independents, he fished our demo out of the pile, and liked what he heard.

I thought it was a kick that out of all the record companies, Capitol was the last one I wanted to go with, because I just knew they were going to be shoving my dad down my throat. Capitol had been Dad's label."—"The House That Nat Built." Larkin hardly even mentioned him, and often told me—and the press—that he would have signed me even if my name had been Smith. He became my biggest supporter there for the next six or seven years, and I still have a lot of respect and love for him to this day. The man was and is a true gentleman, innovative and smart. He saw the need for Capitol to have a black R&B department and signed me to this new venture. Not long after he signed me, he also brought in a group named Tavares and a family called the Silvers. A little later came Peabo Bryson, a wonderfully talented singer who would become my friend.

Because Capitol was actually *still* my father's label, we were facing certain built-in problems. Dad's albums continued to pull in millions of dollars, and there was a need to protect "the franchise." Capitol executives joined my mother in their concern that we would somehow devalue Dad's name.

Larkin was well aware of how many of my father's albums were still selling, and how important it was to keep the Nat King Cole legend alive. He also wanted to avoid any suggestion that Capitol was exploiting "the-daughter-of" for mere profit. But he was also sure that he had something good in the material that Chuck and Marvin and I had created. He knew it was a hard sell to the executives in charge, but was willing to go the extra distance because the music turned him on. He thought that two songs from the demo, "I Love Him So Much" and "You," belonged on the album, and he wanted Chuck and Marvin to write another seven or eight songs to complete the package. We were thrilled.

Since Steve Cooper and Kevin Hunter were both Canadians, they'd been able to get me a lot of work north of the border, and I still had to fulfill several commitments in cities throughout Canada before we could start recording.

By stretching the truth, I guess I could say that my heroin habit was manageable. But I liked to keep my heroin close by—for security, you know. I wanted to take a little stuff with me for the trip into Canada, so before we left New York, I went up to Harlem and paid a visit to my old friend Henry.

Henry was a heroin dealer who lived on

113th Street, and we were friends. You know, your dealer is kind of like the neighborhood bartender who you can talk to about all your problems. Somehow you're convinced he's a good guy. All the while, he's killing you and you're paying him to do it. Henry was a good listener; even though I was a customer, we talked about real-life stuff. Periodically, we'd have these high kinds of conversations, about how we were going to get ourselves together—eventually. Henry always talked about how his grandmother had some land and how he was going to develop it and move down south and give up drugs. His ex-wife, Mattie, lived across the street from Henry, and she was a pal, too.

The band drove to our first show in Toronto at Adam's Rib, a nightclub on the Queensway, and I was going to fly in to meet them. We would then use our beat-up Volkswagen van to drive from one gig to another—honey, Canada is a big country. I called that old orange van *Shitty Shitty Bang Bang*, because of all the noise it made. We had just arrived in Toronto and I was settling into my room at the Lake Shore Boulevard Motel when there was a knock at the door. I opened it and what seemed like a platoon of Toronto police rushed in—both two-legged and four-legged. Between the uniformed officers, the detectives, and the German shepherds, it got real crowded in there real fast. The cops started tearing the room up until they found what they were looking for. And from the moment they arrived, it was obvious that they *knew* what they were looking for. Eventually they unearthed a little $25 bag of heroin along with my hypodermic needles and various paraphernalia from my suitcase, and I knew I was in deep shit. To make it all a little worse, the bust came right on my birthday, February 6, 1975.

One of the members of the band was with me in the room at the time, and he seemed to be in shock. In hindsight he might have been too much in shock, and I've often wondered whether he didn't drop a dime on me. Perhaps he himself had gotten busted, and then turned me in to get himself off. By the way the cops behaved, it's almost certain that someone had tipped them off that I was carrying, and I think they expected to find a lot more than they came up with.

I was put in handcuffs and taken to police headquarters. The laws are deadly regarding drug possession in Canada. After I was booked, fingerprinted, and photographed, they brought me into an interrogation room, shined a bright light in my face, and kept asking me, "Where are the kilos? We know you've got some kilos..." The captain or head detective really thought I was a big-time pusher. Of course, I couldn't tell them anything because I didn't know anything.

I was kept in a holding tank until it was time to transfer me, along with some other female prisoners, to the women's prison: I think most of the others must have been hookers; they knew the names of the guards, and what the drill was. Eventually, we were all herded into a paddy wagon and taken to the women's prison. One of the most incredible things about situations like this is the kind of people you meet along the way. Here I am in a jail cell. That's bad enough. And I am with some pretty hard, tough-looking women who are looking at me crazy, too. So I'm terrified. Yet, they knew that I didn't belong there and that I had bitten off a little more of life than I could chew. They treated me kindly and were sweet to me in their way.

We pulled up to the prison door, which, I swear, looked like those massive doors with steel knockers that squeak and groan before they close with a resounding clang. We were all put in a waiting room. One by one they called out the names of the other women in the group. Each one was given a set of jail clothes and told to hit the showers. Finally a matron bellowed out, "Cole," handed me a prison uniform, and pointed toward the shower stalls. It was just like it happens in the movies, only worse, because it was real. As I headed to the showers, I offered up another bargain to God. I said, "Lord, if you get me out of this one, I'll never do it again."

So I'm sitting on a cold steel bench, just outside the showers, contemplating suicide and praying feverishly and crying like a baby. Just as I finished removing my left boot, this woman called out, "Cole! You got visitors." God had delivered me. As it turned out, the guys in the band had gone to the owner of

Adam's Rib, where we were about to open. We hadn't gotten paid yet, but when they told him what had happened, he was kind enough to give us an advance—and fired us. They came straight to the jail and got me out. I was a very thankful little girl!

Eventually I had my arraignment before a judge, and a very pissed off one at that. In hindsight, I believe that man took my getting arrested as a personal insult and thereby took it upon himself to chastise me like I was his daughter. I had been given a court-appointed attorney and I expected the worst—and deserved it. Even though he could have ended my career before it started, he decided to give me another chance and put me on probation in the province of Ontario. But to make sure that I did not leave the country, I had to sign in at the Toronto police station every Wednesday for the next couple of months.

Well, the good news was that I wasn't headed for the slammer. The bad news was that I wasn't headed back to Chicago anytime soon. I was stuck in Canada.

While I was adjusting to my new circumstances, my manager had his own part of my mess to handle. He called my mother and asked for help. She sprang into action and managed to put a blanket on media coverage. It was about damage control. Between God and a great attorney that she found, the story of my arrest never made it to the States. (Couldn't happen that way today.) Everything stayed under wraps, except there was a small article in the Toronto press that ran in the back pages, which began, "an entertainer billed as being the daughter of the late Nat King Cole..."

The probation was good news from a felony standpoint, but rotten news from the album-obligation-to-Capitol standpoint. Everything was on hold while I was marooned up there, and we had to figure out a way to fool Capitol into believing that I was stuck there on show business, not legal business. We also had to come up with a way to make a living for the next few months. Kevin scrambled to put together a series of gigs that had me crisscrossing Canada like a hockey puck from one end and to the other. Strangely enough, the bad publicity seemed to make us popular in Canadian music clubs, and we worked almost every day during the time that I was stranded on probation. Every so often we'd hear from the record company—"When are you coming back?" But Kevin kept dancin', making dates and making excuses.

By then I was straight, scared straight, and feeling very alone. I hadn't had any problem with withdrawal, since I hadn't been using all that much. Marvin and Chuck, of course, were understandably upset to hear that I was still up in Canada. They were anxious to get started on the new record, but I couldn't bring myself to tell them the truth. Nevertheless, I surely needed a shoulder to lean on. I needed someone to talk to.

That's when my cousin Janice came into the

picture. Janice was the daughter of my father's sister Evelyn, Aunt Bay, and I'd not had any real contact with her since before Dad's funeral. Janice and I had met in Los Angeles when I was about nine or ten, and again at our Uncle Eddie's funeral. But I was desperate for someone to help who wouldn't tell my mother, and Janice was that someone. She didn't ask any questions. She didn't lay a guilt trip on me. At the drop of a hat, she put her own life on hold and came to Canada to travel with me for a couple of weeks, just to get me back on the right track. We were true vagabonds, but every Wednesday I had to get to Toronto—by train, boat, or plane—so I could sign in.

While I was in Canada I had a dream. In it I was in a hallway where I could hear footsteps. I was walking into a room and the windows were open. It was nighttime and two angels came and lifted me up and carried me out over the city. When I told Janice about the dream she said, "That was your father, coming to protect you." That was twenty-five years ago, and I have not had a dream about my father since. But that doesn't bother me, because he is inside me. I believe that I have his spirit with me always. There are times when I sense him as a presence, but I never see him; sometimes I wish I could.

Janice was as wide as she was tall (she was short), with a big old smile that would light up a room as soon as she walked in. Everybody loved Janice, but she was tough. Before she came to Canada to join me, she'd been driving a cab in the Loop, Chicago's business district. With her support, I got through a really humiliating period in my life. The time passed quickly enough, and Janice left for Chicago before I did, and the band left, too. By the time I got to the end, there was no one left but me and the van, *Shitty Shitty Bang Bang*.

The day that I was released from my probation was the day that I got the hell out of Canada—for good, I thought. I was banned from entering that country for three more years, which was fine with me. Now let me tell you how God works: Within the next year my first single, "This Will Be," was such a big hit that the Canadian government made a special provision for me to return and give a concert for five thousand fans. I've been coming back ever since and Canada has become one of my favorite places in the world.

Go figure.

Blame Canada? I can't. All things consid-ered, I'm surprised that I don't hate Canada, because the whole thing was such a horrible experience. But the judge was actually won-derful, and he did me a great service by allowing me to pursue my career. He was really another of my angels, and as they say, as one door closes, another opens.

I was done gypsying all over Canada and was finally free to return to Chicago—but return to what? I knew I'd be there for a while working on the album, and I needed a place to stay. It took only one phone call to Janice to find out that her mom, Aunt Bay, was more than happy to give me a roof over my head—family *is* family—all I had to do was get there.

CHAPTER 11

Expect a Miracle

The idea of driving alone from Toronto to Chicago, more than six hundred miles, was a big deal to me, and *Shitty Shitty Bang Bang* and I eyed each other warily as I got behind the wheel. The back of the van was full of amps and other band stuff, but very little else. By this time my entire wardrobe fit into a knapsack and a small suitcase. It's funny, although I'd been driving for ten years, I'd never really driven this long a distance by myself. As it turns out, I was not alone. I had a very important passenger; it was the Lord. I could see Him, because God gave me spiritual eyes for that trip and it was the most memorable drive of my life.

That was the best drive I've ever taken by myself—I was singing and humming all the way through Michigan. At one point there was a guy hitchhiking by the side of the road. I pulled over, but only to tell him, "I'm sorry, I can't pick you up. I already have a passenger." He looked at the empty passenger seat, then looked at me like I was some kind of loony soon as I drove away. I didn't care. I was completely and utterly happy and I was free at last—thank God Almighty. In no time at all, I found myself on the Chicago Expressway.

Aunt Bay was waiting for me, along with cousin Pam, Janice's little sister, who was in her early teens. I was greeted like one of the long lost (which I had been) as they wrapped their arms around me. When I stepped across the threshold of that little apartment, I knew I was home. There was so much strength there, so much love, and so much safety in such a small, unpretentious place.

Aunt Bay lived at 83rd and Martin Luther King Drive, right next door to the Tastee-Freez ice cream stand. She was a hairdresser—Dad's side of the family didn't have a lot of money; they were just regular folks. Pam had to give up her bedroom so that I could have a place to sleep. That was quite a sacrifice to make, because there were only two bedrooms in the house. But even if I had had the money to live else-where—and I didn't—they wouldn't have wanted me to be anywhere else. That's the kind of people they were. They weren't rich by any means, but they would give you the shirt off their backs. Money was always tight, and I was con-scious of being an extra mouth to feed in a household where there was nothing to spare. But there were always these little miracles that seemed to happen. I remember there were many times when that refrigerator was empty when I went to bed at night—I mean *empty*. There might be a big bottle of water, and maybe a plastic bag of carrots, but that would be it. Aunt Bay would sit at the table praying, as she did every night. The next day the fridge was so full you couldn't even close the door. I don't know who brought the food or how it actually came to be there, but somehow we were always provided for.

Janice and I had bonded a little in Canada, but now we had an opportunity to get really close. Janice was something else. She had what you call a hotline to the Lord, and she made it her lifelong goal to pray for me and pray with me. It was a shame I hadn't gotten in touch with her sooner, but after Dad died, Janice and Bay had dropped out of our lives. Mom just never brought us all together like Dad had done, and I suspect it was because she didn't really approve of Bay. These next few months in my relatives' company would prove to be a significant spiritual awakening for me and I learned a new phrase: "providential arrangement."

It was finally time to get back to some real business. Chuck and Marvin, of course, were happy to see me back. I had done my best to keep the real reason for my extended stay in Canada from them, and I was hopeful that they wouldn't press me for too many details. But once we started working on the album, the connection we had started to develop only got stronger, and Toronto seemed a million miles away.

We became great friends, and we were a trio, like the Three Musketeers. We had a real rapport with one another, and I enjoyed watching them work together. Chuck was suave, and very, very gorgeous (still is). The two of them loved one another like brothers, yet they were opposite in so many ways—in their appearance, in their lifestyle, in their clothes. I used to laugh about the fact that Marvin was single but acted like he was married, and Chuck was married but acted like he was single.

We worked together on the album through the spring. After they had a song roughed out, they'd bring it to me. I'd sing a little of it, and if it felt like it was going somewhere, I'd keep on singing, right there in the studio around the piano. Chuck mostly did the lyrics, and Marvin mostly did the melodies, but there was a wonderful dynamic interplay between them. Chuck would start a sentence and Marvin would finish it, and vice versa. They just knew each other so well. They had happy spirits, and happy spirits make for great lyrics.

I was growing a lot musically, not only because Chuck and Marvin were teaching me so much, but because they were writing songs specifically for me. Their music catered to my voice, and that made all the differ-ence. It was through working with them that I found my true voice. I had no idea what I wanted to do, but somehow Chuck and Marvin did. As an adolescent, I had spent a lot of years in front of a mirror, pantomiming to all of my favorite groups from the Motown days. I would also pretend what it was like working in a recording studio. Now I was getting ready to bring that fantasy to life in Chicago.

It was just ridiculous how much fun we had. It was not at all like working. Janice came to love Chuck and Marvin as much as I did. She attended all our recording sessions, and eventually became our "spiritual advisor." After we completed the recording, Chuck and Marvin saw to it that she actually got credited as our "spiritual advisor" on the album.

We recorded mostly at Curtom, which was Curtis Mayfield's studio, and at Paragon and Universal. Everything was done in Chicago, because that's where we came up with this kind of Chicago sound. It was a combination of Chuck and Marvin's songs, the way the musicians played, and the attitude they had. It was distinctive, just like the Motown sound or the Philly sound. It was unmistakable, and they created this sound for Natalie Cole. Whenever a Natalie Cole record came on, everybody knew right away what it was, and I was very proud of that.

Frequently, Janice and I and Chuck and Marvin would all go out to dinner after a working session. One night we went over to the house of Gene Barge, a horn arranger who was one of Marvin and Chuck's good friends. He would eventually be one of the arrangers on the album, along with Richard Evans. Besides his work as an arranger, he was

153

also quite an actor, and a lot of fun to be with. I don't know if he is still doing arrangements, but he certainly is in the movies a lot. In 1989 he did a Gene Hackman film, *The Package*, and has also been in some of the Bruce Willis films. He's always playing the role of an FBI agent or chief of security, and I grin every time I see him onscreen.

When we didn't go out for dinner, we would go over to Chuck's house, where his wife, Cheryl, who is a real sweetheart, would cook. Or sometimes we'd just hang at Bay's—now this was a lady who could cook, *burn*, I mean *throw down*. I learned to make some of my best dishes in that little kitchen—everything from cornbread to potato salad to short ribs. It became a very social thing for us, because all of us hung out together creating this beautiful music.

One night after one of Bay's amazing meals, Marvin sat down and started playing some beautiful chords at the small upright piano my father had given Bay a long time ago. He composed the music for a song that would end up being a signature tune for me. He was looking at me and I was looking at him and the result was "Inseparable," which soon became the title song on our first album. I couldn't believe it. Marvin was not as much of a lyricist, but he felt so deeply about the song that he started writing it right there in front of me, and later turned it over to Chuck to finish it. I was sitting on the couch, and I remember that this was the beginning of something else for me.

The recording process was the first and most important learning experience of my early career, mostly because this was the first time I was working with top notch musicians. They were consummate professionals. Of course, I had been around some of the world's best musicians already, because I practically grew up with the greatest composers and instrumentalists in the industry. But despite those early piano lessons, I didn't read music all that well, so I was in awe of any musician who could just come into a studio, sit down with a sheet of music, and start playing. I especially envied those background singers who could come in and start singing a part cold from a sheet of paper, but these were the kind of people I was recording with in Chicago.

There was one musician we worked with named Tennyson Stephens, who played piano parts on several songs on the *Inseparable* album. Marvin, of course, did the majority of the piano on the album, but Stephens sat in once in a while to do the organ work. I think he was one of the first people, besides Marvin and Chuck, to pick up on what I could bring to the music. Even if I didn't see it at the time, they did. They lent a certain sophistication and sensuality to the arrangements that would make my work stand out in the world of R&B.

Gene Barge arranged all the horns. He was just so reliable and dependable that he was very much like the rock of our team. He was sometimes the voice of reason, because Marvin and Chuck and I were always trying to create

155

things and take risks. Gene would sit back and he'd listen and then say, "Okay, now, let's come down to reality here," and he'd help us map it out a little better.

Another great musician we worked with was Richard Evans, who is now a professor at the Berklee School of Music. He had worked with Ramsey Lewis before doing the arranging for us. Eventually he went on to do the arrangements for Earth, Wind and Fire. He was just so incredibly rich in his arrangements, especially with the rhythm section, which was what we always recorded first.

There's nothing more thrilling to a musical artist than watching a song take shape, come to life, and then take flight. And here I was in the middle of it. I still was not sure how I got here, and really wasn't sure if this was where I was supposed to be. But I was willing to try anything, and I think I did try everything. We all got a tremendous kick out of working together. Chuck and Marvin and Gene and all of these classical string players and these funky R&B artists and me. It was like a musical adventure every day. That's why each song on the album has its own character. Each song called for a different little story. Everyone was excited by what we were able to do.

As executive producer, Larkin Arnold gave us breathing room to create and be creative. No pressure. We were free to try something and have it not work. He might suggest what would work better. When we had something for him to listen to, he was supportive because he saw potential. Then he'd tell us to go back and write some more. It's very different when you are doing something artistic or creative (you hope), because you are so busy enjoying the process that having a hit is not the primary concern. I was just happy to be in the mix.

One evening we were at Chuck's home, and Larkin was with us. He said, "Look, you've got seven or eight really good cuts here, but we just need one more something. Maybe it should be up-tempo, with a little more energy."

Chuck rose from his chair and said, "I've just been working on this song." He pulled this little raggedy piece of yellow paper out of his pocket and handed it to Marvin at the piano. Marvin played a few chords of what became "This Will Be," and Larkin said excitedly, "That's it! That's exactly what we need."

I didn't think so at all. My first reaction was, "I can't sing that! All the 'hugging-and-squeezing-and-kissing-and-pleasing'—forget it!" I said. "I'm never gonna get that right." What did I know? "This Will Be" became our first single.

The day we wrapped the album, we were all excited, and no one more than Marvin. We went out and had a little celebration, and I came back that night as full of joy as I'd been in a long time. Every night when I went to bed, one of the last things I saw was Aunt Bay's little sign on the dresser that said, "Expect a Miracle." I fell asleep believing it.

The very next morning Marvin called and

asked me out, just him and me—no Chuck, no Janice, just us. "It's Good Friday," he said, "There's somewhere I want to show you."

It was a given that we'd be going to a Baptist church on Good Friday, which by now was fine by me. I'd been raised as an Episcopalian, which was my mother's faith, but since I'd been in Chicago I'd been attending Baptist services every Sunday with Aunt Bay and Janice. It was just what you did on Sunday morning. Dad had been raised a Baptist—he was from a throw-down, hoe-down Baptist church, and his own daddy, my grandfather, was a preacher, but the few times I'd gone to Baptist services as a little kid, they'd scared me half to death. I remember being a little girl and holding on to someone real tight because the Baptist church is high-energy—every-thing is kind of overwhelming for a small person accustomed to dignified Episcopalian proceedings.

The evening of that Good Friday, Marvin picked me up at Aunt Bay's and took me to the Fountain of Life Baptist Church, located at 43rd Street and Cottage Avenue on Chicago's South Side. He led me to one of the pews and said, "I'll be right back."

Honey, did he ever come back! The next thing I saw was Marvin Yancy striding down the aisle in flowing robes. If he'd jumped out of a phone booth in a Superman get-up I wouldn't have been more flabbergasted. He was not just Marvin, but the Reverend Marvin Yancy,

Baptist preacher, producer-songwriter extraordinaire, and I was sitting amidst his congregation for Good Friday services.

God had said to expect a miracle, but He hadn't said what kind.

CHAPTER 12

This Will Be

Marvin was a revelation, and I was dumbstruck. I don't remember a word of what he preached that evening, but I do remember that he sat down at the piano and sang. Looking at him in this new light and in these surroundings, he was absolutely transformed, as was my opinion of him. This was the church that his father, Robert Adam Yancy Sr., had started; Marvin had taken over as pastor after his father died in 1968. He'd studied at the Dwight L. Moody Bible Institute. The name rang a bell: Dwight L. Moody had been the founder of a place from my childhood, the Northfield School in Northfield, Massachusetts.

Marvin was a man who was able to step out of his robes and back into the secular world. Some questioned whether a person could serve the Lord as a preacher and make record albums at the same time. But there was no contradiction as far as Marvin was concerned. It was all rather seamless. He served God no matter what he did. He was so multi-talented, and so modest. He could sing, compose, play the piano, and preach. And he was handsome, to boot. He was looking better to me all the time! This was the kind of man I knew I could spend a lifetime with.

After the service was over, he apologized for springing his other life on me. He'd deliberately waited until after we'd finished the album, because he wasn't sure how I felt about him, and he didn't want anything personal to get in the way. He wasn't ashamed of it, and he hadn't been trying to keep it from me; he was waiting for the appropriate time. And I guess I was ready, because I couldn't get that smile off my face.

Our relationship started developing then and there, and it had Aunt Bay's seal of approval, except that every Sunday I had to fight my way through all these other women. There's something sexy, almost magnetic, about a dynamic preacher, and after a service, the women would just line themselves up in front of Marvin's office waiting to see him. There were times when I could hardly get near him, and that bothered me.

One Sunday I got sufficiently aggravated that I went instead to the Third Baptist Church, where Aunt Bay went. The Third Baptist was pastored by a much older gentleman by the name of Reverend Fowler. I just loved him, like Aunt Bay did. And in June it was here, with Janice and Aunt Bay at my side, that I finally gave myself to the Lord and got baptized. Marvin hit the ceiling when he found out, because he felt I'd stolen that honor from him—he'd wanted so much to baptize me. Marvin was glad in a spiritual sense that I had come to the church, but he wasn't happy that I had done it outside of his territory, so to speak. Even preachers get political.

Nevertheless, we started to become an item, although it was a long-distance item. Between his music and his ministry, Marvin was pinned down in Chicago. I was working pretty steadily. I no longer traveled alone. I took my spiritual advisor, Janice, with me.

Larkin Arnold and all the top executives at Capitol were ecstatic with the album, and Larkin helped Kevin put together a show for me—now I had a regular band, and two backup singers, Sissy Peoples and Anita Anderson. Larkin was very savvy about promoting the records. He made the rounds of influential black disc jockeys with "This Will Be," but he didn't have to do much sweet-talking; the record began to take off.

I had been on the road for about two weeks and upon returning to New York, I went to visit my friend Henry. Drugs were not on my mind; I just wanted to have dinner and a good talk with him, like the old days. As I walked toward Henry's building on 113th, I noticed all these flashing lights and police cars. They were right in front of Henry's apartment. Something wasn't right. There was a small crowd around, and Mattie was there, too. She was crying. My mouth went dry when she told me that Henry had been shot up real bad. He was alive, but just barely, when they'd taken him to St. Luke's, but it didn't look good.

The next day I went to the hospital to visit him. Henry was well built, in his middle thirties, kind of handsome and healthy—at least for what he was doing, but he sure didn't look it when I got there. He looked pretty bad. His skin was a dull gray, and there were tubes coming and going everywhere in his body—out his nose, his mouth, his chest, his arms. He'd been shot four or five times. He couldn't breathe on his own, and he couldn't talk.

Mattie was there, and I pulled up a chair next to her over in the corner and started talking to Henry very quietly. I couldn't even tell if he heard me, because he was basically comatose. She told me that the doctors had pretty much given up on him. Just before I left I said, "I'm going to pray for you," because it surely looked like he could use a little help from that direction.

Two days later I came back for another visit and it was like seeing an apparition. Henry was sitting up, and all the tubes were gone. His skin had a glow to it—somehow he'd been healed overnight, literally. And he was speaking. "Hiya, Nat! How ya doin'?" He gave me a little crooked smile.

His recovery was a gift from God, and I

wanted to make sure he knew it. "Henry," I said, "you really should thank God that you're alive."

"Well, you know, I'm tough. I can take it," he drawled. "I've got a strong constitution and a great body...." I was thinking, "Lord, this man has gone from almost dead to acting cocky and stupid."

I shuddered involuntarily—basically Henry was giving himself the credit that belonged to Someone else. I looked at him and shook my head, saying to myself, "You know, he's talkin' crazy. He's truly grateful, Lord, truly. He really doesn't mean it. He really is grateful, Lord, truly."

Even Mattie said, "Henry, you ought to be ashamed of yourself. You need to thank the Lord for giving you back your life."

I had this funny little feeling inside when I left him, and I just couldn't shake it. When I got back home a couple of weeks later, I was anxious to check on Henry, since surely he was out of the hospital by now. I knocked on his door, but there was no answer. I figured he was out, so I went across the street to Mattie's. She was sitting in her little picture window, looking out onto the street. "Hi, Mattie. You seen Henry?"

"Didn't you hear? Girl, he died. Henry up and died right after you left."

I was stunned. I couldn't believe it. There's a saying that goes, "God don't like ugly, but He ain't stuck on pretty." In the back of my mind, I knew that God had snatched that

man's life away, because Henry did not give
Him the praise for his recovery.

This was a man I really cared about. He was
my friend and now he was dead. There was only
one way to deal with my pain.

"Mattie," I said through my tears, "you
gotta find me some stuff."

I weaved my way down the streets of Harlem,
high as a kite, crying like a fool. It was a hot
summer day, the kind where the folks up in
Harlem sit out on their porches, sipping
lemonade and trying to keep cool. They've got
their radios on and the city is just alive. As I
stumbled down 113th Street, I heard "This
Will Be" on the radio for the first time, coming
out of a little portable on somebody's front
stoop. I was too out of it to appreciate the irony.
It was the thirteenth of August, 1975. The
reason the date burns in my memory is that
I was due to open that night at a club called
Buddy's Place. Buddy's was owned by jazz
drummer Buddy Rich, and it was a major
prestige gig in New York.

Opening night was quite a scene. Cookie,
Marvin, Chuck, Aunt Bay, and Janice were
there, as were lots of my friends and a lot of
press, and they could tell that I was a mess even
before the first show. Everyone was horrified and Marvin was in shock. He'd never
seen me this way. He had no idea that I'd ever
used heroin.

Kevin was wondering whether I'd be able
to perform at all, and was debating the merits
of canceling the performance. With the press

out front, the last thing we needed was another Shepheard's incident. This was my first big public appearance since the record came out, and even though it wasn't exactly a theater, it was a well-known Manhattan hot spot, and how I performed would be noticed—especially if I bombed because I was obviously wasted.

It's funny that even though I was out of it, I remember what I was wearing. It was a black pleated chiffon dress, and I had a rhinestone necklace and earrings. I also had on this big Afro wig. I did two shows, and after the first show, Kevin and the rest of them couldn't believe that I'd even gotten through it, much less pulled off a musical triumph. I tore the place up for the first set, and then I went out and did it again. When we left the stage, the entire joint was stompin' and cheerin'. I got rave reviews. (Go figure.)

When I got to my dressing room, there were twenty pairs of eyes staring at me in amazement. My performance that night was nothing but God's intervention. He orchestrated it, He made it happen, and He saved my behind—again.

Janice was furious at me because of the state I was in, and once she helped me back to my apartment, I got violently ill. It was awful. I was throwing up and I thought my insides were going to come out. I was sweating and cold and my body was aching really badly.

I was miserable, but Janice couldn't have been happier. The way she saw it, each time I vomited, I was ridding my body of some more of the devil's work. Whenever my head was in the commode, she was in the corner on her hot-line to heaven shouting, "Oh, praise the Lord! Glory Hallelujah!" The more I retched, the louder she prayed, "Thank you, Jesus!... Just get out of here, Satan. Go away, Satan." It was quite a scene.

But it was the final scene. That was the last time I touched heroin.

From New York, it was on to other cities— and by now, "This Will Be" was racing up the *Billboard* charts. Things were taking off in a big way. I had a show at a well-known club in Los Angeles. It was an engagement at the Coconut Grove inside the Ambassador Hotel. I was the opening act for Herbie Hancock. One of my first celebrity fans was a famous young singer sitting in the audience named Stevie Wonder.

As it turned out, I met Stevie after the show and we liked each other immediately. There was a party being given for me up in my suite, and I invited Stevie to join us. At the end of the evening, after everyone else had left, Stevie stayed and sat at the piano, singing and playing for me into the morning. The piano was in a little alcove with a portal window that perfectly framed the moon shining through. That was magic.

By the time I played at the Kennedy Center in Washington, the Grammy nominations had already been announced. It was a sold-out show. That night onstage, I was dancin' and prancin' and shakin' my booty for all it was worth. I shook to the left, to the right, then I spun around and was shakin' to my band. I turned back to the audience, and that's when the unthinkable happened: my tube top slipped down. Honey, I got a big ovation that night. But, trust me, it was for all the wrong reasons.

The Grammys for 1975 were held at the Hollywood Palladium in late February of '76 and I was in my dressing room trailer when we got the news that I had won in the Best New Artist category. The next category I was nominated for was Best R&B Female Vocal Performance. This was a category that Aretha Franklin had won every year for the past nine years. I took away what would have been her tenth. It was a bittersweet moment because this was a woman I totally idolized, and if I'd been a little more together, I would have thanked Aretha from onstage, but I was too shocked. It was the beginning of an unfortunate period in our relationship.

Up until that point, we were on our way to becoming friends. Aretha had even put "This Will Be" in her show at Carnegie Hall. She was really upset with me because someone told her that I had really begun to believe that I was the new Queen of Soul, which was a big joke; I never believed I was queen of anything. The press had a field day, and for years they pitted us against each other and said a lot of things about me that just were not true. Aretha didn't know how devastated I felt over this rift, and we never got on the phone to say "Forget the press, let's you and me meet somewhere and talk this mess out, woman to woman." Even though Aretha was an idol of mine, I had something to say, too. I simply wanted to tell her that I loved and respected her, and that I wasn't the arrogant bitch that the press was making me out to be.

It was horrible. I spent the next several years being snubbed by her. She would get upset if I was on the same TV show with her, and she would walk out of the room if I walked in. That really hurt. Thankfully this has changed. Aretha and I are now friends, but it took a tragic event to bring us together.

CHAPTER 13

Marvin

After those Grammys, my life would never be the same. I had a Grammy-winning hit record in "This Will Be," and people started treating me differently. I was the same person, of course, but what changed was the way others perceived me. Even the postman and the customers at the corner market start treating you like you are someone special. I knew what it was to be treated special, but until now it was because of my father. I was slowly starting to shed the blessing/burden of being "the-daughter-of." Step by step, I was becoming "Natalie Cole" in my own right. It seemed as though just yesterday I was singing to folks who were more interested in drinking and eating than in who was behind the microphone. And all of a sudden, I was performing in giant venues where thousands of people were sitting there for one reason only: to listen to me. It was a rush to have people out in the parking lot hawking tickets and crowds of fans asking for your autograph. Plus, I now had an entourage—bodyguards, wardrobe assistants, secretaries, and all kinds of backstage assistants hired for the sole purpose of making my life easier.

The trappings of stardom are pretty amazing. Designers want you to wear their clothes, merchants want you to shop in their stores, and chefs hope you will eat in their restaurants. You get invited to all the big parties, and rub shoulders with other celebrities that you've admired for years. They treat you like family, even though they've just met you. And bankers are suddenly willing to cash your checks. Doors just open, like magic. They wave you on through or say, "Just step this way, Miss Cole," or "It's good to see you, Miss Cole."

I'm telling you, it's a real trip, but it's not for everybody. But I wish everyone could experience it at least once in a lifetime, just to see what it's like. Of course, that's not all being a star really is. I wish it were, but there is so much more that comes along with having your picture on the cover of a magazine, or having a hit record. Adulation from fans or being recognized at the supermarket is only a small part of it. Along with playing those giant venues, and having your name on billboards, come the record company executives, the business managers, accountants, press agents, and promoters who feel that they own a piece of you. It's like having a husband times ten, except that they try real hard to keep you happy. You have a new name: "Meal Ticket." As long as you are delivering, the world will beat a path to your door. And in those first few months after the Grammys, I had all the attention I ever wanted—and then some.

During the time from 1975 to 1979, the writing team of Chuck Jackson and Marvin Yancy turned out some great songs. Every day, it seemed, Marvin came up with a new tune on the piano, Chuck wrote the lyrics, and we went into the recording studio, putting it all down on tape with a full orchestra and arrangers. My contribution was growing on a daily basis, and eventually I even started writing my own songs, which I always had dreamed of doing. People were paying attention, and I loved every minute of it.

Natalie, our second album, went gold within a month of its release, and I eventually got my third Grammy—once again for Best R&B Female Vocal Performance—for a song I co-wrote, "Sophisticated Lady (She's a Different Lady)." "Mr. Melody," the first cut on the *Natalie* album, became a hit single. I also recorded "Good Morning Heartache," a Billie Holiday song about heroin addiction. It was one of my personal favorites because it spoke to that part of myself that I was trying to put behind me.

By now, I had moved out of my Upper West Side apartment to a Midtown high rise on 53rd and Seventh Avenue that came complete with a uniformed doorman and a beautiful view of the city. But none of it would have mattered if I didn't have Janice to share it with. I came to appreciate her even more. She was not just like an adopted sister, she was my best friend and she continued to fill the crucial role of spiritual advisor. Presidents have their ministers that they travel with, and a lot of stars travel with their guru. I had Janice. No matter where we were or what kind of show we were about to do, she would gather us all together, and we would hold hands and she would say a prayer. It really made a difference, because we were reminded that it wasn't any one of us who was making this thing happen, it was God. He was getting all the credit.

Perhaps the biggest change that year was all the performing we did in Europe. Larkin set up the concerts, and he always stayed one or two steps ahead of us, meeting with the press and seeing that everything went just right. I worked all over Germany, Denmark, Sweden, Brussels, and London, which has become one of my favorite cities. I loved the European audiences. They didn't care whether I was Natalie Cole or Natalie Jones, they didn't care whether I was black or white, they just wanted to hear me sing.

In Japan, I was invited to participate in a competition called the Tokyo Music Festival in June of 1976. I took first prize for the song "Mr. Melody," which was very popular in Asia. This is also how I became friends with a singer named Chaka Khan; we had met in the airline lounge at Los Angeles International Airport before getting on the airplane to fly to Tokyo. Chaka was singing with a group called Rufus, and I was already a big fan of their music. She was, to me, one of the greatest singers around, and I still consider her one of the best soulful voices I've ever heard. I sang with Chaka on a television show in Japan, and we thought about going on the road together at some point. Ironically, it was through Chaka that I met two people who would later play large roles in my life. Her personal assistant, Benita Hill, became one of my closest friends and is now my personal assistant, and her musical director and drummer, André Fischer, became my husband more than a decade later. (Actually, he did ask me out in Tokyo, but I was already holding the torch for Marvin by then.) During that same trip to Japan, I also became friendly with the Pointer Sisters. It was a special time, and the backstage meetings turned into friendships that are still strong today.

Janice, of course, continued to provide friendship, laughter, encouragement, and support, and without her I would never have been able to enjoy the success I was experiencing. But I was at a point in my life where I wanted someone next to me, someone to call my own.

I couldn't stop thinking about Marvin, and every time we were in the studio together, or working on some new song, I would always be so excited that my heart would begin to race. I would steal a glance over at him and he would be looking at me, too—we knew we were in love. All Marvin had to do was to play a chord or two and look up at me with those big brown eyes.

You can hear the love in those first few albums. He and I truly did make beautiful music together, but ours was a complicated relationship. Neither of us had been married before, and in a large sense, we had been married to our work. We both had full-blown careers; Marvin had two. He had his own church and a congregation, of which he was the pastor. I knew him, of course, as my songwriter, producer, and trusted musical advisor—and now, my boyfriend. That's a really complicated thing when you think about it.

Marvin had another problem in his life. He was trying to extricate himself from a relationship with another woman he had met before me, and she wasn't making it easy. She was determined not to lose him, no matter what. The situation between Marvin and me didn't get much better after *Natalie* was released, and we started putting the songs together for the next album, *Unpredictable*. The cuts on that album say it all: "This Heart," "Still in Love," "I Can't Breakaway," and "I've Got Love on My Mind." We loved one another, but we couldn't get it together. By now, everyone else could see how strongly we felt about each other. Chuck was thrilled, Aunt Bay considered it a "providential arrangement."

In the meantime, the music was only getting better. I wrote two of my own songs for the *Unpredictable* album, "Your Eyes" and "Peaceful Living." My writing was very different from Chuck and Marvin's, but they went with it anyway, even though my work had more of a pop sound to it. My songwriting ability could have developed faster if I had had the courage to make more quality time with the arrangers.

For the time being, I was content and happy just to get one of my own songs on an album. I guess I just didn't want to overshadow Chuck and Marvin, or try to take away their glory because they were riding high, and each of my own songs on the album was a space taken away from them. However, as my star began to rise, all the attention was on me. I was the one being invited all over the world. But the extraordinary part about Marvin—which is why I came to love him so much—was that he was not a jealous man.

One day, and I remember it well, Janice and I were sitting in my hotel room in Saginaw, Michigan. The year was 1976, and it was summer. Conversation turned to Marvin.

"Now, this has gone too far," Janice declared. "The two of you know you need to be together. So whatcha gonna do?"

I didn't have an answer, because recently I had found out that Marvin was planning to be married—but not to me. The girlfriend who had wanted him in her life so badly had gotten pregnant in an effort to keep him. Marvin was a pastor of a church that was beginning to get a lot of attention due to his success in the secular world. He was feeling the pressure to do the right thing and make this lady his wife. The wedding was only a few weeks away.

Even Chuck had called me to persuade me to talk him out of it. Now, I don't usually go around telling folks to call off their wedding plans, but Janice asked me two things that really struck me: "Do you love him? And, if so, how much?"

Well, there was a song on my first album called "I Love Him So Much"—till it hurts me... There was my answer. I was petrified picking up the receiver, and had no idea what I was going to say. I don't remember how I started the conversation, but I do recall him saying to me that he was getting ready to send out the wedding invitations. They were sitting on his desk.

When I heard this I said, "Marvin, you and I have to talk. I don't care where, but it's got to be in person, and it's not going to wait. I'll get on a plane to Chicago tomorrow. Meet me at the airport."

After my show the next night, I caught a plane to Chicago so that Marvin and I could talk face-to-face. I came prepared with this whole speech, but to my surprise, there wasn't a lot of talking. Marvin just took me in his arms and asked me to marry him.

"Natalie," he said, "I love you and I want to spend the rest of my life with you." Of course I said "Yes!"

I didn't have another engagement (I mean the musical kind!) for two days, so I didn't have to get right back on the plane. Marvin and I spent those two days in each other's arms, whether it was in bed or on the floor or at the diner around the corner from Marvin's house. On the third day, we decided on the spur of the moment to just go and do it.

Forget the big wedding ceremony. Forget the fancy dress. No invitations, no fancy dinner, no big media event. All that mattered to the two of us was the two of us. That was more romantic than anything we could have arranged. My wedding dress was loaned to me by a dear friend named Albertina Walker, who was also a famous gospel singer. She and her husband, who was also a minister, picked me up at Aunt Bay's house. I sat at the window overlooking the parking lot waiting for my future husband. This is one of my most delicious memories: seeing Marvin step out of the car and look up at me. I can honestly say it was one of the happiest days of my life.

Albertina and her husband, Reverend

Reynolds, picked us up on July 30, 1976, to take us down to the courthouse, where we got our license. With Reverend Reynolds reading from the Bible, we took our vows and became the Reverend and Mrs. Marvin Jerome Yancy in the back seat of their Cadillac. I had to get back on a plane; Marvin had to go preach a funeral; and we didn't see each other for ten days. But we knew much of our marriage would be lived over long-distance wires, and we were too happy to worry about distance.

CHAPTER 14

Robbie

Our marriage was a well-kept secret for about six months. The only people who knew were Aunt Bay, Janice, Pam, and Marvin's mother. I felt like a little girl, even though I was twenty-six years old. I had gone off and gotten married and didn't have to ask anyone's permission. I hadn't even told my mom. It was a giddy and a guilt-ridden feeling—but I got over it! This marriage didn't need her blessing—or anyone else's, for that matter. It was between me, Marvin, and God.

My working life did not let up. I performed for an entire week beginning November 23,

1976, during the Thanksgiving holidays at the Winter Garden, in New York. It was a sold-out performance every night in that 1,500-seat theater. Ramsey Lewis opened up for me. Can you imagine? That event was the beginning of my relationship with stage designer Stig Edgren, who created the look for the show. Stig had the whole thing animated, with the scenery moving in the background and an intricate lighting system that added to the overall ambience of the night. It was all perfectly beautiful. There is nothing like New York audiences. It's a make-or-break situation. If they don't like what you're doing, they'll let you know it.

My mother was in the audience on the first night, and so was Marvin. They met for the first time in my dressing room. My mother didn't know anything about this man other than that he had just married her daughter. I think she had been of the opinion that I would never get married, so naturally she was appre-hensive and suspicious. I suppose the whole thing was difficult for her. To me, there really couldn't have been anything more perfect than me marrying a producer-songwriter. I don't know what was going on with my mom and me that night, but it was just one more thing in a growing list of troubles that the two of us were having. I was beginning to feel that I just couldn't win with her. I didn't let her spoil the moment for me, though. Marvin and I were in love and nothing else mattered.

I discovered I was pregnant in January of

1977, while I was taping *Sinatra and Friends*. Frank and I sang "I Get a Kick Out of You," and I was baaaaad. At fifty-two, Frank was still very much in his prime. I may have been intimidated by his legend, but I wasn't intimidated musically. I was only twenty-seven years old, and I'd never sung that song before in my life, but I knew what to do. Even though we'd only rehearsed it once, it seemed to come naturally to me. When we were finished, he looked at me and said, "You're going to go far." We had just finished the song when my doctor called me on the set with the news: "The rabbit is dead." I was ecstatic. In fact, I was just so excited and proud to be carrying Marvin's baby that I began wearing maternity dresses way before I needed to. I was probably the only expectant mother in America struttin' around in sequined maternity dresses singin' R&B. Even with morning sickness, those nine months of my pregnancy were the most special and happiest of my life.

I remember one time when I was performing down in Georgia. Marvin and I were sitting eating breakfast early in the morning, getting ready to either get on the bus or catch a plane to the next place. I ordered some grits and they didn't stay down for two seconds. I couldn't make it to the ladies' room, and ended up in the men's bathroom. Everyone was so concerned, especially Marvin. The waitresses were nice about everything, considering the mess I made in the restaurant, but concerned that everything was all right with the baby. What made the moment so special for me was that this was when I first started feeling move- ment inside of me. That's really got to be one of God's greatest mysteries: knowing that there's a person living inside of you. Although I was throwing up grits, here was our child sticking his elbow in my side. The funny thing about the whole incident is that grits came to be what my baby loved best. He still does.

Eventually, we had a real wedding cere- mony at Marvin's church, with a lovely recep- tion at the Ritz in downtown Chicago. The date was February 6, 1977—my twenty-seventh birthday. My mother did not attend. A few weeks later, we had yet another reception in Los Angeles at the Beverly Hills Hotel. We kept an apartment in Chicago, and an apartment in New York, and eventually we purchased a house in Los Angeles.

Our new home was at 2920 Hutton Drive in Benedict Canyon in Beverly Hills. Marvin lived there during the week, and then every weekend he would return to his church. He didn't leave all of his pastoral duties in Chicago, though. He baptized Wayne, my conga player, and Stella, our housekeeper, in our swimming pool. I was still working, of course, and kept working until my seventh month, although I did take things a bit easier. Once Marvin and I bought the house on Hutton Drive and I was expecting, I made good on a promise I'd made to myself—and to God—back when I was in Chicago making *Inseparable*. Aunt Bay never realized any financial benefit from my father's will, and she'd been entirely unselfish in giving me her love and support at a time when I really needed it. I vowed then that I'd try somehow to give back a little of what she'd given me. I moved her (and Janice and Pam, too) out to Los Angeles and set her up in an apartment right near her church. She never had to worry about money again; I took care of her right up until she died.

While pregnant, I also recorded my fourth album. I called it *Thankful*. *Thankful*, like *Unpredictable*, would eventually go platinum, giving me the distinction of being the first female artist to have two platinum releases in the same year. "Our Love," the second cut on the album, would become my fifth consecutive number one single.

There were a few other things that made *Thankful* a special album for me. The most important was that three of the cuts on the album were my own compositions. I wrote "La Costa" with Linda Williams, my piano player and conductor when I was on the road. She was a brilliant and gifted musician, and in those days a lady conductor was a rare sight. "Annie Mae" and "Keeping a Light" were entirely my own creations. "Annie Mae" was my favorite because it was a ballad of sorts, inspired by the true-life story of a young woman I knew, our housekeeper, Stella.

Stella had come to work for Marvin and me in our home in Los Angeles. She was a little younger than I was, but she'd had a really rough life, and she didn't have any kind of stable background whatsoever. She had left home when she was fourteen and didn't have much of an education, if any. To survive she had to hustle for everything. She worked for us for about two or three years. One day, Stella sat me down and talked to me about her life. It inspired me that she had gone through so much and didn't hold any bitterness. She held no grudges. You could see the hard life in her face, but she had such a good heart.

That inspired me to write a song for her. I went right to the piano that evening after talking to her. Instead of calling the song "Sarah" or "Jane" or something, I called it "Annie Mae," because to me that name is a symbol for girls who are looking for a better life than what they have. There might be abuse in the home, or their mothers are too busy doing whatever they're doing, so they're kind of on their own. On my travels, I had seen and heard lots of those kinds of stories. There are so many young people like that out there. Homeless kids, just trying to find their way. Funny that this should be the first song that I wrote without help or encouragement from anyone. I found out later on that my mother-in-law was called Annie Mae, and she loved that song. It also turns out that Tina Turner's real name is Annie Mae, so I think God was helping me out in choosing the song's title.

My pregnancy was beginning to be pretty obvious, so when *Thankful* was released, the cover was a painting of me instead of a photograph. It was done by an artist named Craig Nelson. I still love that painting, as I love the album itself. It really is one of my favorites. *Thankful* was absolutely what that was all about, and how I felt.

I recorded an album called *Natalie...Live!* and we taped several shows from the Latin Casino in New Jersey as well as the Universal Amphitheatre in Los Angeles. Live shows with the right audience are a win-win situation. There are no holds barred. You can just go crazy if you want to, which is something you can't do in a recording studio because you need to stay within some boundaries. Plus, the cheering from the audience is invigorating. It feels like electricity is in the air and it's infectious. Everyone's in love with you and you are their guru for as long as they'll follow—very empowering, indeed.

I think that those who do their best work in a recording studio and are also able to take that best onstage are rarities. My father was one of those people, and I have learned so much from watching him—this dual talent is what I've always worked toward as a performer. For me, interaction with the audience is everything. And not only with the audience, but with the musicians. I like to look them in the eye, and everyone is a player in this musical journey. I remember watching Sly & the Family Stone when I was in college. Sly could just kick ass on the stage; so could Kool and the Gang and the Rolling Stones. I learned a lot watching people like Chaka Khan, Janis Joplin, and

Patti LaBelle, because they grab the audience and they don't let go.

We had a real tight group by the time we went live. Everybody knew what they were supposed to do. There wasn't any hesitation or any anxiety. The recording people also did a very good job, considering what they had to do. It's very clever how the album sounds like everything was done on one night, but it's actually our best songs from different nights. The *Natalie...Live!* album contains some songs that I never recorded in the studio. I've always enjoyed experimenting with different styles, so I took the old Doris Day tune "Que Sera Sera" (which had already been done by Sly Stone) and put a different spin on it. The Beatles' classic "Lucy in the Sky with Diamonds" is a particular favorite of mine. I stole a little bit of their style and Elton John's version gave me some ideas to re-create this unique song. "Cry Baby" is my tribute to Janis Joplin. She is my favorite rock 'n' roll singer of all time. All of these tunes are wailin' songs. Wailin' is good for the soul sometimes, and I guess that's the rock 'n' roll inside of me trying to come out.

I remember the night at the Universal Amphitheatre well. We were in high gear from the first note to the last, and the audience was fired up. I jumped around on that stage like a crazy lady. Billy Dee Williams was sitting in the audience and looking at me as if any moment he thought I was going to have that baby...right there. By now, I had been on the road so much, and traveled to so many places, that I was certain my baby would be born with wings. Actually that wasn't far from the truth—we were about to give birth to an angel.

The only time I got scared about the pregnancy was one night after doing a show in Canada, before I came off the road. I was reading—of all things—Stephen King's *The Shining*. I was reading this book and I was three months' pregnant, and I had to put it down because it scared the hell out of me. It scared me so much I was afraid it was going to affect my baby.

I came off the road in my seventh month, and Marvin and I began attending Lamaze classes. What a hoot that was. The way he was acting, I had to keep reminding him that *I* was the pregnant one and not him! But he was great. He wanted so much to do the right thing and he was trying so hard.

In our Lamaze classes they told us to keep a bag packed with everything you were going to need, along with a photograph of a happy time, something you can focus on to conjure up warm and relaxing feelings. I chose a picture of Marvin and me from our wedding reception in Los Angeles. Of course, when the real time came and I was in labor, I wanted to throw darts at it.

On October 13, 1977, we were on our way back from Lamaze class and had stopped to pick up some Kentucky Fried Chicken because I had this incredible craving. I really needed the Colonel in a major way! Janice was staying with us, so when we got home, all three of us were in the bedroom watching TV. I hadn't eaten more than two bites when the labor pains started.

Marvin was calm and collected. He called the doctor and he agreed to meet us at Cedars. Dr. Brooks ended up driving from Palm Springs to the hospital, bless his heart. He's my doctor to this day. Before I left, I called my mother to tell her that the time had come. Mom told me: "Okay, I'm coming. But first I'm going to the World Series. Don't have the baby until after the game." I couldn't believe it. I knew she was a baseball fanatic, but really! It was the World Series, the Yankees vs. the Dodgers, and I thought she was kid-ding—she wasn't. She said, "Try to hold on until I get back from Dodger Stadium." Mom eventually made it to the hospital on time. In fact, my entire family was there. All of them made it. There were about twenty people sit-ting outside in the lounge waiting for the big moment. And you know what? My son didn't get here until absolutely everyone else arrived. It was 8:59 P.M. on October 14, 1977.

I ended up being in labor for almost nine-teen hours, and it was worth every second. Except that everything I learned in Lamaze went right out the window. I wouldn't let Marvin touch me.

I thought I could do this without drugs... By the thirteenth hour, I was calling for an epidural. I wanted that baby out, and right away.

"Let's get going with that spinal," I was shouting.

Robert Adam Yancy came out perfect. He was six pounds, four ounces, healthy and beautiful. The cutest little thing—with a mop of black hair—just like a little papoose, like a little Indian baby. My little angel.

I was in the hospital three days. The day that Marvin and I took Robbie home, I had him on my lap, and he was looking up at me and he gave me this little wink. I swear I saw it on his three-day-old face, and he looked just like my father. And I thought, "He's got the spirit of Nat in him." My boy was going to be just fine. Dad was part of this, God was part of this, and Marvin and I were part of it. Robbie was to be our greatest blessing.

CHAPTER 15

In the Public Eye

A day or two after Robbie was born, my doctor said something along the lines of, "Don't change your schedule to accommodate your child, let your child integrate into your schedule."

I thought that was a very profound suggestion, because most young mothers take the opposite tack and start building their lives around their children. That is not nec-essarily a bad thing to do, but it does not always work out well. I may not be the best person to dispense child-rearing advice, but I will say that this was one thing I got right. Robbie is very comfortable with our household's hectic, fast-paced lifestyle. I'm always going, going, going. It was that way before his birth, it was that way when he first arrived, and things haven't changed. And spoiled? You bet. The first couple of months, Robbie's cheeks were pink with rashes from people kissing him constantly.

Robbie was not just a wonderful baby. He was a precious baby. I hovered over him, even when Marvin and I hired a nanny, which we needed because both Marvin and I had careers that couldn't be put on hold indefi-nitely.

I had hired a young woman named Etta McCrae to work for us just before Robbie was born, and when we began to think about a nanny, she had a suggestion: "I have a sister, Drue, who has been with Sarah Vaughan for many years. She basically raised Sarah's daughter, Paris. Would you like to meet her?" Marvin and I ended up at a concert a few nights later with Sarah Vaughan opening for Frank Sinatra at the Greek Theater. How fabulous was that? After the show, we went backstage and met the great Sassy—I never had a chance to really thank her because when she introduced me to Drue, I knew that she would be perfect for us. She had obviously done a good job with Paris, who was already a charming young woman, and I think I probably offered her the job on the spot. Drue became such a cornerstone in our lives and she stayed with us for many years. She helped me run my home and raise my son—and she helped raise me, too.

Robbie was a good baby, a beautiful child, inside and out. To this day, he's a very sweet young man—and he still makes me crazy. He wasn't mischievous, as boys go. He wasn't like a Dennis the Menace. He loved music right away, of course, but then I guess he got it honest. He was on the road with me inside my tummy that whole time I was singing all of those songs, so when he heard my voice after he was born—that was the same voice he knew so well. That is a special kind of connection to have with your child.

Along with becoming a mother, I also had to learn how to be a minister's wife. I don't know if I really fit, but I did what I could. I was a performer through and through, but at least on Sunday mornings, I became a pastor's wife. I made sure that I wasn't doing any concerts on Saturday evenings (that wasn't an easy task), and that I was in Chicago, dressed in my Sunday best. I sat in the front-row pew with Robbie on my lap. It wasn't a sacrifice. I enjoyed it and my own relationship with God was very important to me on a daily basis.

With a new baby, our home life became

very important to us. Together we worked to try to create an environment that was comfortable, whether it was our choice of furnishings or how we made up our schedules. And the home we created was also great for entertaining. Everyone wanted to come over to our house to hang out or play music—and there was always plenty of that to go around. Living with Marvin, I came to appreciate more and more just what a unique artist he was. He would sit at the piano for hours on end, and it was a joy for me to watch and listen. Marvin had a great sense of humor and a great laugh. He was so very passionate about his music and didn't care very much about writing hit songs. That was more Chuck's way, which is probably why they worked so well together. Chuck always had a feel for what was going to work, and if it hadn't been for Chuck, Marvin perhaps would never have had any hits.

When Robbie was about three months old, I prepared to go back to work. Marvin and I agreed that I should keep Robbie with me and we would work out being together as a family. It was a hell of a schedule and, in hindsight, I can't say it was the best way to go. But for a while, it worked.

In April of 1978 I had my first television musical special. Dick Clark was the producer, and I was delighted because he had been so helpful at the early stages of my career when he invited me to appear on his show, *American Bandstand*. It was the MTV of its day, and many black acts got their start because of his show.

I was on it twice. I am grateful to people like Dick Clark, Mike Douglas, Dinah Shore, Casey Kasem, Merv Griffin, and so many others who believed in my talent. They contributed to my confidence as a singer and a recording artist. *The Natalie Cole Special* was a very sophisticated presentation, thanks to Dick Clark. My musical guests were great: Johnny Mathis (nervous and cute); Stephen Bishop (brilliant); and Earth, Wind and Fire (awesome). To top it off, I had the opportunity to work with Nelson Riddle and his orchestra. Nelson Riddle had been my father's conductor and arranger for about fifteen years, and a kinder, more solid man you've never met. He and my father were good friends, and during those rare times I was able to be at a recording session, it was obvious that there was a lot of love and respect between the two of them. The fact that he made time to be part of my television special was a highlight in my life. What a sweet way to pay tribute to my dad, his friend, who I know he missed dearly—as did I.

Nelson conducted while I sang "Mona Lisa." This was the first time I had ever performed a song of my father's on television. Everyone, including Riddle, got teary-eyed. I was emotionally overcome on camera, but I made it through. Just as it had been back in Amherst, there was something about doing one of Dad's songs that seemed to invite a heavenly presence into the room. It was both frightening and exhilarating. It would be thirteen years before I would take the next step, and pay tribute to Dad in another way, but I wasn't ready—not yet.

The rest of the show was filled with really great music. Each performer did a song, and then I sang one of their songs with them. Johnny Mathis and I sang a lovely tune called "Small World." Stephen Bishop and I sang a great song that was a big hit for him called "On and On." I did a dance number with Earth, Wind and Fire called "That's the Way of the World." I was not a great dancer, but I was cute.

Thank goodness my break from touring didn't hurt the box office. My fans were still there for me. In October of 1978, I sold out the Metropolitan Opera House. I was the first black female pop artist to ever sing there, and I was pretty wild onstage, which was something that they weren't used to at the Met. My father knew that he was making history when he got into a new theater, but me, I made history without even knowing it. It was easier for me, of course, because the racism wasn't as blatant as it had been then. Although I was breaking new ground as a female black artist, I really wasn't that conscious that I was making any kind of racial breakthrough.

I suppose one of the signs of success is when people don't see you as black or white or whatever. In a way, you transcend color. People see you first as a star. Then, as a talent. And, somewhere down the line, if you're lucky, it's more like, "Oh, by the way, she/he is black..." My father's music was like a bridge between races. This bridge was responsible for my comfortably integrated childhood.

But transcending color means more than just crossing over, because there have been many black artists who have crossed over in a commercial sense, but can't get over the fact that they are black. It doesn't happen to everybody who is black and makes it in the white world, or who is white and makes it in the black world. In some instances, when you do cross over, everyone does seem to forget. But it's still not the norm. One black artist who has achieved greatness, who has transcended, is Bill Cosby. When Bill Cosby tells his jokes, they are universal. There's something about those jokes and the way he tells them that sound like they could be about any family. That's transcendence. That's the example and spirit that Marvin and I tried to infuse into Robbie.

In February of 1979, I was presented with a star on the Hollywood Walk of Fame. It is only a few feet down from the front doors of Capitol Records, which was perfect, because my father's albums had built the building and my albums were now paying the electric bills, and perhaps a lot more. Unfortunately, my mother was a bit uptight about it. She made a terribly unkind remark about me to an aunt, who then told me. I couldn't get over it. We got through the ceremony, but later, when she was back at home in Massachusetts, I called her up in the middle of a dinner party she was hosting. I really let loose on her, and Mom accused me of ruining her dinner party. The incident caused a major rift in our already strained relationship, and it would be a long time before we spoke again.

Not long after this, I went through my disco phase. Disco was red-hot, and Capitol Records thought they could make me into a Disco Diva. Anything was better than the press calling me the new Queen of Soul, so I agreed to go with what everyone wanted. The result was *I Love You So*, which should have been called, *I Love You So, but I Don't Love Disco At All.* I never fully embraced it. The album didn't do badly from a sales point of view, but it was not as successful as my previous albums had been.

The disco craze had an energy and a fury that kept feet dancing and heads spinning. The music has its own high and it was about as potent a narcotic as the new drug that was also the rage: cocaine—my newest drug of choice. Wanna dance?

CHAPTER 16

Divorce Hollywood Style

I don't remember the exact moment when I got back into drugs, but I definitely shifted back into self-destruct mode. I must have been restless or bored. You know, you get bored if things are going too good, so you screw things up, and you start sabotaging your own happiness. Anyway, I got distracted. My focus changed and I forgot what was important. The life and the love I thought I cherished began to slip away. Things got messy. I don't fully remember this, but Larkin said I started locking myself into the ladies' room at the recording studio. He would know, because it cost him and the record company plenty. It cost me even more.

I started snorting cocaine at one of the parties I was invited to, and then I turned Marvin on to it. Hey, misery loves company, as they say, so I spread it around. All our friends seemed to be doing it; important people in this business were leading the pack. Virtually overnight, cocaine was everywhere. It was like a snowstorm had descended on Los Angeles, and they needed plows to clear the streets. The quality of cocaine was exceptional in those days. Nobody seemed to have bad coke. And our pockets were fat with our

new success. My motto for that period was:
If you got the time, I got the dime.

For Marvin it was a new experience. He may have smoked a joint, but he'd certainly never tried anything like this. We went from experimenting with it at parties to bringing it into our home. And now we had some new friends: slick dealers from the streets who would bring over their friends to join in the fun. We lost touch with all our old friends. If they didn't want to party with us, to hell with them!

I once read somewhere that if you are feeling far away from God, guess who moved? Our home went from Heavenly Heights to Dante's Inferno. This was yet another ugly and painful lesson in my life. Even now, as I recall some of those times, my eyes fill with tears and I find myself marveling at the sickness of it all.

Cocaine started off being the best fun. It's not like heroin, which fills an emptiness. It's the opposite—a celebration of excess. Plenty of food, plenty of good wine, plenty of everything. I think it was Robin Williams who said that cocaine is God's way of telling you that you're making too much money.

I remember we were at a party at Redd Foxx's house, and there was this big bowl of coke on the coffee table. Everyone helped themselves and kept on steppin'. It was like it was a damned dip for crackers or something. Coke was the thing of the day, as commonplace as having a martini or a beer.

Cocaine is like making a new friend who enters your life and is really fun to be around—

at first. A couple of months later, they're getting a little more of your time than anybody else, because they have a way of manipulating you—but you don't see it. They are exciting and fun, and they start hooking you up with a different group of people, or they always seem to be able to find you the best dress or the best restaurant, and you end up really liking that person. Soon, they become your best friend, and your other friends start getting upset that this new friend is getting all your time. Silent, but deadly. Your new friend has become a part of your life and next, it *is* your life. It is demanding and it is possessive.

You can do cocaine for a while and it doesn't really have quite the same kind of slam-bang impact that heroin does. It's a different kind of feeling, an invigorating shot of powerful adrenaline. But when cocaine becomes more important than the people you are with, then you are in big trouble. Gradually you find yourself preferring the company of the white stuff to the company of your husband or your child. One day you wake up in the morning and you are looking for cocaine in the medicine cabinet, under the bed, in the kitchen, and then God knows where else. If you've ever been down this road, you know what I'm talking about.

Marvin and I were very vulnerable. He of course was trying to maintain his life in Chicago. This was particularly hard for my husband because he was a minister. The question begs to be asked: How could a man commissioned to spread the word of God be doing drugs? The best way I can answer that is to say this: God's preachers are His when they are in the pulpit. But once they step down—they are only men.

Eventually Marvin and I didn't just snort cocaine, or roll it up into cigarettes, we started freebasing it. That's a complicated and dangerous process which requires a lot of apparatus and a lot of preparation. I had nearly flunked chemistry in high school, yet I became a practicing chemist making this stuff in Beverly Hills. We had friends who had nearly blown up portions of buildings making freebase—because they didn't know what they were doing. I used ether and other chemicals to crystallize the cocaine so that I could put it in a pipe and smoke it. I bought the best coke, the best chemicals—oh, I was a pro. They call it crack now, but then we didn't really have a name for it.

I set up my own little laboratory in our home (much like the one Marty had to make LSD back in college). I got so good at the process that I developed a reputation as a "gourmet cocaine chef."

By now, the proverbial you-know-what had hit the fan. There were rumors going around about me doing cocaine. I reacted by denying everything. In fact, I gave a *People* magazine interview in which I said, "Everything's fine, nothing's wrong," but of course, everything was very wrong. At this point I think Marvin and I had actually tried dealing. Not that we made good dope dealers, because we didn't. You can't use the stuff and deal it. Needless to say, we were awful at it. We would smoke up half the inventory before we ever got around to selling it. We were really pitiful.

It was around that time that Marvin started to get paranoid. That's a typical effect of cocaine use. He got this idea in his head that I was cheating on him with a member of my band. It was never true, but the devil was busy working at killing this marriage, and us.

Things were falling apart around us because we weren't paying attention. We were twenty-eight, successful, and rich—and dumb. That's just how it was. We had access to just about anything we wanted. And sadly, we couldn't handle it.

I don't remember a specific argument that led to Marvin's and my breakup. I just recall that I was the one who wanted this marriage to be over. I had my attorney draw up the divorce papers and on New Year's Eve, 1980, Marvin was served at our apartment in Chicago. We didn't even have an argument. I didn't tell him ahead of time. It was like an ambush. I was quite a piece of work, and my life was a total mess.

Marvin didn't contest the divorce. We were able to walk in and out of court. We were divorced within a year, because there was no contest over money or over Robbie. It was almost amicable in the sense that he didn't resist, and I ended up kind of backing off. Robbie was a preschooler at the time, and he went to see his dad every couple of months. Marvin's family never turned their back on me or really got angry with me. They continued to love me and Robbie continues to have a close relationship with Marvin's family.

If I had to regret anything about my life, it would be divorcing Marvin, because I believe, deep inside, that he and I were truly meant for one another. We made beautiful music together. That's why it was so ridiculous. I don't know what I was thinking, except that once the drugs entered into our household, everything changed. I lost sight of how happy I was in the beginning. It was the biggest mistake of my life, and I made it not only for myself, but for Robbie as well. That's something I'll always have to live with.

It was not just the end of my marriage. It was the end of an era. My career was starting to show signs of wear and tear. And so was I.

CHAPTER 17

Near the Edge

I'm amazed at how many times I have brought myself to the brink of death in my lifetime. God was working overtime to save my butt, and I marvel that He never gave up on me.

The years between 1980 and 1983—right after my breakup with Marvin—were the worst years of my drug use, before I ended up at Hazelden. My career gradually went into the toilet because of my drug use. During this time, I wouldn't even hire someone who wasn't on drugs. How could I tell? I wasn't exactly subtle during the interview. I'd kinda pull out my pipe while I was talking, and I'd pretty much know from the reaction I got whether or not this individual was with my program. And if they weren't, they were underqualified. Easy as that.

Even in the midst of my drug-induced self-absorption, I knew better than to expose close friends and family to my habits. I never lit up right in front of Cookie, Bay, or Janice. Rather than confront their disapproval, I isolated myself from the rest of my family, my business people, and my old friends, as much as possible. I stayed home a lot if I wasn't touring. If I went out, it was usually with people like me—fellow druggies. Mostly we were freebasing cocaine. My world became very small. The dope man became my best friend.

I became friendly with strangers, anyone who sold to me. One night, I was on the other side of Los Angeles, far away from the lights of Beverly Hills, buying some powdered courage. The house was like a mini-factory, with a room that was just for cutting, preparing, and packaging cocaine. The workers were all women ranging in age from fifteen to sixty-five, wearing colorful scarves around their heads.

It was sort of a cross between an assembly line and a sewing circle. They were all very friendly, sitting around chatting and working. It was almost surreal, and in the next room you could smell chicken frying. It was disgustingly homey, with kids running around and a TV set on.

I didn't stay any longer than I needed to. In the back of my mind some part of me had to be wondering what these people were wondering—about me. Here's "the-daughter-of" down in the 'hood in Compton, picking up cocaine at a dope factory. What a concept! Anyway, I guess it didn't bother me all that much—see, having your dope is like getting your life saved. You become immune to stares, whispers, and anything else that might make you think about how demented you really are.

As I was getting into my car and pulling away, I saw a sight in my rearview mirror that I could not believe. A large black van pulled up on the sidewalk and a swarm of men appeared wearing dark clothes and helmets. They were vaulting over the fence surrounding the house, and running toward it with guns pulled. I saw big yellow letters across the backs of their jackets: It was the L. A. SWAT unit. That whole house was busted. They took everybody—babies, men, women, and grammas. Everything told me that I should pull away, but I couldn't take my eyes off the scene. A few minutes before and I would have still been in there.

I could see it:

DAUGHTER OF NAT KING COLE SNARED IN DRUG BUST

I couldn't believe my luck. I drove home almost peeing on myself. How did I manage such a narrow escape? There's that angel again.

One of the only bright spots of this time period was my eighth album, *Don't Look Back*. I worked with songwriter Michael Masser, who came to my home and sat at my piano and played a song he wrote, "Someone That I Used to Love." It made me cry. I couldn't wait to record it. Although Chuck and Marvin were producing the album, Michael insisted on producing his own song.

We hit it off as soon as I met him. Michael was sweet, talented, and rather eccentric. His intensity reminded me of Schroeder, the *Peanuts* character, playing Beethoven. He had this very interesting-looking blond Dutchboy haircut. Once we started to record the song in the studio, I must have done the vocal twenty times. Literally. Michael ended up using the third or fourth take, which I had tried to tell him to use anyway. I was ready to kill him.

We worked all night at the Lionshare recording studio on Beverly Boulevard in

Hollywood. Chuck and Marvin were not allowed to interfere. They had to nervously sit by and watch him work everybody into a total frazzle, while he tried to produce this record.

One particular night in the studio, we had a young black guy working as the recording engineer. This was his first major session, and Michael was giving him an absolute stroke. Michael had played about seven or eight piano tracks for this song.

He wanted the engineer to edit all eight tracks together, which is a nearly impossible task. We didn't have the technology back then that exists today, so this was an extremely laborious process. Michael was playing like Ferrante *and* Teicher all across the keyboard—how was this kid, a novice engineer, supposed to edit all that into one meaningful piece?

In the midst of all this craziness, my friend, Melissa Tormé, Mel's daughter, had snuck into the engineering booth and was hiding under the console. Michael hated to have anyone in the studio except the people working on the recording, and when someone ratted her out, he just went wild. He went crawling under the console and tried to drag her away, but everyone was laughing so hard—including him—that when he got Melissa out from under there, he had to chase her all over the studio before she left.

I swore I could not possibly work with Michael ever again. Of course, I did. Never say never.

Don't Look Back, released on May 15, 1980,

was a good album by my standards and was respectable by commercial standards, but there is no doubt that I was slipping down in the eyes of the Capitol Records executives. "Someone That I Used to Love" made an appearance on the charts, and I was particularly pleased with my version of the Ella Fitzgerald classic "Stairway to the Stars," which I dedicated to my mom.

In between singing and getting high, I found time to become completely obsessed with my appearance. I would be home all day and change my clothes three or four times every couple of hours. All dressed up with nowhere to go. I was a skinny little thing, almost anorexic. But I was described in print as "model slender."

I received an offer to be the spokeswoman for Posner Cosmetics and did my first TV commercials for them. Posner was a line of beauty products for black women. I was high as a kite during most of the shooting sessions. Typically, I was so tired from being up all night freebasing that I would come in early in the morning and lie down while the makeup man did my face. At the last minute, he would make me open my eyes so that he could do my eye makeup. Then I'd get on the set and I'd do my perky thing in front of the camera, and in between takes I'd nod off. I don't know how I did it, but Posner sold a lot of makeup that year.

There is a curious bit of history to another advertisement I was involved with at about the same time. J. Walter Thompson created a television spot for the 1981 Thunderbird featuring the song "Unforgettable." An image of my father is superimposed over a 1955 T-Bird; an image of me is superimposed over the 1981 model. You can hear both of us singing, and the ad gives the impression that we are alternating verses. I had completely forgotten this commercial until someone reminded me of it during the *Unforgettable* tour in the 1990s.

In the fall, I worked with singer Lou Rawls at the Las Vegas Hilton and then we went on to Carnegie Hall. Lou was a great admirer of my father and was also signed to Capitol Records. The show was divided in half, with each of us doing our own thing. However, we did a few dynamite songs together. We opened with an up-tempo song called "It Takes Two, Baby," and did a medley of songs from *Porgy and Bess* that was lovely. There was some discussion about the two of us doing a *Porgy and Bess* revival on Broadway, which I would have loved. I'm sorry we never recorded that music. This was also the first show in which I did a medley of my father's songs with a background screen that showed photographs of him and me when I was little. My behavior was very erratic and it really annoyed Lou when I made the show late. But when I got onstage, I was good, and we pulled off standing ovations night after night.

Applause from strangers helped me hide from the fact that I had few real friends left. There were a lot of people I gave hundreds or even thousands of dollars to buy cocaine for me and they simply never came back. Others ended up hanging around my house for months. There was this little posse of people that all hung out together. Honey, this was the seediest collection of friends I'd had since Peaches and my felon buddies back in Springfield. I had this group of women I called my "friends." They brought coke all the time—they seemed kind of cool. A week later, all my furs were stolen and all of my gold records and some of my father's were off the wall. Now that I think about it, it was almost funny, because they must have thought that the gold was real. I guess they intended to melt it down. But if you see a plaque in somebody's home that says "Presented to Natalie Cole" and they claim that I gave it to them, they're lying.

DAUGHTER OF NAT KING COLE DIES IN LAS VEGAS HILTON INFERNO

God was constantly giving me signs—the next one was a real wake-up call. Bill Cosby and I had just finished a date at the Las Vegas Hilton in February of 1981 when I almost lost my life in that infamous fire when I was trapped in my room for several hours. The fact that I suffered no physical consequences from that incident is no small miracle. But it still didn't stop the insanity.

In June of 1981, I was asked to step in at the last minute for Aretha at the Kool Jazz Festival in San Diego because she had a throat problem. I was honored to be her fill-in and glad to have the opportunity to perform in front of thirty or forty thousand people. This was a young R&B audience, and I was anxious to cut loose in a way that you usually can't do in Vegas or the other places I had been playing with Lou Rawls. It was a great night, the crowd was with me, and I sang all my best stuff, from "This Will Be" to "Lucy in the Sky with Diamonds." I don't usually pay much attention to reviews, but I took a special pleasure in Robert Hilburn's L.A. Times article about the festival, titled: "Natalie Cole at Kool—A Star Is Reborn." I'm glad that I gave that a strong performance that night, but I knew that I was a long way from reborn.

Happy Love, which was released in August of '81, was my first project without Marvin and Chuck. But I didn't feel inspired and, looking back, I'm sure that my producer, George Tobin, didn't either. George had a horrific obstacle to rise above and he spent most of the time sitting around waiting for me to come out of the bathroom. We worked from April through June at Studio Sound Recorders in North Hollywood trying to get it right. The only song I really liked on that entire record was my rendition of the Percy Sledge classic, "When a Man Loves a Woman." Sometimes I still do it in my show, but the album got only a lukewarm reception commercially. My lone success at the Kool Jazz Festival was not enough to compensate for the string of disappointing performances and blown concert dates that I was starting to pile up. The bloom was starting to come off. Shortly after the figures started to come in, Capitol informed me that they were not going to renew my contract.

Amidst the bad times, there was some good. The first time Robbie ever came onstage with me was in September of 1981 at the Greek Theater in Los Angeles, when I was still touring with Lou Rawls. Robbie had started drumming when he was a baby. He could barely sit up when he began tapping his feet on the wall. I would sit behind him and he'd sit between my legs and beat the wall with his feet—I mean real rhythms. The first drumsticks that he ever held in his hands were two cardboard cylinders from wire coat hangers, and after that he was just beating on everything. When I brought him out onstage in his little suit, he was four years old. We brought out a stool for him to bang on during "Our Love," because that's my song to Robbie. He tapped away and the audience went crazy. He was just the cutest thing. And then he took a bow with me. It was fun for both of us. I don't know who was more thrilled or more proud—him or me.

I was never afraid to take my son around in public. Some celebrities are very protective of their kids; they won't even let the press see their faces. I never saw it as much of an issue. Perhaps it was because my dad sometimes included my siblings and me in his public appearances. I think it probably might have helped us to understand how he dealt with fame by sharing a little of his limelight. I certainly never had a problem with it, so I figured Robbie wouldn't either.

I started dating again and I was introduced to a cool, gorgeous Italian guy called Dino. The truth is that he was the right guy at the wrong time. He was a thoughtful, decent man from a nice Italian family. But everything was all wrong. We were together for about a year, and during that time I lured him into my style of life, but he really couldn't handle it. He cared a lot for me and Robbie. He was fearful for me because I was so reckless, and I also had incredible stamina because of the drugs. I could stay up for hours and hours, sometimes days. I don't know how many times he had to put me to bed after I had passed out on the living room floor. There were some good times—when I was straight long enough to enjoy our time together. He would cook for us. We would swim and travel, and he really loved Robbie. He was one of the few good guys in my life.

As if I wasn't getting enough clues that I was in serious trouble in my life, I was arrested for several traffic violations in a short period of time. One of these was just after I made a drug buy on Sunset Boulevard. I was anxious to get back and cook it up, so I pulled out of the parking space without looking and cut off a police car. They stopped me and checked my

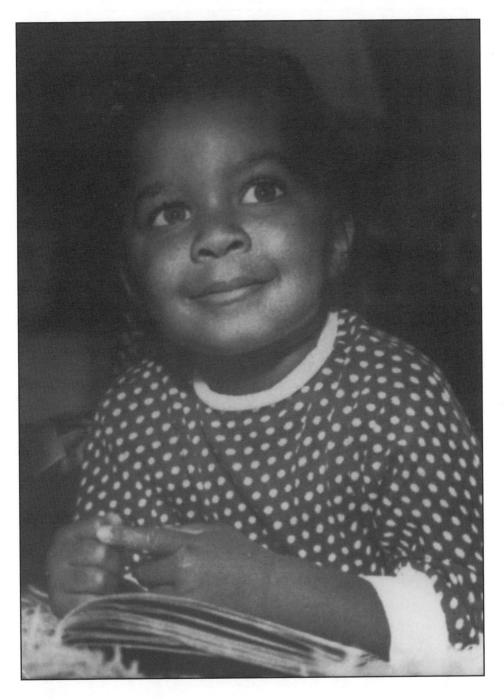

Here I am—Natalie "Sweetie" Cole at age four—"and
when she was good, she was very very good, and when
she was bad, she was horrid!
COLE FAMILY ARCHIVE

Ignore the pout here—Cookie and I loved when we could get Dad all to ourselves. MICHAEL OCHS ARCHIVE/VENICE, CA

Dad and I prepare in the studio for the Capitol recording "I'm Good Will, Your Christmas Spirit." I was six years old and dad was coaching me on my first record, lisp and all! MICHAEL OCHS ARCHIVE/VENICE, CA

I joined Dad, Debbie Reynolds, Eddie Fischer, and
Cookie in the studio, circa 1950.

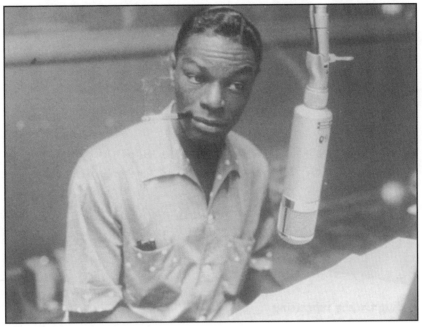

Dad in the studio with his very sophisticated
cigarette holder.

Dad and Bing Crosby rehearsing in Capitol Records' Studio A.
PHOTOGRAPH COURTESY OF CAPITOL RECORDS

Dad and Sammy Davis Jr. reach out at the Villa Capri in 1955.
PHOTO BY BERNIE ABRAMSON/MPTV

Dad and Dean Martin ham it up.
PHOTOGRAPH COURTESY OF CAPITOL RECORDS

Dad, Frank Sinatra, and good friend Glen Walicks at the Friar's Club in New York, undated. PHOTOGRAPH COURTESY OF CAPITOL RECORDS

Dad chats with John F. Kennedy at the Palladium, L.A. in 1963. PHOTO BY DAVID SUTTON/MP TV

Dad with some of the greats of all time—Count Basie, Ella Fitzgerald, and Joe Williams, 1955. PHOTOGRAPH COURTESY OF CAPITOL RECORDS

On the set of the TV show *This is Your Life* with host Ralph Edwards. It was supposed to be a surprise for Dad, but they had to keep it from me too…gee, didn't they think I could keep a secret? PHOTOGRAPH COURTESY OF RALPH EDWARDS PRODUCTIONS; PHOTO BY PAUL BAILEY

Me at age ten, singing with my first professional group, "The Malibu Music Men," at the home of a friend, 1960. PHOTO BY WAYNE WILCOX

Here I am, sitting with Aunt Betty, Cookie, and Mom in 1962. See where I learned how to dress with style?

From the *Inseparable* album photo shoot, around
1975—no comment on the hairdo, please.

Here I am clutching the Grand Prize trophy for "Mr. Melody" at the 1976 Fifth Toykyo Music Festival International. The prize was $10,000—which was a fortune back then! AP/WIDE WORLD PHOTOS

My first Grammy—for Best New Artist of the Year, 1976...one of many miracles to come... AP/WIDE WORLD PHOTOS

Pensive during a 1975 interview—doing way too much thinking!
MICHAEL OCHS ARCHIVE/VENICE, CA

Johnny Mathis and I strike a pose before performing the duet of his popular song "Small World" on my Natalie Cole Special on CBS in April 1978.
MICHAEL OCHS ARCHIVE/VENICE, CA

Mom joins me to celebrate my star on the Hollywood Walk of Fame—1979. The star is located a few feet down the block from Capitol Records, still known as the House that Nat Built. Very cool.
AP/WIDE WORLD PHOTOS

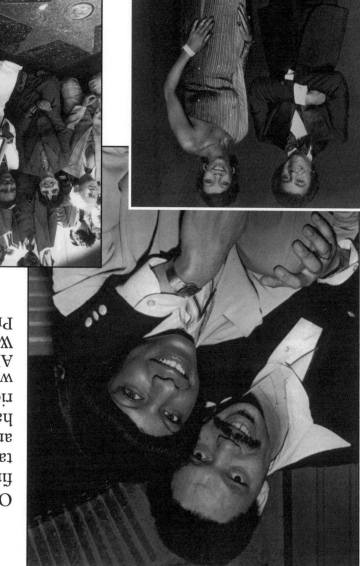

One of the first pictures taken of me and Marvin as happily married man and wife.
AP/WIDE WORLD PHOTOS

Earth, Wind, and Fire were also special guests on the Natalie Cole Special. We performed their hit, "That's the way of the World." Great costumes! RAI (A NATALIE COLE COMPANY)

Celebrating my third Grammy win with the Jackson Five at the 1978 Grammy Awards. MICHAEL OCHS ARCHIVE/VENICE,CA

The victorious team—Marvin, Chuck Jackson, and me—after winning the Female Favorite Soul Award at the 1978 American Music Awards. AP/WIDE WORLD PHOTOS

Barry White and I at the 1979 American Music Awards. MICHAEL OCHS ARCHIVE/VENICE, CA

Me and Robbie—my little angel!
PHOTO BY DALE WITTNER

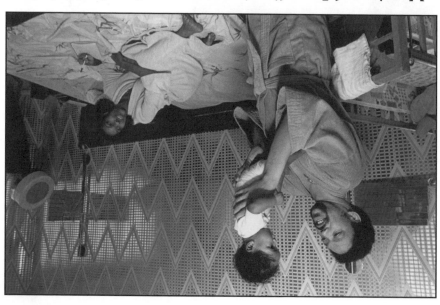

Marvin and I reveling in new parenthood with baby
Robbie in our high-rise Chicago apartment in 1978.
PHOTO BY DALE WITTNER

A quiet moment in
Marvin's office—just the
two of us.
PHOTO BY DALE WITTNER

Singing at the
Cambodian refugee
benefit in L.A. in 1980.
AP/WIDE WORLD
PHOTOS

One of Robbie's first
onstage appearances—
he took to it like a
duck to water—now
where could he have
gotten that?
MICHAEL OCHS
ARCHIVE/VENICE, CA

Mom at the recording studio during the *Unforgettable* project. Like everyone else, she was often moved to tears due to the emotional impact of this event. PHOTO BY LESLEY BOHM

Opening night at the Universal Amphitheater in L.A. This gorgeous dress was inspired by a Lana Turner film. It got more attention than I did! PHOTO BY LESTER COHEN

Rehearsing "Mona Lisa," just one of the twenty-two songs included on the Unforgettable CD. PHOTO BY LESLEY BOHM

A rare photo of the Cole daughters and Mom at a Capitol Records Tribute in 1991, Los Angeles. Standing left to right: Me, Mom, Casey, Carol, and Casey's twin Timolin. A good-looking family if I do say so myself! PHOTO BY BILL JONES

I call her my "baby sis"—Whitney and I at a fundraiser fo diabetes in Los Angeles, circa 1997.
PHOTO BY BILL JONES

"Songstress extraordinaire" Anita Baker and me at her first Los Angeles concert in the early 90s at the Beverly Theatre.
PHOTO BY BILL JONES

I'm feeling a bit over-dressed alongside Tracy Chapman but she understood!
PHOTO BY BILL JONES

Me and my girl Patti Labelle at the 1988 Soul Train Music Awards.
MICHAEL OCHS ARCHIVE/VENICE, CA

Robbie joined me at a charity race for Multiple Sclerosis at UCLA in 1997. Hey, we had the fifth highest score out of thirty-six teams—not too shabby! PHOTO BY ALEX BERLINER/BEI

Performing "Mr. Paganini" at the 1997 Grammy awards at Madison Square Garden. Extra bonus: I had just won for "Best Duet" for "When I Fall In Love." PHOTO BY RON WOLFSON

Luther Vandross, Quincy Jones, and I at who knows where. The important thing is we were having fun. PHOTO BY JERRY PFAFF

Steve Case and Gerald Levin were in the audience when I performed at a Global CEO event in Manhattan in early 2000—just after the AOL Time Warner deal was announced. PHOTO BY DON POLLARD

Tony Bennett presented me with the Song-writers Hall of Fame Hitmaker Award in New York in 1999. PHOTO BY SAM TEICHER

Me and a very grown-up Robbie at the Universal Amphitheater in June, 2000. PHOTO BY ALEX BERLINER/BEI

Good friend and supportive fan, Kevin Taylor, from the BET Network. PHOTO BY KATHLEEN BEALL

car, where they found a bottle of pills, but the prescription was in somebody else's name. They made me walk the line, which I couldn't do very well, so they handcuffed me and drove me down to the new police station on San Vicente and Santa Monica. The packet of coke I'd just bought was still in the cuff of my sleeve, but they hadn't searched me. It was a sure bet that I'd be searched at the station. I was gonna have a big problem. Clever girl that I am, while I was sitting in the back of the patrol car with my hands cuffed behind me, I eased the packet out of my sleeve and stuffed it down the crack between the cushion and the back of the seat. And didn't I try my best to read the number of the squad car so I could go back and get the cocaine later? How sick is that?

All they found on me was a little pipe for marijuana and they didn't really have anything else. They knew who I was, but instead of arresting me, they put me in a holding cell and let me sleep. Meanwhile, everybody working with me was freaked, because they didn't know where I was. We had a gig the next day in St. Louis and I was supposed to leave town early the next morning. Randy, my bodyguard, was looking all over for me. I called my assistant when I woke up and she came to get me about six o'clock the next morning. Miraculously, I made the plane. No harm, no foul.

One night, Dino and I had had an argument and I got very upset with him, so I took my keyboard and a six-pack of Moosehead beer and jumped in my hot little Datsun 240Z. I had just dropped some Quaaludes, which obviously impaired my judgment, because as I came down Benedict Canyon Boulevard to where Alpine intersects with Sunset, I took the corner too fast. I bounced down Sunset, hit-ting three concrete lamp posts—*bam, bam, bam*—like the ball in a game of pinball. The Datsun flipped over and skidded to a stop on its crumpled roof. I was conscious, hanging upside down from my seat belt, and I remember asking myself out loud, "Am I dead yet?"

CHAPTER 18

Ready or Not—I'm Ready

**DAUGHTER OF
NAT KING COLE
DIES IN DRUG-INDUCED
CAR CRASH**

S o I'm asking myself, "Am I dead?" (I knew I certainly should have been.) To my amaze-ment, I swear I heard a voice on the radio saying, "No, not yet." I felt myself and checked to see if I was still in one piece. I had cut my finger, but as far as I could tell, all the moving parts were still moving. I crawled out the window, and passed out.

When I came to again, I was positive that voice on the radio had lied to me. As I opened my eyes, I saw the stars, felt hands all over my body, and heard women's voices asking Jesus to help me. I thought I was dead for sure. What had happened was that the first people to come upon the flattened remains of the 240Z were four women returning home from a prayer meeting at their church. When they saw me on the ground, they began to pray and lay hands on me. As the cobwebs cleared from my brain, I heard the police and ambulance sirens and looked over at my poor little crumpled Datsun. It did not look as though a human being could have been in that car and survived. But there I was.

The police found the smashed bottles of beer, but did not charge me with drunken driving. En route to Cedars Sinai, the paramedics radioed ahead for my doctor, who checked me in under an assumed name. (When you need an alias to go to the hospital, that, too, should be a clue.) He marveled that all I required was a couple of stitches to close up the gash in my finger. From the minute I got to Cedars, I couldn't wait to leave—I kept telling them that I had to go. It wasn't like I had a hot date— all I wanted to do was to get to my girlfriend's house and get high.

I imagine that God was sitting up in heaven with his hands over his face and saying, "Oh brother, here we go again. Get her out of there. It's not time yet." The angel taking care of me was working double duty in those days, and I wasn't even grateful.

Despite these heavenly wake-up calls, I kept smoking, so God tried something else to get my attention. In July of 1982, I was head-lining at Caesar's in Atlantic City, when in the middle of the show I suddenly couldn't sing. I had lost my voice, something that had never happened to me before in more than a decade of performing. I was petrified.

I immediately flew home to have my doc-tors confirm the worst: I had nodules on my vocal chords that were causing me difficulty in singing. They would have to be surgically removed. There was some small possibility that I could lose my voice entirely as a result of the surgery. There was also a chance that with rest, the nodules might disappear on their own. So I rested.

But there was more bad news. I got a phone call saying that Marvin was in the cardiac unit at St. Joseph's in Chicago. Despite the fact that we had now been apart for two years, and the fact that I had ambushed him with divorce papers, despite the fact that we had moved on with our lives, we still loved each other. I took the first plane from L.A. to Chicago. Marvin had been hospitalized with chest pains and arrhythmia. In the back of my mind, and in the core of my being, I believed that somehow we would get back together.

During the years of our separation and

divorce, Marvin and I gradually became better friends. We worked together through two more albums, and he came frequently to Los Angeles to see Robbie. Marvin was getting a hold on his drug problem, but I wasn't. Whenever he urged me to get help, I only dug my heels in deeper and rejected his attempts to reach out. We continued to talk on the telephone despite the fact that he remarried. I even thought he might divorce his second wife so we could remarry, but then she got pregnant. By this time, we both realized we'd made a mistake in leaving each other, and I held out hope that someday we could fix this mistake.

Our little son paid quite a price for our mistakes, and I am so grateful that we had Drue as his nanny; if it hadn't been for her, the consequences could have been disastrous. Robbie could have died, because I got to a point where I stopped paying attention to anything or anyone but myself. There was one day when he came close. I was in the back in the bedroom with some "friend" getting high. Robbie was riding his tricycle around outside, and somehow he fell right into the pool. I had a couple working for me who didn't know how to swim. They jumped in after him anyway. Bless them, for they certainly saved his life; he had sunk right to the bottom. After they pulled him out, he was all right, but it was a terribly close call. And typically, I barely reacted. I didn't snap out of it. I didn't stop doing drugs right then and there. I didn't really change anything. I just stopped what I was doing for the moment and went and got my son.

I had become a negligent mother. I remember my son knocking on the bathroom door as I stayed in the bathroom for hours, just getting high. He'd knock on the door, "Mommy, Mommy, please come out. Mommy, are you coming out?" I knew enough that I didn't want him to see me. Actually, in my insanity, I believed that if he didn't see me getting high, somehow that made it not so bad.

One day I sank to such a low that I took Robbie with me to go pick up drugs. I was to meet my dealer at nine o'clock on a Sunday morning, and I didn't even take the time to get us dressed. I just got in the car with my son—Robbie in his PJs, me in my PJs and robe—and drove off to make the score. After-ward, I put the drugs in his diaper bag for safe transport.

The first truly public revelation of my personal struggles came in October of 1982, when my mother petitioned the Los Angeles Superior Court for conservatorship of my finances. I did not object. (It was one of the few times I did not put up a fight.) She explained that I had been under "severe mental strain" since I had discovered that I might lose my voice because of the nodules. She was quoted in the *Los Angeles Times*: "If you are a singer and you think you are losing your voice, that causes great mental stress. I think that she was just frightened, and now we know the reason. I don't think it is too bad."

Of course, she knew by now that I had a drug problem, but she was trying to protect me. Dear mother—she could really go to bat for you if she was protecting you from others. She was afraid that the same kind of business management vultures who took advantage of my father would try to take advantage of me in my addicted condition. And she was right. After a half dozen years at the top of the charts, I had earned millions of dollars in recordings and concerts. The most that the court auditor could find was $300,000. My accountants at the time couldn't explain where the money went. It didn't *all* go to drugs.

Behind the scenes, my mother, my sister, my brother, and pretty much anybody else who cared about me were begging me to go into drug rehabilitation. All kinds of people were trying to talk to me, but no one could get through. I knew that I was totally screwing up. I cussed a few people out, including my sister Cookie. My family tried to perform an intervention, which was kind of pathetic. It was so uncomfortable and embarrassing for my family to have to deal with this. Even though I didn't want to go into rehab, finally I agreed to go, mainly to get everybody off my back.

I had no intention of giving up drugs. How could I tell? Before I left, I put a little stash in my safe for when I returned.

Meanwhile, I went along with the program, so to speak. My destination was a cheery, sunny place on the California coast. My mother had already taken over my affairs, and she must have been desperate to find a place that could deal with me, because I don't think anyone researched this place very well. This was a facility that treated all kinds of mental problems, and drug addiction was the lowest priority on their totem pole.

Even as late as November of 1982, there was a lot of ignorance about how to treat drug addiction. Many people really didn't want to deal with the fact that drug addiction is an illness, not a crime. It is not about willpower. In some cases, it appears to be hereditary, like alcoholism. Many facilities for rehabilitation were being run by people who had never taken more than an aspirin.

This joint was sort of a catch-all loony bin, where they distributed pills for people with every kind of mental problem. The patients were doin' the Libri Shuffle, the Thorazine Waltz, and the Vali jiggle as they danced down the hall-ways. Druggies were sittin' there right next to people who'd slit their wrists the night before. The treatment was one-size-fits-all—everyone was getting something dispensed to them, and if the drugs didn't work, they gave you shock therapy.

I didn't take any pills or get shock therapy at this facility. Instead, they sent me to sem-inars. I met with a psychiatrist once or twice a week for an hour, and he was older than Methuselah. He told me that I was sick, which in essence was true, and he told me that the cure was a combination of pills and a good talkin' to. You know, let's talk about my childhood. I didn't know much about my problem, but I knew that this was not going to help.

You don't really have withdrawal from cocaine. You just walk around pissed. You could call it some kind of withdrawal, but it's certainly not anything like withdrawing from heroin. I hated every minute of my time there. I just wanted to leave. The doors were locked at night; we were in a ward and it wasn't very much fun. Worse yet, I was still having severe problems with my voice. When I arrived, I could barely talk.

After the thirty days, it was, "Bye, see ya." Maybe I had some follow-up treatment afterward with a doctor of some kind, but I don't remember doing any of that. Frankly, the best I could say was that they kept me locked up and dry for thirty days and gave my voice some rest. They didn't know what to do about my addiction. At that point, I didn't want to do anything about it either, so I can't entirely blame them.

Cookie and John came to pick me up on the day I was released and were being so sweet to me. I asked if they didn't mind if I drove home, and they said fine. Well, I peeled out of that parking lot and onto the freeway like a rocket. I don't think the gas pedal ever left the floor of the car until I pulled into my own driveway. Cookie and John were still sitting there, crushed into their seats like that guy in the ad for audio speakers—totally blown away by the little ride. I was in a big hurry to get back to the stash in my little safe. I couldn't wait, my mouth was watering, I just couldn't wait to get high.

The only really good thing to come out of my first stay in rehab happened to somebody else. My friend Vinnie and I had bonded over the coke pipe. We got high together—he was like my little Italian brother.

Vinnie was always a very generous and honorable person, unlike the other lowlifes I was hanging around with. When I went into rehab, he was so frightened that he stopped doing drugs. I wasn't scared straight by rehab, but he was. Go figure.

As soon as I came home, I decided I had to deal with my throat nodules. Mom took me to Dr. Edward Cantor, a Beverly Hills surgeon, who operated on my vocal chords. My mother was there for the surgery, and it was one of the rare times I could see that she was worried—really scared. When I opened my eyes after the operation, I remember seeing her sitting there. I am not ashamed to admit that I was almost glad the surgery had been necessary; I was happy to have some sign of her maternal concern, even at the cost of some physical pain. While I was locked up in rehab, counting the days until I could get back to my coke pipe, the whole world was learning about my drug problems in lurid detail. The November issue of the *National Enquirer* carried a piece titled:

SINGER NATALIE COLE
FIGHTING A
MASSIVE COCAINE HABIT

They said I was called "The Base Queen" because of my obsession with freebasing. (I was also called the Cook, the Chemist, and the Coke Gourmet, but they didn't know that.)

When I came out of rehab—supposedly clean and sober—there was so much rejoicing that I didn't have the heart to admit that I had gone right back to it. Now that I was "cured," everyone was anxious for me to rehabilitate my image. The press was just dying to hear the minutiae of my drug confessions and the joy of my redemption, so who was I to argue? The people-pleasing facet of my personality really took charge. I said what everyone wanted to hear. In a series of interviews with national magazines, big newspapers, and TV shows, I lied like a con artist. I confessed my sins, begged forgiveness, and preached the virtues of the clean life. Meanwhile, I kept right on smoking cocaine. I can remember thinking at the time that maybe I really would give it up. But I just wasn't ready. I was still deeply addicted.

My mother was starting to get a grasp on what was happening to me. She wanted me to clean house and rid my life of certain people who she felt were aiding and abetting my drug habit and were profiting while I was going down the tubes. The number one head she wanted to roll was that of my manager, Kevin Hunter. My mother had never liked Kevin, and the feeling was mutual. Kevin and I had worked together for eleven years, and there is no doubt that he was the most important person in the early days of my career. He introduced me to Marvin and Chuck. He was absolutely instrumental in getting me signed with Capitol Records when everybody else had turned me down. He advised and protected and helped me in many ways. He had tried to get me away from drugs. We had been through a lot together. He had been a good friend. But as I had grown more successful, Kevin had grown more abrasive and imperious in his dealings with people in the business. At the moment when I was messing up the most, he seemed to be more interested in being important than in helping me. With a lot of emotion and uncertainty, Kevin and I parted.

With Kevin out of the picture, my business manager, Ralph Goldman, suggested that I talk to a friend of his named Dan Cleary as a possible replacement. (I must have a thing for the Irish!) Dan had started out as an agent at GAC, which became CMA, and that was my father's agency. As a young man, he had met my father on several occasions, and had even met me as a little girl. Eventually, he went into management with a partner named Sherwin Bash and had represented not only the Carpenters and Olivia Newton-John, but the Commodores, Chaka Khan,

Anita Baker, and a few other acts. I was always amused that he represented so much R&B talent. I guess he just has good taste. He had seen me perform and had been there in 1976 when I won my first Grammys.

Dan and I met at my home and I liked him. He had spoken with my mother and could see that I was in a lot of trouble. It didn't take a genius to see that. But it took a great visionary like him to see beyond my affliction and believe that I still had the potential "to hit some home runs," as he put it. He could see that it was going to be difficult. But, God bless him, he decided to take me on.

Before Dan came on board, I had been working on an album called *I'm Ready,* and it already had all the early warning signs of a disaster. Capitol had dumped me when the *Happy Love* album did not do big numbers. So I went to Larkin Arnold, who had moved to Epic Records. Of course, he knew that I was in bad shape. He just didn't know how bad. As I was trying to record the songs for this album, my voice was not what it was. On top of that, I just couldn't keep it together. Sometimes I showed up late to the recording sessions; sometimes I didn't show up at all; sometimes I showed up and did the old lock-myself-in-the-bathroom-for-hours routine. It was a nightmare for everybody.

By that time, the company was having a hard time finding good people who wanted to work with me—hell, truth be told, they were having trouble finding *anyone* who wanted to work with me. Stanley Clarke, a wonderful jazz musician and producer, had the thankless task of producing this mess. Larkin knew that Chuck and Marvin were the kind of friends who would still do anything for me. So we got together and tried to rekindle some of the old magic. But it wasn't happening. For one thing, I couldn't focus. And for another, we had barely a month to pull together some material for this album. To their credit, Chuck and Marvin wrote five songs in that short time. But it was far from their best work.

That didn't stop Epic from releasing *I'm Ready*. Larkin was more concerned with my standing with the professionals in the music industry than with the public. He argued that it would be worse for my professional reputation to dump the album than to release it. Besides, Epic had invested nearly a million dollars in this disaster, and they needed *something* to show for their money. Shameless, shameful, pathetic, embarrassing, humiliating—what words can I use to describe the disappointment I felt about this mess? It's decisions like this that bother me about the way record companies deal. If you have a bad product—not up to snuff—why would you want to sell it? I'll tell you why: first, because they don't care; and second, they're not worried about anyone suing them for releasing an inferior product. As much control as they had, they could have shelved that embarrassment. And they should have. It didn't do anything for them, but it hurt me like hell. "Too Much Mister," the first and only single from the album, generated modest interest, but the album sold a disappointing forty thousand copies. To no one's surprise, Epic announced that they would not renew my contract for another album.

On the morning of August 13, 1983, I appeared on *Good Morning America* and sat there glassy-eyed, telling the host, David Hartman, how wonderful it was to be free of drugs. I told him, "I was forced to learn and to relearn the meaning of life, and I never had that happen to me before.... I haven't done anything wrong to anyone. That is what is so great about being able to sit here and talk about it. I've done all the damage to myself and I came through." How arrogant I was and how incredibly dumb.

Lying like that, it's amazing my nose didn't start growing right there on national television. The fact is, I had been up the entire night before smoking my brains out. This is one of those film clips that refuses to die. It is a haunting reminder that follows me everywhere, even all these years into sobriety—to this day I cringe when I see it.

As is typical of cocaine addicts, I became very paranoid. One evening in November of 1983, my doorbell rang. Three men in dark suits arrived unannounced. This is a drug user's nightmare. Narcs? FBI? Jehovah's Witnesses? Peering out the door, I recognized my manager, Dan Cleary; my business manager, Ralph Goldman; and my attorney, Jeff Ingber. I assumed it was a business call—but not this time. They sat down in my living room and got right to the point.

Dan spoke first: "Natalie, we really care a lot about you, and we're afraid that you are going to lose your life. We don't want that to happen." Ralph and Jeff added similar words of care and concern. They didn't threaten. They didn't raise their voices. They just talked sense. And for the first time in years, I listened. This clearly wasn't about money. In fact, they'd all been deferring commissions and fees or taking less than they were entitled to because they knew that I was struggling finan-cially. Dan had been my manager for less than a year at that point, and it had been hell, but he still believed in me. Someone was still cheering for this broken, screwed-up woman that I had become. And they were decent and loyal enough to tell me the truth. What a concept! How strange that I would respond to their pleas. You will look long and hard to find three other suits in the music business with that kind of heart.

That night had an impact on me and I felt another emotion I thought I had kept in check: fear. Powerful...heart-pounding...stop-you-dead-in-your-tracks fear.

Dan said that there was a place in Min-nesota—Minnesota?—that Kitty Dukakis had told my mother about. The plan was that after Thanksgiving I would go to a place called Hazelden. I had never heard of it, but it was about to change my life...forever.

CHAPTER 19

Hazelden

As the days got closer to leaving, I started getting nervous, and I'm told I made Dan's life pretty miserable (most of this time period is a little hazy for me). I called him several times in Mammoth, California, where he was skiing with his family, to tell him I wasn't going.

Of course Dan ignored me, and at the appointed hour on November 29 he showed up at my door. But I didn't make it easy for him. At the last minute I decided to go back for my keyboard. I had to have my keyboard. What if I wanted to do some writing while I was up there? In addition, I had no intention of arriving at Hazelden sober, so I'd gotten high before I left for the airport, and I brought some supplies with me. I didn't want to just go quietly into the night on this trip, and you know I had to have a *little* something to fortify myself. Hey—old habits die hard—real hard.

The flight was horrible. And who should we run into on the plane but an old friend of mine, Lindsay Wagner. She was going to Minneapolis to work and wanted to know what I was doing. She looked at me real strange when I told her I was going for a little R & R to just sort of hang out for a while. Yeah, right, on the ice-covered prairies.

We arrived in Minneapolis in the middle of a snowstorm. It was only November but it felt like the dead of winter, and it was 20 below zero. Our flight must have been the last plane cleared to land that day. When our luggage came down, my keyboard was nowhere to be found. Since I wasn't in any big rush, this looked like a golden opportunity to stall. I whined to Dan, "I have to wait for my keyboard. If I don't have my keyboard, I'm not going anywhere."

We stood around the baggage carousel for a long time waiting for it. Everyone else had pretty much gone and they were shutting down the terminal when Dan finally said he'd found the keyboard and got a skycap to load everything into the back of the limo. I had one foot in the back seat when I caught sight of it being loaded into the trunk. It had been completely mangled. Dan was obviously hoping that in my drugged-up stupor I wouldn't notice.

Now I was really upset, and I threw a class a hissy fit. By this time the blizzard had wors-ened, and there was thick snow and wind whipping all around us. I don't know how, but Dan finally stuffed me into the car.

The driver told us that on a good day, it was a forty-five-minute drive to Center City, where Hazelden was located. Good day, my ass. It was already dark, and all we could see was white. Then the limo ran into a ditch. We were in the middle of nowhere. About that time, I was *really* hating Dan. I told him, "Hiring you was the biggest mistake I ever made."

Dan was getting desperate and I was the bitch on wheels because I had run out of my "white courage." He got out of the car, and I watched as he waded through the snowdrifts in his Gucci loafers toward a light that was off in the distance. It looked like a farmhouse. Finally a tractor appeared out of nowhere. They hooked up the front of our car and pulled us out of the ditch.

It was at least another hour driving through the snowstorm before we finally got to Hazelden. What was supposed to be a forty-five-minute drive had turned into a three-hour trek, and I was feeling downright homicidal. When we pulled in, it was about nine o'clock at night. Even though the place looked all shut down, they had been expecting us to be late because of the snow and were waiting for us.

They brought us in and took us to my no-frills room. Sitting on a little table next to the bed was the worst-looking plate of food I had ever seen. It was hours old and it consisted of a piece of roast chicken, broccoli, and some potatoes—obviously stone cold. I turned to Dan and said, "You can't do this," just as he was waving bye-bye and going out the door. "What the hell have you done to me?" I yelled after him, even though I had the sneaking suspicion that he knew *exactly* what he was doing. I don't remember whether or not I told him he was fired.

I can't tell you much about how I spent my first few days at Hazelden, but I can tell you this. God has a way of putting a hedge around his children. You can't get out and no one can get in. He knows how to get our attention. You will have to deal with Him—sooner or later. But for someone like me—stubborn and hardheaded—it was just my nature to fight like hell and resist the inevitable. And you couldn't tell me nothin' because I was still trying to swim upstream in that river called Denial.

I wish I had a picture of what I looked like when I first got to Hazelden. I was very thin—nearly emaciated—and my skin had taken on a greenish hue. My hair was dull and brittle. I spent about three days in detox. By the first morning I was there, the drugs were out of my system, and I had a mean headache, but they wouldn't give me so much as an aspirin. The detox area was located in a separate section of a rather large building. Other than that, it was a week before I really took notice of my surroundings.

The Hazelden facility is like a college campus, with probably two hundred people in residence at any one time, housed in about ten dormitories. Each dorm had a great big middle room, where we'd do all of our group therapy sessions and group talks. The girls and guys were kept separate, but we all gathered together for general assembly.

My fellow patients were a mixed group of people from all walks of life. We were not allowed to mingle with anyone outside our section. This was called "fraternizing," and it was strictly enforced to help protect patient privacy. I was not the only black person, but at the time I was the only entertainment person that I knew of. There were other famous folk, mostly athletes and sports figures, but since we weren't allowed to fraternize, I didn't really get to know them. Of course, some people did recognize me, but thankfully it was not an issue. It was important that we all feel safe without having fingers pointing at us.

This was a different kind of place. There were no doctors and no psychiatrists. There was no shock therapy, no medicine, no dispensary, and no mother's little helper in the middle of the day. We had rooms where we could read and spend quiet time, but it was not encouraged—rather it was discouraged to have too much quiet time. In the early stages of recovery, it's the quiet that can get you in trouble. Most activities were done in a group.

The schedule was a tough adjustment for someone accustomed to a show business timetable. By nine at night we were brushing our teeth, and by ten or ten-thirty—when I'd normally be starting to party—we were in bed. We rose at seven. Nobody banged on the door, but it was recommended that we get our butts out of bed, get down to breakfast, and be ready to start the day. Even though our routine was determined for us, it was up to each individual to follow it—one of the keys to a successful recovery is that you have to want it. Some people at the Hazelden program had been ordered there by the court, so they had

231

no choice, but otherwise anyone was free to leave—an interesting and effective use of reverse psychology. We weren't allowed to make telephone calls for the first two weeks, which was probably a good idea, because it would be like kids going to summer camp for the first time and calling their parents every five minutes, begging to come home.

The grounds of Hazelden were actually quite beautiful, even in their snowy state. Nobody was going outside, however. On some days the windchill factor was 60 degrees below zero. I saw icicles outside my bedroom window that were six to eight feet long.

There was a woman there named Joanne who ran the dorm. She was real tough and a recovering addict, as were most of the counselors I was there:

working there. Three things I learned while I was there:

Number 1: They don't take no mess;
Number 2: They've been there, so they know all the tricks; and
Number 3: They're some of the most wonderful people you'd want to meet.

But you have to get by Numbers 1 and 2 before you find out about Number 3. The first week, I went to my first AA meeting—Alcoholics Anonymous. I didn't know what the heck the meetings were, but they were a required part of the program. People would get up and say, "Hi, my name is Mary and I'm an alcoholic." And then they would start telling their story. At first, this was frightening and uncomfortable for me. I didn't want to stand up and say my name—I just wanted to be left alone. But everybody felt that way, and it created a strange sort of camaraderie inside this very exclusive club.

At Hazelden they talk about us coming in as onions. Their job is to help you to peel away the layers down to the core and really find out who you are. Then you can begin to build again.

You're not supposed to understand the process; you just do it. This is about surrendering your will to strangers. People who you have never seen before and might never see again—these are the people who are going to try to help you save your life. And Lord knows I needed saving.

I needed to begin to do something *for* myself instead of *to* myself, and I had to make sure that I was getting help for the right reasons— not for my mother, not for my dad, and not even for my son. I had to start looking at a lot of things about myself that I didn't want to examine—and I didn't know if I could do that.

It would be a long way back if I decided to go for it. I had a lot to think about. I'd become totally unreliable and irresponsible, both personally and professionally. I had a six-year-old son to support, and my career was in serious jeopardy.

And I was basically broke.

My mother had taken control of my financial affairs at about the time of my first rehab. When it came time to pay for Hazelden, she was understandably reluctant to foot the bill. The attitude she expressed to Dan was, "Come on. Not this again." Dan had to go to San Jose and talk with her business manager, Harry Margolis. I was told some years later that he said some very unkind things about me. I had met this man maybe twice in my life. He said something like, "She should be thrown out in the streets like a dog." Gee, how do you really feel about me, Harry?

Meanwhile, Marvin and I had agreed that our son would stay with Drue, his nanny, during the time I was away. Robbie was comfortable around Drue and truly adored her, and she loved him like her own. In fact, I had gotten so bad in the last couple of years that Drue was clearly more of a mother to Robbie than I was. Sometimes he'd call me Nana and he'd call her Mama. That hurt. Nevertheless, she was a godsend.

Marvin and I had agreed that Robbie's life should not be disrupted just because mine was. He didn't insist that he take custody of Robbie. My mother, though, tried to step in and asked that Robbie come live with her. We thought it was curious that my mother wanted him, because up to this point, she hadn't displayed much effort to have a relationship with him. Robbie didn't really know her, and now that he was old enough to go to school, we were afraid that she'd send him to boarding school. To be fair, there was no obvious indication that she planned to do that, but Marvin and I just didn't feel right about it. Despite the divorce and all our problems, Marvin and I had remained close. We loved our son, and we were united in our decision: Robbie would stay with Drue. I don't think my mother ever got over that.

When I started feeling up to it, I wrote to Robbie and told him that Mommy was sick, that I loved him, and would be with him as soon as I could. My cousin Janice wrote me back to tell me that when she read it to him, he took the letter over to the corner and stood there and looked at it for a while. God, the shame of it all—when I pictured him doing this, my heart broke all over again. I realized what a mess I had created. I felt helpless, hopeless, lonely, and tired, but I finally stopped fighting against the program.

I was supposed to fulfill at least thirty days at Hazelden. My earliest phone calls to Dan had started off with, "I can't wait to leave." However, toward the end of the thirty days, on Christmas Eve, I told him, "I'm not sure when I'll be coming home. I'm doing better, but I don't think I'm ready yet." I had gone from hating Hazelden to being afraid to leave. That was the best Christmas present I ever gave myself.

CHAPTER 20

Jellinek

The walls of denial were starting to crumble around me. I realized that the fantasy was over. I absolutely knew that if I didn't get my life back on track, I was going to lose every-thing—my son, my career, my life. In fact, Marvin had seriously considered filing for custody of Robbie unless I got myself together. I was a world-renowned celebrity who was getting ready to become a statistic. I was depressed and very sad. In AA, they talk about hitting bottom, and I had finally gotten there, but in my case, my bottom came up to hit me—smack in my face.

In recovery, your priorities become very simple. You want to live. You want to be with your son. And you'd like to keep your job. It's very basic. You really have to do it for your-self. That's the bottom line. Then no matter what, they can't take that away from you. You may give it away, but they can't take it away from you.

Toward the end of the first thirty days, my counselor called me into her office and told me that she was going to recommend me for a long-term program—anywhere from four to six months. I swallowed hard but agreed. She said, "We want to give you the opportunity to get back on track. Maybe, if you put in some time, you might make something out of your life and get back at least some of what you've lost." I found myself keeping my fingers crossed that I would qualify to go to the House of Jellinek. In Swedish it means "House of Recovery." I was praying hard that I would be accepted—but I needn't have worried. All one had to do was take a look at my drug history and honey, I was *over*qualified!

The House of Jellinek was a separate building located on the Hazelden property about a quarter mile from the main buildings. It was a fully equipped home, totally self-sufficient, so that we had little contact with others outside the group, which consisted of twenty-five men and women. Some of us had roommates—mine was a sweet lost soul a bit younger than I. Now that I think of it, she kind of reminded me of Winona Ryder. We were cool right from the beginning, although I ended up being a little more responsible than she was—fancy that! We lost contact when I left, and I've always wondered whether she made it.

I was just amazed at the kinds of people that ended up here. There was an alcoholic airline pilot, a college professor, a young woman who was bulimic-anorexic, and a heroin addict who'd been in rehab going on nine times. There was a young man named Sean from Northern California who looked like a surfer. He had smoked so much marijuana and taken so many pills that he had been in detox alone for three months, for the mere reason that he was unable to walk or talk. And then there was me. I could go on, but suffice it to say that we were some messed-up folks—we were "special." This was my family for the next five and a half months.

Many of us were in relationships that they recommended we get rid of immediately. Some of us (like me) were even told to get rid of our homes (pretty drastic). This was about a new life, and you couldn't have a new life if you were still holding on to the old one. Otherwise recovery could never happen. Some people were even told to leave their spouses. In another context, this might be amusing.

In Jellinek, the therapy was extreme and confrontational. There was no screaming, though, and these people were never mean. They knew exactly what we were going through. I spent many months crying. I cried hard and long—I cried every single day.

In recovery, we learned about "progress, not perfection." Well, that was a relief. One of the glaring characteristics of addicts is that we are so hard on ourselves. We beat ourselves up, we underestimate ourselves, and we undermine ourselves. We are a case of extremes, from low self-esteem to overconfidence, cockiness, or arrogance. I think that's what gets us in trouble. The "progress, not perfection" theme gave us permission to be flawed.

I had a lot of ground to cover to make any progress. I had to deal with the problems I was having with my mother. I had to deal with the shame of what I had done to my father's name. And then there was the closure that I had never really had after my father died, or the grief that I was unable to express after all these years. When a counselor said I was still grieving for my dad, I resented it bitterly.

"What do you mean when you say I'm 'grieving for my father'?" I responded indignantly. "He died almost twenty years ago!" As I said it, I remembered with sharp pain that I had always felt that a piece of me had died on that day, too. As we talked, I recalled how, as a child, I hungered for his infrequent visits home and for the warmth of his unconditional love. He was a powerful balance to my mother's well-meaning, but austere, parental behavior. I treasured those memories of baseball games and car rides and family evenings when he smiled at me and I just glowed. But the sudden tragedy of his death had cut all that off. I was an even more lonely little girl when I was forced to return to Northfield, and I suffered all my life with the deep lingering regret that I had never been able to say goodbye.

Of course I was grieving for him! I was finally able to admit it. And as soon as I admitted it to myself, the emotional floodgates broke. I wept tears of grief about those childhood years of missing him at home, about being kept away from him when he was dying, and about the early death that never allowed me to tell him how much he meant to me.

From the weeks of tears and long postponed confrontations with grief at Jellinek, a new insight emerged: By denying my grief and denying the trauma of my father's death, I had blinded myself to the truth that Dad was very much with me. His spirit, his love, his gift of music—all were there inside me. I can hear his voice now—singing, joking, and talking. Even more powerfully, he had been there in my darkest hours, guiding me, protecting me, and forgiving me—an angel on my shoulder. Hazelden was very much like school, and I found I liked being back in an educational environment. I embraced it because I was a good student and liked to learn. I started filling myself up with information, including the Big Book, which is a cornerstone of AA. Once I got into the rhythm of things, I truly wanted to understand what was going on inside myself. It wasn't fun, but I discovered that I was in a place where I could feel safe. I was surrounded by people who knew what I needed, knew what it would take for me to get it, but would walk the plank with me for as long as they could. Each of us was assigned a personal counselor. Mine was named Vicky. She was only twenty-six years old. She had become an addict when she was twelve, had gotten sober when she was nineteen, and had then become a counselor. I'd say to her, "This isn't going to work, and you're too young to be telling me anything." But Vicky was wise way beyond her years, and she was good. She helped me to articulate my real feelings. One of the things I was learning about myself was that I was a people-pleaser to a fault. I was afraid to say no without feeling guilty. I handed out the benefit of the doubt like candy. And when I was wronged, I didn't know how to express my anger. As I was growing up, I was not allowed or encouraged to disagree—especially with my mother. I had opinions, but I learned to keep them to myself.

The program at Hazelden is built on the AA twelve-step program, and we began to go to meetings daily. I'm not going to pontificate on all twelve steps, but the first and most important step is "We acknowledge that our lives have become unmanageable. We are out of control." It's really hard to acknowledge this, because it means that you have to start taking a look at all the stuff you've done to yourself and others, and that doesn't make you feel very good. Some people handle not feeling good by taking a walk or taking a nap, or maybe they go and exercise like crazy. Others, like myself, need to feel better *fast*. Hence, we look for a way out, and the way I had chosen was self-medication, consequently self-destruction. It starts off very innocently, but for those of us who have a natural addiction to things, whether it's to drugs, alcohol, sex, gambling, bad relationships, whatever—we inevitably end up getting into trouble. We don't know *when* to stop, and after a while, we don't know *how*. I never intentionally tried to kill myself. I thought about it, but I never tried to do it. In fact, it's about the only thing I didn't try.

The second AA concept is that "We believe that only a power higher than ourselves can help us." AA does not promote religion, but it does promote the need for a spiritual perspective, not merely a physical one. In AA they say you come into the program emotionally, physically, financially, and spiritually bankrupt. For many addicts, the first thing they lose is spirituality, and in recovery it is the last thing they get back.

I think the hardest step for me was the eighth one. I had to make a list of everyone I could remember who I'd harmed with my drug use. That was a long list. I was surprised at how many people I could find that I hurt. And then I was supposed to attempt to make amends with each and every one of them, knowing there was no guarantee they would forgive me. There is no guarantee they're even going to respond, but I still had to do it. I was really resistant, and asked, "Can't we take the list and maybe just pray over it?" I hated this step, because it forced me to feel humiliated all over again. But I had to do it—I had to see this through.

I decided to write letters. They offered some kind of physical evidence. However, the staff recommended face-to-face discussions with certain people, and obviously I needed to resolve some major issues with my mother. They asked my mother to come to Hazelden, but she wouldn't. This was not a really great time for my mother, either. She was not too happy about my situation, and most assuredly she was embarrassed, but her refusing to come didn't make it better. There are certain things that she could have done. My counselors felt that at the appropriate time, it would have been helpful to me for her to participate in some of my therapy, if only for a day or two, but she wasn't able to do it. She really wanted the blame to stay right where she thought it should be, and that was with me. I never got around to asking her why she didn't make the effort, and I daresay many parents might have reacted similarly. Curiously enough, my mother had sent me a beautiful and loving card for Valentine's Day. But that was before she was asked to come to my therapy. Sometimes I just couldn't figure her out.

As a mother myself, I can't imagine not being there for my child at such a critical, sensitive time. (I hope I never have to find out.) But I can't blame my mother. Certainly there were things in the past that had happened between us and we had both been affected. But ultimately, I made my own choice. It was more important that I take responsibility for my stuff and my mistakes. Blaming someone else at this point was going to get me absolutely nowhere.

I think my drugging and recovery was a learning experience for my entire family. My younger siblings were easily influenced by the things that they heard. To them, I guess I was the black sheep in the family. My sister Cookie was very upset when she heard that the Hazelden people had asked my mother to come and she had refused. She had her own issues with my mother, and it drove even more of a wedge between the two of them. Cookie and I got very close at this time. She was incredibly supportive and continues to be one of the major angels in my life today.

I think my mother just didn't want to deal with examining the part of herself that was Natalie's mother. When you look at a child in trouble, it feels like a reflection on you, whether it is or not. Even if it's not, there's still a connection that has been broken, and that's what my mother didn't want to acknowledge.

I wish my mother could have had the vision and the courage to be able to put everything aside and say, "Whatever it takes, I'm going to be there for my daughter." But she wasn't that kind of mom, so I keep hoping, and try to leave the door open.

There were other parts of the process that I didn't like very much. I had to keep a journal every night. I hated seeing my thoughts on paper—it was so invasive—and I hated having my counselor look at them. However, toward the end of winter, I had a breakthrough. Vicky was excited, and said, "I think you're starting to learn about forgiveness—starting with yourself."

This is a crucial and powerful tool. Forgiving myself was painful, but once I started, I was able to do something that was also very important—I could start to forgive my mom. As I continued to write in my journal, my perspectives started to change. I needed to forgive her for not being there for me as a child, and for not being a more nurturing parent. I had never thought about forgiving my father for dying, because I blamed everything on her. But Vicky helped me realize that I needed to focus some of that forgiveness on him, too, because many times he was not there for me either, but I made excuses for him. Forgiveness is one of the hardest virtues to attain. It's not part of our nature. It's not human to forgive. It is divine.

By now I had been clean for three or four months, and some of us were allowed to take day trips to the big city (Minneapolis) and go to the mall. I'd been getting high for about five years nonstop, and being sober for this long was almost an out-of-body experience. I didn't know what it felt like not to be loaded. I didn't know what it felt like to be, well, *normal*. The words "being clean" took on a new meaning. It was funny. We all had different recollections of what it was like or how we had felt when we were previously in similar situations but under the influence. And we would exchange stories—by now we had become friends. We were with each other twenty-four hours a day. You know everything about them and they know everything about you, so you decide to become friends. Basically, we were a pretty good group of people who had the common desire to get well. So it was only natural that we bonded together.

The trip was a joy for me, but not everyone had it so easy. Sean, the young man who had smoked so much marijuana that he couldn't walk or talk, came to the mall with the rest of the group. But on our first trip, he had an episode of sensory overload in the car. It was too much for him. It was the first time he had been in a car sober in over a year. He was hyperventilating so bad we had to pull over so he could breathe. He was really in a panic, just from being in a car. Eventually he got to the point where he could ride in the car for more than fifteen minutes and go to the mall. Sometimes it was the little things that meant so much.

During the first few months, I was virtually without music. For the first time in my life, I had no desire for it. I don't remember even listening to the radio much. Whatever was happening on the charts, or who had the latest hit song, I had no clue, and I didn't really want to think about it. There were a couple of Michael Franks cassettes that I did bring with me—that's what I listened to in those pre-CD days. *Michael Franks's, The Art of Tea,* and *Passionfruit* were the tapes I was listening to. They were so comforting and soothing. I needed that. I really loved Michael Franks, and I want to say thank you right now to Michael. (If you don't know who Michael Franks is, go ask somebody.)

It was kind of a conscious decision to be as music-less as possible. I think that in many ways, I was more normal during that time than I probably ever had been. I had grown up with so much music around me that I didn't really have to think. But when I made the decision to get sober, I was able to take advantage of an addictive characteristic, which is to go from one extreme to the other.

The first time I cried tears of joy at Hazelden was when I saw my son. I was just really, really happy. About a month before I left Jellinek, they let him come visit me, and he taught me the meaning of unconditional love. I felt so guilty about what I had done; I had made such a mess of his life, as well as my own. He didn't care—he just wanted his mom. He came with Drue and we all stayed in a hotel room together and went to lunch and dinner. He was so cute. We walked and I held his little hand and looked down into his beautiful face. On some level, I had almost forgotten I was a parent. But I was a mom and there wasn't anything physically wrong with me—so what was I doing there? I was making progress, and that was what counted.

Toward the end of six months, my counselors at Hazelden started getting ready to kick me out. They felt it was time for me to step back into the real world. All of a sudden, six months didn't seem long enough. Was I scared? You bet, but I had been given the tools to make it, and if I was willing to continue to "work the program," I could change and improve the quality of my life…or I could chuck it all and throw those six months right out the window, take my chances, and probably end up very dead.

Sadly, some of the people I went in with did not make it. I heard that the brilliant woman who had been my AA sponsor and had completed the program one month before me committed suicide. Another man who I thought was going to make it also ended up commit- ting suicide not long after he left. I had become really close with the guy who had been in rehab nine different times for heroin, but he couldn't get it together. I heard that when he got out, he became involved in var- ious criminal activities. (Guess I wouldn't know anything about that.)

There were some good reports: When Sean finally "graduated" and left Hazelden, we kept in touch for a bit. Last I heard, he was working in a pharmaceutical company, of all places. How hysterical is that? He wrote that he couldn't believe it himself, and he was never tempted to take even one pill. It is awe- some to see how God works in other people's lives. There are some you know are going to make it, and others you just hope that they do. No one imagined he could ever be totally whole again. But he made it—another walking miracle. Not all recovering addicts are in the facilities. They're still walking down the street, leading decent, productive lives.

Leaving Hazelden was a bittersweet depar- ture. Undoubtedly, it helped to shape, or should I say reshape, the woman I am today. To use the tired but true cliché, it was both the best of times and the worst of times. When I left there, that's how I felt. I graduated from Hazelden on May 16, 1984. When I had arrived six months earlier, it felt like I was entering a frozen wasteland—everything looked and felt like Siberia, which was a good reflection of what was going on inside me. And now, the timing for my departure could not have been more perfect. It was spring, the land was thawing, and flowers were starting to blossom everywhere. The world was full of color. The contrast was amazing. My own appearance had also changed drastically. My skin was glowing and my hair was growing out, but I was thirty pounds heavier. I hadn't been this heavy since I was pregnant with Robbie. But I could lose the fat. It was how I felt about myself that had changed, and I wasn't about to lose that.

As I walked out the doors of Hazelden, hopefully for good, I carried my six-month commemorative "chip" in my hand and a new word had been embedded in my heart—gratitude. It was the best thing I ever did. The best, the best, the best!

CHAPTER 21

Starting Over

Recovery is a lot like life. You're always growing, but never fully grown. And you don't say you are "healed" or "cured." You just say, "Today I did not use, by the grace of God." And you take one step at a time.

There's so much of your life that begins again when you're sober. When I came out of rehab, I felt alive in some ways for the first time in a long while, and I didn't want to lose that. Even though I was back in the "real world," there was still a feeling of *unreality* about coming out of Hazelden, and part of that feeling stayed with me for years.

It seemed like I was being watched—and I was. You know how it feels when you're just driving along, and then you look in the rearview mirror and see a cop? And he's not really following you, he's just going in your direction? It's a weird feeling. Post-Hazelden, I would be driving, see a cop in my rearview mirror, and get serious shakes and dry mouth. I had to fight the urge to pull over and surrender. There were "cops" in the rearview mirror within my own personal circle as well. My family, people who worked with me, Robbie's Nana, and everyone around me—especially my son—were kinda lookin' out the corners of their eyes, wondering if I was okay, and watching for clues that I was screwing up. After all, they remembered all too well what had happened the last time I was "cured."

They weren't the only ones. Within just a couple of days of coming back to Los Angeles, I went to my first AA meeting. It was in the Pacific Palisades, and I was stunned when I walked in. All the AA meetings in Hazelden had been rather small, groups of thirty people at the most. There must have been almost a thousand people there in the Palisades. It looked like a convention—or perhaps a premiere. Most of the attendees were industry people. Music, movies, television—lots of familiar faces.

As soon as I walked in, an older man came up to me and said, "Hi, Natalie, nice to meet you. We've been waiting for you..." I shivered—right there a chill went through my body. In that crowd, there was nothing "anonymous" about Alcoholics Anonymous, at least *I* was not anonymous. It was the final assault on whatever remained of my denial or any other lingering delusion that I'd slipped off to Hazelden without anyone noticing.

I was so astonished that I don't remember anything else about that meeting. It wasn't easy to stand up and say, "Hi, I'm Natalie and I'm a recovering addict," although later, at future meetings, I sometimes said, "Hi, I'm Natalie and I'm happy to be a recovering addict." What a difference a day makes.

It's a humbling moment to be able to say, "Yeah, I've been there." Unlike Martin Luther King saying, "I've been to the mountaintop," your testimony is: "I've been to hell and back and I'm still here."

When you get up at a meeting to tell your story—to encourage or to inspire other recovering addicts or recovering alcoholics—there are three things that you talk about: what happened, what it was like, and what it's like now. And even if you're only recently sober, the what-it's-like-now part is always the most inspiring. There were so many should-have-beens in my life—all those obituary head-lines that ran through my brain every time the angels pulled me out—and you don't begin to experience gratitude until your life starts to unravel and then gets put back together again. As they say in AA, one day at a time. You are never done, and in treatment they remind you to "always leave the door ajar—just a little—so that you can look back and see how far you've come."

In the early days of recovery, I still had dreams about drugs. I dreamed about getting high, and the first dream I had is one I remember well. I'm in what looks like a dor-mitory room, with minimal furniture and no rug on the floor. In the room is a tall wooden dresser, and on top of that dresser is all of my paraphernalia. The window is open, the sun is shining, and there are beautiful clouds in the sky—it's a gorgeous, gorgeous day. I'm looking at the bright blue beautiful sky and I'm trying to get to the drugs on that dresser. Everything is in slow motion, and I'm saying to myself, "If I could just have a little bit...no one would know." And then this voice says, "God will know." At that point I wake up. I've actually had that dream a number of times in all different variations. In all situations, In all of them I'm trying to get back to all that stuff. But I never do.

The fact that I didn't get to the drugs, even in my dreams, was a statement to myself of my determination to stay clean. I was determined to stay sober; I was determined to be a mother and take responsibility for raising my son; and, somehow, I was determined to get the music back in my life.

The first thing I needed to do was work on rebuilding the broken pieces of my relationship with my son. If I couldn't have a relationship with him, nothing would be right. Robbie had come to see me in Hazelden not long before I left, and he met me at the airport upon my return. Children are very vulnerable and very sensitive, and Robbie surely knew there was something going on with his mom that was not quite right. What a blessing that children are very forgiving—the heart of a child is just so wonderful—and once I was home, Robbie's needs were quite simple: He just wanted to have his mom back home again.

That was going to take some arranging, because I came out of Hazelden literally homeless. My home on Hutton Drive had been sold while I was away. Not only did the sorry state of my financial affairs demand it, but my counselors at Jellinek had told me I needed to give it up. There were too many things about it that were connected to my old life, right down to my old address books, which were burned. I had to get rid of my relationship with Dino for the same reason. When I got back to Los Angeles, he was no longer in my life. He had been told, rather unceremoniously, that it would be best if we parted.

Even though he had been one of the true good guys in my life, he was an enabler.

For a short while, Robbie and I lived with my Aunt Charlotte, bless her heart, who had a lovely home near Hancock Park in the old neighborhood where I had grown up. I was just so grateful to be back together with my little six-year-old boy, I dedicated myself to solidifying my relationship with him. We spent every day together—it was like being a kid again. We went to the amusement park. (He loves roller coasters, just like me.) I took him to the movies, I cooked for him, I did everything I could just to renew our bond. We were stuck at the hip, giving a new depth of meaning to "inseparable." I wouldn't go anywhere without him, and he would not leave my side.

That initial joined-at-the-hip phase must have been emotionally hard on Drue. Robbie had lived with her while I was gone, and she was the one who had been there for him even before Hazelden, when I was too out of it to mother him. Despite the pain of being displaced in his affections, she was genuinely happy because Robbie was happy. Drue had spoiled him terribly, but I loved her for the love she had given to Robbie.

My mother had made no bones about her displeasure with Drue's close relationship with Robbie, and she was still carrying a grudge because Marvin and I had decided that Robbie would stay with Drue while I was in Hazelden. She was determined to communicate her feelings in a way I could not comprehend: Unbeknownst to me, while I was in Minnesota, she had chosen not to pay Drue's salary. Thank God for my friend Vinnie—the guy who was scared straight by my first rehab—who stepped in and paid Drue every month for six months until I got home. That's a real friend.

My mother is not very good with money, and that's putting it mildly. She never has been. But she knows how to spend it. When I had gone into Hazelden I was close to broke, but when my mother turned my financial affairs back over to me, I was *really* broke. In fact, now I owed her money.

I needed to be back on my own, the sooner the better, and Dan, Ralph, and Jeff—my business team—scrambled to set me up in a place to live. By borrowing from Peter to pay Paul and pulling rabbits out of the proverbial hat, my son and I moved into a townhouse in Studio City, and for the next ten years I was a Valley Girl. They found me a car, too—a little black Fiero. Only Robbie and I could fit in the car, but at least I had wheels, and, honey, beggars can't be choosers.

The place on Hutton had been lovely and spacious, but now I had this big furniture left over from it that I had to stuff into the town-house. I jammed most of it in there, but it didn't really fit, and everything was out of scale. Since I didn't have any money for new furniture and didn't know how long I'd be there, I had to make do, but I was not always feeling as grateful as I should have been. I was ashamed

of my home. The reality is that there wasn't
a damn thing wrong with that place, and to
someone else, it would have been a palace.
Mostly I hated the townhouse because it was
a daily reminder that I was starting over.

When I moved in, I had to go through a lot
of my belongings that I hadn't seen in a while.
When the house on Hutton was sold, everything had been boxed and put into storage—
well, not quite everything. Sorting through the
debris of my former life was another unpleasant
experience—and it was made even more miserable when I realized how many of my things
were missing. Because she had control of my
affairs, my mother had access to my house while
I was in Hazelden. I think it is safe to say that
she had gone through my stuff and thrown away
some of my belongings. Although Cookie did
what she could to protect my possessions,
the damage had already been done.

Now that I had a place to live, I had to get
back to work. Dan was convinced that now that
I was clean and sober, I could make a comeback. At first, I wasn't so sure. In darker
moments, I imagined myself flipping burgers
or answering telephones. I don't know what
kept me going other than my Aunt Bay. She
must have worn out several sets of knee pads
praying for me. She was my inspiration, my
courage. We talked almost daily, and she
refused to let me fold. And within six weeks,
I was on my way back to work—but with
great angst and trepidation. For several years
after Hazelden, I was borne along by other

people's faith in me, and not by my faith in myself. If it had been left up to me, I'd probably *still* be sitting in a little hole somewhere, scared to death. And I was not just career-scared; I was life-scared—flat-out deer-in-the-headlights petrified. I was consumed with basic survival issues.

God bless Dan, who was as much a cheerleader as he was a manager. He just kept saying, "It's going to be fine. You're going to be fine." He pushed and pushed and he kept saying, "You can do this," and "This is how we're going to do it."

By July of 1984, I was working for Steve Wynn, appearing at the Golden Nugget in downtown Las Vegas. Steve was my employer, good friend, and a dear man. I am still so grateful to him for taking me on when nobody else would. The good news was that I was alive and sober, and I was working—and I hoped I could still sing my butt off. The bad news was that I was gonna *have* to sing my butt off, because it had gotten so enormous.

Hazelden had done a great deal to restore my self-esteem, and it also restored my sense of vanity. I became very self-conscious about how I looked onstage. I cared again about my appearance. My size presented a practical problem—I couldn't get into any of my clothes. I didn't have the money to go out and buy new ones, so we found a seamstress who could run up a few things for me to perform in—real cheap.

The gig at the Golden Nugget was not a fancy

showroom—after years as a headliner, I was back to working the lounge. It was a big comedown from where I'd been playing before, but nevertheless, it was a place to start, and it was pretty cool being back onstage—any stage. I wasn't real happy about the way I looked, so I compensated by singing the house down.

I was delighted to be singing again, and even more delighted when I realized that I hadn't lost my ability to connect with the audience. It's a skill I learned as "the-daughter-of." I remember someone saying that people want to be sung to, not at, and that was one thing Dad was very good at doing. It was also one of the best gifts he ever passed on to me. By being open and revealing his humanness every time he went onstage, he taught me the most important lesson about performing—without saying a thing. Whatever kind of music you're singing, you must connect with the people in the audience—and once you connect, you can do anything you want, because they are there with you.

I connected with a few members of the audience in particular, including a guy who might be considered my first boyfriend since Hazelden. He was a professional gambler. I sure know how to pick them, don't I? Butch was much younger than me, and was actually quite a nice guy. At least he wasn't into drugs. It turned out that he traveled with a posse—there was Grandpa Bad, Markers, and a guy named Munchies. The head guy—the God-father—was named Willie "Flukey" Stokes.

They all wore those broke-down hats and big ole fur coats. They were mack daddy to their hearts. (For those in need of a translation, a mack daddy is a guy who dresses fly. He doesn't have to be cute—he's got a pimp look, but not necessarily a pimp mentality. He is generous, he is *soave bola*—you never know too much about him, and he's always surrounded by women.)

Butch and his friends all dressed in orange or yellow or turquoise or lavender color-coordinated suits—right down to their silk underwear. Even their socks matched. You had to question their taste, but everything they wore looked expensive. I never had seen anything like it before. They looked like throwbacks to 1969—but a nicer group of guys you've never met. And they treated me like gold.

I had met them when they came to one of my shows at the Golden Nugget. After that, they came almost every night—five or six of them—and they would make requests. Butch and his friends just loved watching me perform. After the show, they would sit with me and talk, and then they would go gamble. I only went gambling with them once. Thank the Lord, gambling is one addiction that I missed. It held no attraction for me at all. In fact, I disliked it so much that I would run instead of walk whenever I had to go through the casino.

Not these guys. When this group walked into the casino, they were there on business, and they were expected. The pit bosses had a table waiting just for them—they shot craps at their own private reserved table. They would typically bring in half a million dollars in cash, lose it one day, get it back the next, and then add an extra three or four hundred thousand dollars the day after that. They were serious gamblers, and they knew when to quit, so they did make money. The casino bosses didn't seem to mind, and the whole posse seemed well thought of.

They were nice people, at least to me. Unlike the typical slicksters, I was really the only lady these guys had around them. One or two had a girlfriend come with them occa-sionally, but they didn't have a bevy of women hanging around them, at least not when I was there. They showed a lot of respect for me and they thought I was the bee's knees. Butch took me to dinner, behaved like a gentleman, and treated me like a lady.

My instincts told me, however, that Flukey led a double life—and so he did. (What a surprise!) It turns out that Butch's boss was more than a professional gambler. He was also a money launderer, drug dealer, and debt collector. He kept most of his money underneath his kitchen floor. When Flukey was gunned down on Chicago's South Side in 1986, more than seven thousand people turned out to give him a folk hero's funeral. He was buried with his ever-present cell phone held up to his ear. Two years earlier, Flukey had buried his son, Willie "the Wimp" Stokes, in somewhat more flamboyant style. Willie Junior had been propped up in a coffin built to resemble a Cadillac Eldorado convertible, complete with blinking headlights and taillights, a windshield, whitewall tires, a Cadillac grille, and his vanity license plate, which read "WIMP." His hands holding the steering wheel had $100 bills woven between the bejeweled fingers. I just knew that someone was going to dig that thing up eventually.

My engagement in the lounge lasted about two weeks. Vegas paid well, but Dan didn't want me to play there for too long. (I wasn't wild about staying longer, either. Although I'd been well paid and well treated at the Golden Nugget, the Vegas of 1984 was a lot seedier than the Vegas of today.) He wanted my career to move forward, and he had a plan.

Dan was very smart and he had a lot of ideas, which was good, because at that point I didn't have any. It was all I could do to put one foot in front of the other. My career aspirations, to the extent that I had any at all, were modest. I would have been happy to get even halfway back to where I'd been. I had no idea that going further was even possible—it just wasn't in my brain. The core of Dan's strategy was to book me *out* of the limelight, so I could build up my little purse and also get my chops back. Smaller venues, smaller cities, but bizarrely enough, these gigs still paid fairly well. A successful singer's life is truly amazing: You have the potential to make a hundred thousand dollars in a couple of weeks. Although I was just starting back to performing, I was paid $20,000 to $25,000 for each appear-

ance—and that was low money for me compared to what I'd made before.

I worked for almost a year in places that you
ain't never heard of, but I was able to build
myself up financially. Honey, at this point I
was in it for the money as much as anything.
Nothing else was going to work until I was confident that I could provide for Robbie and me.
I started to travel again—a lot, and I put in a
tremendous number of days away from home.
My May graduation from Hazelden was good
timing from one standpoint, because for the
summer of '84, Robbie was out of school and
could travel with me. We spent July and
August together. In September, when he
started first grade, I took him over to Drue's
on weekends, which was mostly when I worked.
During the week he was in school and at
home with me.

After I left Las Vegas, Butch came to visit
me in Los Angeles occasionally—although
he stayed with other people, not with Robbie
and me. I must say he was a gentleman, and
he was very friendly to Robbie. When Butch
came to visit, Drue would cook for him. She
was a great cook and the guys were really
nice to her—and actually to everyone who
worked for me. Butch and I saw each other for
about six months. He bought me nice gifts, but
we had more of a friendship than a relationship—we were rarely intimate sexually, in
part because I was still much too fragile to get
involved with anyone.

It was important to concentrate on my

work. Dan chose my gigs carefully. There were no big shows, nothing more than he thought I could handle. He made sure I moved up gradually, so that I was able to get well and get better, not in front of giant crowds but in front of smaller audiences, at least until I lost some weight and got back my confidence. It was about work, work, work, focus, focus, focus, and staying the hell out of places like L.A., New York, or Chicago, where the press might eat me and my fat butt alive.

My job was to show up on time and sing— two things I'd been unable to do before I went to Hazelden. Dan took care of everything else. He rode herd on all the messy details, including the mundane (but endless) touring and contractual arrangements. The hardest part, of course, was just getting the bookings. He went through almost as much hell as I did. There may have been a lot of nice people rooting for me out there, but not many of them were in the music business. He got a lot of doors slammed in his face and hang-ups in his ear, and I'm sure I don't know the half of it. He shielded me from all that rejection, because he knew I wouldn't be able to take it. At a time when I was vulnerable, Dan was very protective, and that's probably one of the things that was, and still is, most valuable about him. Dan understands integrity. He understands morals and ethics. And Dan has never judged me.

Little by little, the master strategy started to pay off, but recording was something I didn't dare do again until early 1985, when a man named Paul Fishkin came to us. Paul, a recovering addict himself, had started a new label called Modern Records that was being distributed by EMI. It was a small independent label, and they were willing to take a chance on me. The result was *Dangerous*, my first album since the dreadful *I'm Ready*, and a semi-hit single by the same name. This reentry back into the music industry was to be my first sober album in six years.

Doing *Dangerous* put me back into contact with a lot of people in the music business I had worked with before. That was embarrassing and it was scary, because I didn't know how they were going to react when I walked into a room. The music industry was totally disgusted with me. It was as if I'd written them a bad check. I wasn't the only one going through this stuff, but my story stuck out somehow, because a lot of people had put a lot of time into backing and supporting me. I guess my screwup was more special than other folks'. My first five years after rehab were marked by having to prove and prove again that I was back. In these early stages of recovery, I discovered the truth about how people saw me when I was still using drugs. Some of them just couldn't wait to remind me of how wasted I was, or what a bitch I was, or how I'd let them down. Hell, I wasn't just famous—I was notorious. Listening to their accounts, I was forced to confront my mistakes. I gritted my teeth—I was determined to get through this somehow.

It's funny, because I almost got used to people saying, "I've been really praying for you," or "It's nice to have you back," just as if I'd been away at war, or was out on parole. It was like having leprosy. Sometimes it felt good, and other times I wanted them to shut up. It did confirm that people know more about you than you think they do.

We started working on *Dangerous* at the Music Factory, a studio on Melrose Boulevard in Los Angeles. Marti Sharon and Gary Skardina wrote and produced the material. I think we found Marti and Gary through Paul Fishkin. I liked Marti—she was crazy and fun. And she pushed me a little, too. To this point, I'd been much more confident onstage than I was in the recording studio, but Marti thought my voice was this incredible instrument, and she had me doing things that I didn't think I could do.

My voice was actually in better shape than ever. After the nodules in my throat were removed and before going to Hazelden, I'd worked briefly with a vocal coach named Seth Riggs. He had been very concerned about my voice at the time, because the combination of the late nights and trying to work around the drug smoking amounted to terrible abuse. Now I started working very seriously with him again. I was diligent, and it paid off. I became his pupil, the person he would refer to as an example to follow. He was so proud of me for hitting notes that I hadn't hit in a long time, and he was proud of the power that I had.

On March 22, 1985, I was getting ready to go onstage in Dallas when I received a telephone call to tell me that Marvin had had a stroke and had died. I didn't know what to do, so I walked out and told the audience what had happened. They were stunned. I was devastated. I couldn't believe that Marvin was dead, and I couldn't believe that anybody would give me the bad news right before a performance. I don't know how I made it through that show. When I got offstage, I called Drue and told her to fly Robbie to me from Los Angeles. When he arrived, I had to tell my sweet little seven-and-a-half-year-old that his daddy was dead.

Marvin had loved his son so much—oh, he loved his little boy. Robbie had been with his father just a week before in Chicago. Marvin was only thirty-four years old. Robbie took it okay, at least at first, but I was a mess. Although Marvin had remarried, I continued to think of him as my soul mate.

Marvin's lifestyle during and after our marriage had contributed to his death. He had a heart murmur, which I didn't even know about until after we had divorced, and of course, doing drugs with a heart condition is dangerous.

Before he died, he had come to Los Angeles, and it seemed like something was starting to rekindle. We had even talked about getting back together. I joked with him and said, "Just don't get your wife pregnant." He seemed to be under a lot of pressure—possibly some of it was financial. Professionally, he and Chuck were never able to hook up with anyone of great significance after their success with me—they never found that next Aretha. Some say he died of a heart attack, others say he died of an aneurysm, but I've always believed that Marvin really died of a broken heart.

Going back to Chicago for the funeral was horrible. Lord Jesus, it was awful. The services were held at Fellowship Baptist Church, and the Reverend Jesse Jackson, Chuck's half-brother, officiated at the services. The funeral was huge, and the church was filled to the rafters with people standing in the aisles. Even more outside came to mourn or to stare. The street in front was closed off and the police had to be there to direct traffic.

From the ruckus everyone made when I walked in, you'd have thought that I was still Marvin's wife. (At the bottom of my heart, in some ways, that's what I felt, too.) Everyone knew that my career had been born in Chicago, and that it had started because of Marvin and Chuck.

Gospel singer Albertina Walker sang. She had witnessed our marriage and had loaned me the wedding dress when Marvin and I got married in the back seat of the Cadillac. After the service, we drove forever to the cemetery, and it all came back—I was flooded with memories of my father's funeral, with all the crowds and the ceremony and the press everywhere taking pictures. It was tough—really hard. That was a sad time, a really, really sad time.

Robbie went to the viewing, but he did not go to the funeral. I wasn't going to put him through that.

Robbie was now a boy without a father, and I knew that I could never fill those shoes. I felt very much alone, grieving, and still trying to find my own way in recovery. Marvin's death was like a door that had closed. Little did I know that it was the first of many.

CHAPTER 22

Be Careful
What You Pray For

More than ever, my first responsibility now was to Robbie, and I was thankful that I was healthy enough to be able to take care of him. Marvin died less than a year after I got out of rehab. Before Hazelden, I could hardly take care of myself, let alone take care of my son. I hadn't been a good mom, and Marvin had been concerned that if I didn't get my act together, he'd have to take Robbie away from me. But Marvin would have done that only as a last resort. He always believed that I would still make a good mother if I could just get myself together, and that's where he wanted our son to be. It's weird—he wanted that not just for Robbie, but for me. It's almost like he knew that I needed that, and instead of frightening me, it made me feel good. If he had died before I went in to Hazelden or while I was there, I would have lost my son. There's no telling with whom he would have ended up.

Even with Marvin's untimely death, it was another demonstration of God's grace. God has always been the force that has moved me, ever so slightly to the left or to the right, just in time to allow me to be accessible to the blessing—or to get me out of the way of the oncoming train at the last moment.

When I returned to Los Angeles from Marvin's funeral to resume work on *Dangerous,* there was another piece of Providence waiting for me in the form of a telegram. It was from Aretha Franklin. It was very simple, just, "I'm so very sorry to hear about Marvin—if you need anything, please call." I was touched by her reaching out to me like that. But how sad that it took something so tragic to reunite our friendship. I didn't see Aretha for a while, but we would occasionally talk on the telephone. As far as I'm concerned, they should erect a statue of Aretha. I loved this lady and I never stopped loving her. (She recently came to see my show in Detroit, and let me tell you, it was *such* a good feeling to have her there.)

I knew that Marvin's death would have a profound effect on Robbie, and my concerns about his emotional security just added to the worries I already had about being the sole provider for his welfare. Our relationship as mother and son was back on solid ground, but for the next ten years or so, I worked hard making sure that nothing bad happened to him, and that nothing bad happened to me—and I stocked up on knee pads.

With a heavy heart, I went back to Los Angeles and finished *Dangerous*. Although nothing of huge consequence came of it, at least it sounded good. There is one song on the album called "The Gift," which was written by a friend of mine, Mark Davis. The song is somewhat autobiographical: It's about trying to get control of your life, and it speaks volumes about where my head was at the time. With my first sober album, I proved to myself that I could do it. In the past, I had really believed that I needed drugs to perform at my best. But, of course, I found out that wasn't true. Gradually I began to feel a little of the confidence that Dan had had in me all along. My career didn't come back all at once, but rather in bits and pieces. I saw each piece coming back, got a chance to adjust, and then went to work on the next piece. It was like climbing a ladder, one step at a time. I would say a little prayer in my heart: "Thank you, God, for what you have given me; thank you, God, for what you have taken away; and thank you, God, for what you have left me."

I got a contract to perform at what was considered to be the best of Vegas, Caesars Palace. I was the opening act for Dionne

Warwick. I will always think of her as a good friend because she was always very supportive and encouraging. She couldn't have been more loving. She'd come out and do all of her zillion hits after I did my set—I was a bit more pop, but it worked. As I was finishing up, I'd introduce her and have my moment to stand onstage with Dionne Warwick. I reconnected with some great people, including "Uncle" Bill Cosby, who gave me his big dressing room and took a teensy one instead. I'd known him since my student days, and of course, he'd performed with me at the Hilton right before the fire.

At this point, the Lord must have thought I could take on more. I've learned that God has his own way of preparing his soldiers. He gradually takes away things so that you have to stand on your own. You can't keep depending on other people to be there. And pretty soon you have to depend solely upon Him. I was still dependent upon a lot of other people, to the degree that was unhealthy. So God said, "Okay, this person is starting to mean just a little too much to you, and I need you to move forward. Now watch this..."

And so more people started dying—very significant people. A very good friend died of AIDS before anyone knew what it was. My cousin Janice, my traveling companion and my spiritual advisor, was next. She'd never been the same after the fire at the Hilton in 1981. The walk down the twenty-four smoky flights of stairs had put such a strain on her heart and lungs that she developed cardiac and respiratory problems. She had always been heavy, and with all that damage to her heart and lungs from the fire, she got sicker and sicker. She started losing a lot of weight, and eventually she had a stroke and couldn't move her hands. Aunt Bay and Pam had to take care of her, and she resented the loss of her independence. Janice died on the sixteenth of November, 1985.

Right after that, Robbie was suddenly struck with a frightening and bizarre medical problem. He and I were attending a church event with cousin Eddie and Aunt Bay one Sunday evening when Robbie complained of not feeling well and showed me a bump on his neck, which appeared to be a swollen gland. Taking no chances, we went to the emergency room at Cedars-Sinai Medical Center, where he was given an antibiotic and admitted to the hospital. Within an hour, Robbie went into shock and developed blisters all over his body. As he lay there in intensive care for a week, running a high fever and breaking out in boils and lesions, a small army of specialists tried to determine what was happening to my son. Finally they identified his condition as Stevens-Johnson syndrome, a rare skin disease that can occur as a reaction to drugs such as peni-cillin. Robbie's case was particularly severe, and his body was so covered with painful blisters that the hospital brought in a special type of bed for him that is used for burn vic-tims.

During the seven and a half weeks that he

remained in the hospital, I stayed at his bed-side every day. Drue and I took turns staying with him at night. It was a grueling experience for Robbie, and terrifying for me, because I had to watch helplessly as this strange disease ran its course and ravaged my son's body. Anne Archer, the actress, happened to be at Cedars to research a role that she was preparing to play as an ICU nurse, and I will never forget how compassionate and comforting she was to me and to Robbie. Although he still bears some scars from this experience, through the grace of God, Robbie emerged with his health restored.

In March of 1987, I was in Milan, Italy, when I got a call that Drue, Robbie's Nana, had had an aneurysm. By the time I could make it home, they had taken her to Daniel Freeman Hospital, where she lay in a coma, never to regain consciousness. Her daughter, Debra, and I had to make the difficult decision to take her off life support.

Robbie was not yet ten years old, and the impact on him of all this dying was devastating. Death is not anything you can ever get used to, and that little boy saw a lot of death at a very young age. It started affecting him. He became fearful of going to funerals, because people he loved were dying all over the place. He was afraid to grow up, because he started believing that if you grow up, you're going to die. He thought I was going to die next, and he worried a lot whenever I left town. His father was dead and he had no brothers and sisters, so I was *it*. He didn't want to be too far away, because separation was scary to him. He went to a local school, and every weekend we were together. We were a matched set—except for the hours he was in school, wherever I went, he went.

The question for me was, where was I going to go next? After *Dangerous*, we had origi-nally contracted to make a second album with Modern Records, and although we started work on it, we couldn't finish. Paul Fishkin didn't have enough financial backup, and his company eventually folded, or at least that's what I was told. It could be they just pulled the plug, but didn't tell me. Either way, we were out in the cold, and Dan had to go look for another label, and I was gonna be a tough sell. The truth was that although I had been busy giving myself a pat on the back for making my first sober album in six years, nobody else in the record industry cared. All those doors that slammed shut right before Hazelden were still closed tight, but this time it was for a different reason. Dan, as always, put it to me straight. "Nat," he said, "if an artist is saleable, a record company isn't terribly con-cerned about their sobriety. And if you're not commercially viable [a gracious way of saying that you're not making a lot of money for the company], they don't give a rat's ass that you've turned your personal life around."

One of the places where Dan felt we might have a chance was at EMI, which was headed up by an old friend of his, Bruce Lundvall. At the time, I had a gig at a music festival in Cleveland, and because Bruce was such an old friend, Dan leaned on him hard to get him to send his A&R guy, Gerry Griffith, to Cleveland to catch my act. Gerry responded pretty much as if he'd been ordered to the dentist for a root canal, but he agreed to go. After the show, Dan and I waited around, but Gerry never came backstage. I was disappointed—his nonappearance played to all my insecurities: Was I *that* bad?

As luck would have it, the next morning Dan was at the Cleveland airport, waiting for his flight to L.A., when he spotted Gerry. Knowing Gerry hadn't shown up, and wanting to get to the bottom of things, Dan quickly changed his flight to New York. Gerry never knew Dan was on his flight, and they arrived at the EMI offices at almost the same time. Dan headed straight for Bruce's office, smoke coming out of his ears. He bullied his way in without an appointment, demanding to know what Gerry had thought of my performance. (This is classic Cleary, and the fact that Dan would take off on this kind of dogged hot pursuit on my behalf is one of the reasons why I respect him so much.)

Bruce called Gerry in, and he confessed to his boss that on his way to the show, he had narrowly averted a terrible car accident. He felt that this was God's way of telling him not to go to the show, so he'd turned around and gone back to the hotel.

Dan listened to the story and asked Bruce

if they could have a moment alone. Once Gerry left, Dan turned to his friend and declared, "God was in touch with me, too, and He told me you'd better give Natalie a two-album contract." His will was done.

Bruce is actually a very lovely man, and one of the more subtle angels in the record business. He was very supportive and he, like a few others, saw something in me and my work that made him believe in me and say he'd go for it.

EMI-Manhattan bought a couple of the songs that I was getting ready to record for the second album on Modern. One of them was a ballad called "I Live for Your Love"; the other was a Bruce Springsteen number, "Pink Cadillac." They became big hits off an album I called *Everlasting*.

Both "I Live for Your Love" and "Pink Cadillac" were the brainstorms of producer Dennis Lambert. He'd done the Jefferson Starship hit "We Built This City." When I went to his house to work on "Cadillac," I was nervous. This was a dance song—and you remember how I felt about that disco dance stuff—but then, I'd never worked with anyone quite like Dennis before. He was very passionate about his work, which turned out to be great for me, because his enthusiasm gave me the confidence that I could pull this off. Two very hot mixers named David Cole and Robert Clivilles (known collectively as C&C Music Factory) put a mix on "Pink Cadillac" that was over the top, and it ended up as a huge hit in every dance club around the world. *I* had a dance hit. Me! It was hysterical.

I thought to myself, "I'm too old to be doing this kind of stuff." I couldn't imagine myself on stage rockin' to the music like Tina Turner. But "Pink Cadillac" turned out to be a big song, and it took us all over the place. With "Pink Cadillac," I started playing club dates where the gay crowd hung from the rafters—it was my Grace Jones kind of a vibe. The song became very big in Europe. It was wild, and it was a lot of fun. I was really very surprised. I never got a chance to talk to Bruce Springsteen, but word got back that he was blown away by it. He thought it was very cool that a woman could do this and it would come out so great.

The next single was a beautiful ballad called "I Live for Your Love," which was also a hit. The third hit from the album, called "Jump-start My Heart," was produced by two brothers, Reggie and Vince Calloway. It was a big deal for me when it hit number two on the R&B charts. I also did a few Burt Bacharach songs, and had a chance to spend a lot of time with him and his then wife, songwriter Carole Bayer Sager. The two songs they did for me are "Split Decision" and "In My Reality."

One of the difficult things for me about recording is that I want every song to be really good. Often on albums, there are one or two hits, and the rest is filler. For me they didn't all have to be hits, but they all had to be good. Even when I was first starting out,

I was always considered to be an "album artist"; I was never just a singles girl. People wanted the whole enchilada, which was a real compliment to me, so I wanted every song to count.

We really worked hard promoting *Everlasting*—I performed at a lot of dance clubs, and visited or phoned over 250 radio stations and even made appearances in stores. Sometimes I hit seven of them in a day, and believe me, that was rough. I had to go to places I didn't feel like going, and schmooze with people I didn't feel like schmoozing with—and the stations knew it. They loved being able to jerk me around, because they knew that I had to do it. It was a very humbling experience, but if you disappear for a while like I did, you can't come back and expect your seat will be saved.

The impossible happened! *Everlasting* spawned three hit records and eventually went gold. When it was nominated for a Grammy, I was floored. There were lots of kudos, lots of people saying, "We missed you; you deserve this." Even Robbie was running around the house screaming, "She's back!" As I was nearing the end of my fourth year of sobriety, the cops in my rearview had backed off, and I, too, started to believe, "Okay, maybe I am back"—almost.

When it comes to getting awards, I've always been surprised—starting with the first Grammy in 1976 that I "stole" from Aretha Franklin. Win or lose, however, I was always very grateful, because I knew how hard everyone had worked—not just me. With *Everlasting,* I was actually happier for Dan than I was for myself when we started kickin' some butt, because it's wonderful when someone really believes in you and you don't disappoint them. Indeed, success is the best revenge.

It felt as if another piece fell into place when I won a *Soul Train* award a little later in 1988. "I Live for Your Love" won in the Best Female Single category. There is a funny line black artists have to walk when they cross over to the pop charts, and getting this award from my peers meant that they still felt I was black, too. At the awards ceremony, I felt very grateful, and I got a chance to thank those who had seen me come and go—and come again. The icing on the cake was winning an NAACP Image Award that same year. On both of those occasions I had the great pleasure of sharing the stage with Whitney Houston. Whitney had won the *Soul Train* award for Best Female Album for her second album, *Whitney.* And at the finale of the NAACP Image Awards, we just tore up the stage together.

I had met Whitney while I was doing a show in Boston. At the tender age of nineteen, she had just started touring after the smash "Saving All My Love for You." I was impressed by the way she carried herself, and I knew this girl was going to be a star. I went backstage to introduce myself and tell her how much I enjoyed her work, and we ended up becoming great friends. We exchanged telephone numbers, and we called each other every now and again. Sometimes we lose touch, and have to get back in touch again. It's like we are connected by rubber bands—no matter how long it's been since we last talked, five minutes after we're talking again, it is as if no time has passed at all. She's always so very gracious. Our relationship is mostly over the telephone, because we are both so busy. But we have a nice strong connection. I think she knew right away that I was there to be supportive. Whitney is like my baby sister, and I think she knows how much I am in her corner. She, in turn, showed her support for me in future situations— but I'm getting ahead of myself.

When I think of the people around my mother and father—the celebrity people—I recall how real they were. They were very nice to me, and they weren't just patting me on the head. They invited my family to their homes. I don't recall being around what I would consider phony or fake people. They weren't just drive-bys, they were true friends to my parents. Pearl Bailey, Ella Fitzgerald, Louis Armstrong, and Danny Thomas are gone now, but if they were alive, they would still radiate that sincerity. When I started getting into this business, I looked for the same kind of friends my parents had: the ones that I could count on. But times have changed. I don't have a lot of celebrity pals, but there are a few I am proud to call friends and I would hope they consider me the same way.

I remember a conversation I had with Whitney when she was feeling overwhelmed. We were both in London, and I had called her from my car to say I was headed home to the United States. We talked for my entire drive to Heathrow and she was stressed out. She finally confided that sometimes she felt as though she couldn't trust anybody.

I told her, "Honey, I've been there." I value friendships like this because they are just so damn hard to come by.

More often than not, your *best* friends will be others who are in the business, or people you have known for a long time from before you were a star. These people are the ones who watch your back. They are the ones who know your faults, and love you anyway. I'm glad that I've kept my old friends, because it's taught me how to be one—especially to some people in the business who have a hard time trusting friendships.

The most gratifying thing I'd heard from my good friends in the business since I came out of Hazelden was "Good to have you back." I don't know if all of them meant it, but it sounded good, and it seemed appropriate to call my new album *Good to Be Back*. I worked with an incredible saxophone player and new talent named Kenny G. He joined me on one song on the album, an R&B version of "When I Fall in Love," one of my father's songs. It was a very cool version and it was produced by the talented musician Marcus Miller. Despite the fact that Kenny G. had broken his hand, he still came to put his part on, and he did a great job. That's dedication.

I wrote a song of my own called "More Than the Stars." I had written it with my cousin Eddie and I loved the lyrics. I got to work with Burt Bacharach and Carole Bayer Sager again, and it was great. Burt is crazy. Whenever I went to his house, he just sat down at the piano and started going. Carole had great lyrics and Burt writes wall to wall—in any of the songs I've recorded for him, there's no bridge or instrumental break. You just have to keep on singing forever—kind of like with Michael Masser.

You remember, the last time I had worked with Michael Masser was in 1980, and I swore then that it would be exactly that—the last time. *Good to Be Back* proved that you should never say never, no matter what. For this album I ended up working with him on a song called "Miss You Like Crazy." "Miss You Like Crazy" was like a baby—it took nine months to record.

It didn't take long before the sessions descended into a state of war between Michael and me, and when he came into the recording booth with me, I hit the ceiling. The booth is "sacred ground." It's the artist's turf, and no one else is permitted. No other producer in the land does that, and he had worked with other big stars like Aretha, Whitney, and Barbra. He stood there and actually conducted me, or tried to, which was horrible, as well as unnecessary—I mean, give me a break.

"Get him out of here!" I finally shrieked to no one in particular. Michael left, but stood at the window looking at me, which made me turn my mike and music stand toward the wall, so my back was to the glass. Who says the artist is the only one who gives drama?

One day, during this nine-month labor of love/hate, I was in the studio trying to keep from killing him when Whitney Houston called. I told her, "I gotta be some kind of masochist. I can't believe I'm doing this to myself again! I thought that the twenty takes he made me do the last time was bad—this time it's worse, much worse." The final total was sixty vocal tracks.

She said, "Girl, just go have a drink... because that's what he does." Whitney told me that Michael had made her do 120 vocals for "Saving All My Love." Somehow I got through my sixty still sober.

This time it wasn't just me he pissed off. Michael got so possessive of "Miss You Like Crazy" that he took the master home with him. This was a definite no-no—the master belonged to the record company and they had no sense of humor about it leaving the premises. He had wanted "Miss You" to come out at a certain time, but EMI-Manhattan was not cooperating, so he ran off with it. Up until then, Manhattan had been so enamored with Michael that they had let him call the shots. Now they realized that maybe he was a little bit over-the-top, and they went ballistic. A sheriff was promptly dispatched to Michael's home to demand that he surrender the master.

Don't get me wrong. I still love Michael dearly. He is a good guy with geniuslike qualities, and genuinely sweet. He's so sincere and so passionate. But just like the last time, working with him made me nuts. I vowed never to work with him again. And, guess what? Just like last time, his song was the hit of the album.

By 1988, I was approaching the five-year anniversary of my sobriety. I had not touched a drug since November 29, 1983, and it really took that five years—five and a half years— to get back to where I was before this all happened. These years were not that pleasant, but at least I got through them sober, and that was the most important thing. Most recovering addicts would say that we've been to the other side and have seen the jaws of death. We've looked into the face of despair; we have been to the land of no return. Some of us came back; a lot of us didn't. This is where gratitude continues to prevail.

For most recovering addicts, the last thing that you usually get back is your spirituality. In my case it was the first thing I got back, and it came back stronger than ever. Even though emotionally I was still pretty shaky, I learned to depend on God. No matter what else happened, I was going to be okay. I was able to surrender (but it is a daily process). I began to read my Bible daily—that's where my strength is. The hardest thing for me is to not put so much hope in other people, because I have always been so trusting. This continues to be an issue I have to work on.

As my five-year anniversary approached, there was one big void that I began to feel. Love and romance were missing from my life. Since Marvin and I had separated and divorced, I had had a lot of boyfriends. I don't think I was alone one day—give or take a few weeks here and there. I went through a large number of men, and honey, I can't remember half of them. I wasn't intimate with all of them; it was just a matter of having somebody—anybody.

Frankly, that's the dilemma so many women find themselves in. We've been so brainwashed into thinking that if we don't have a man, there's something wrong with us. That mind-set just begins a whole litany of bad decisions, and it invades other aspects of your life. You find yourself making life choices based on a strategy of how to get another man.

Not long after I got out of Hazelden, there was a big buzz in the media about how after age thirty-five a woman had a better chance of getting struck by lightning than getting a husband. I was about thirty-five at the time, and believe me, all those articles were a boon to the psychiatry and counseling business—every woman I knew was in therapy. We totally bought that idea that we needed a man. For years, I can't count how many of my friends were on this manhunt. And men can smell it... The wrong man smells that and, honey—you are in trouble. Because if you're desperate and he's looking for a free ride—well, you just know how that's gonna come out. All you have to do is take a look at all the women who are on that testosterone safari— they're successful, they've got it together, they've got nice homes, they look kinda halfway good—*and* they're just perfect fruit for that guy who's going to come in and take almost everything they have, including their self-respect. Alas! The joys and pains of being a woman.

In October of 1988, I went to the wedding of a friend and I came home depressed. I remember sitting in the garage in my car and weeping, because I wanted to be with some- body. Those manhunt fumes must have been radiating off me like those little squiggly lines they put around skunks in the comics. I had been single for almost ten years, and I began to pray for a relationship with a man who really loved me. I wrote a letter to the Lord. I said, "Lord, I'm asking you to send me the right person. I'm tired. I've been picking the wrong folks. My judgment is all off. I need a spiritual person and he has to love my son. You know what I need much better than I do," and I put the letter in my Bible. Then I made a promise to fast for three Sundays in a row. I made this commitment to God because I wanted Him to know how serious I was. The truth was I was feeling desperate and I was ready to go for the next man who got off the boat. The Friday before the last Sunday of my fast, a girlfriend called and said, "Do you know André Fischer?" I told her that I'd met him briefly years ago. "Well," she said, "he's trying to get in touch with you because he wants to get a song to you."

André Fischer was a blast from the past—I first met him back in 1976, when I was performing at the Tokyo Music Festival. At the time, he was the music director and drummer for Rufus and Chaka Khan; he was the drummer on those great early songs she did. He had asked me out back then, but since I was head over heels involved with Marvin, I declined.

But this was about music, not about romance, so I gave her the number and he called. He was very nice over the phone, and I arranged to meet him in the parking lot of a film studio, where he had a recording studio inside a trailer. Despite the fact that he no longer sported his outsized Afro, I still recognized his handsome face. André was somewhat larger than he'd been in Tokyo—he now weighed about 250 pounds, and he was wearing a houndstooth jacket and some black pants. It turned out that the music he wanted me to listen to was really beside the point. After all these years, he wanted to ask me out again.

"Would you like to go to dinner?" he asked.

"Sure," I said. "Why don't you give me a call after six on Sunday." That Sunday was to be my last Sunday of fasting, but the phone never rang, and I didn't see him for about a month. In November I went to an awards show with my son and a friend, and I saw him in the parking lot. The white tuxedo jacket was a much better look for him than the houndstooth, but even though he looked nice, I was angry. I called him over and I cussed him out right there in the parking lot. "What do you think? That I have all my life to wait for you to pick up a phone? You said you'd call and you didn't. You don't have any manners and you're rude." I just went off on him and he was mortified, but I didn't care.

"Well," he said, "the reason I didn't call you was that your manager found out that I had given you some material, and he said I had to go through him to deal with you."

"BS," I replied. "My manager doesn't tell me what to do." Dan had a sense of foreboding about André and didn't want me to get involved with him. In hindsight, I should have listened to Dan—hooking up with André would be one of the biggest mistakes I ever made.

He called again a couple of weeks later and invited me to his birthday party the day after Christmas. I couldn't do it, because I was working at Caesars in Vegas. He ended up coming to see me there, and he brought his kids. After one show he came backstage to say hello, gave me a kiss on the cheek, and left.

In January 1989 I was playing at Harrah's in Lake Tahoe, and he came with his children to see the show. They walked into my dressing room all bubbly—Liz was seven and Kyle was five—and proceeded to make themselves at home. They were all bundled up because it was cold. They were really beautiful kids, they were just precious, and I liked them right away. André was clearly very proud of them. I invited them back to the house the next day, and André asked if he could play some music for me.

The house I invited them back to was Bill Harrah's, where I was staying. It was lovely and huge—sixty thousand square feet, with only three bedrooms—I could never figure that out. Robbie had come up with me, and the two of us just rattled around in it. Liz and Kyle immediately hit it off with Robbie, and they all went out to play in the snow. André stayed indoors with me, looking like the Michelin tire man. He sat there with his overcoat on—for two hours. Just looking at him made me uncomfortable. I made some hot chocolate and tried to coax him out of his coat. The next day I had a little party and they all came back again, and I remember that at one point we were all sitting around on the floor and I found myself sitting very close to André—and we were very comfortable. I thought that was really neat, and when he left, he gave me a kiss on my forehead. I was smitten.

The man moved very fast. When I got back to L.A., André and I started dating, and it wasn't much more than a month later that he asked me to marry him. At three o'clock in the morning on February 10, 1989, André proposed to me. After having prayed and put that letter in the Bible, I was convinced that this was the man that God had sent to me.

I was so happy to have somebody in my life that when André asked me to marry him, I think I took about two seconds to say yes. I consulted with Robbie and he said, "Yeah, Mom, I think you should do it." I had noticed also that Robbie would get attached to guys quickly—he wanted a dad so badly. And it was no different with André. He liked him right away. Robbie had been looking for a man that he could look up to, talk to, spend time with, have conversations with, and André seemed to be that kind of guy. André talked to Robbie, and he spent a lot of quality time with him and became his friend.

He also successfully convinced my family that he was the guy. They were concerned about whether he would be able to handle being "Mr. Cole" if it came to that, and the fact that sometimes I would be out on the road a lot. André reassured them that he knew about being on the road, being a star, and being a celebrity, and he was certain he could handle it. It was no big deal, because he'd been on the road and he'd been a star in his own right with Rufus. I saw it as a big plus that he knew and understood my industry so well. In fact, André and I had even started working together at this point. He had already appeared in my life by the time I did Good to Be Back, and he cut his teeth producing both "As a Matter of Fact," and one of the album's hits, "Gonna Make You Mine." So he was a solid guy—he not only had good taste and had wonderful, sweet children, but he was a competent producer. He turned his masters in on time, he almost always came in under budget, and he knew how to put a great rhythm section together. And it was so wonderful to be back in the loving arms of a man again.

We set the wedding date for September 17, 1989. Marvin and I hadn't had much of a fancy wedding, so I wanted something more this time. There were a hundred or so people at the church ceremony, and then we had at least six hundred people at the reception. My brother, Kelly, gave me away, and my whole family was there, even my mom. It was gorgeous, although Janice was deeply missed. My wedding dress was created by Lee Smith, the same wonderful designer who had done all my clothes when I was pregnant. He was perfect for the job, because by now he was making wedding gowns for the television soap *Days of Our Lives*.

The ceremony took place at my church, Bethany Baptist, and we were married by my pastor, the Reverend Rocellia Johnson. My Uncle Freddy played, and our first dance was to "Function at the Junction." Our reception followed at the venerable old Biltmore Hotel in downtown Los Angeles. It was a beautiful wedding and that night everybody but my mother was smiling and happy, especially me. But this was one of those times when my mother's instinct was dead on. Compared to André, my mother adored Marvin. I think she saw through André's facade from the moment she met him. He was a loser,

CHAPTER 23

Unforgettable

My marriage to André Fischer signaled an upswing in my life in many ways—or so I thought. This marriage meant Robbie would now have a father in his life, and, for me, it marked the end of the long, difficult five-year recovery period after Hazelden. It also meant that finally I would have someone with whom to share my personal life and my career. Many pieces were falling back into place.

The only sour note at this beautiful time was my father's absence. It broke my heart that he could not have been there to share my joy. I felt as if he had died almost before life had begun for me. I had never had the opportunity to make him proud, or to do anything for him that mattered. I didn't even have the chance to say goodbye to him or "I love you," because I didn't understand that he was dying. I had just turned fifteen and I didn't quite get it. I was not prepared. I just thought that he would live forever and I never imagined he'd be gone. Here, clearly, was another piece of my life that still needed work. Dad had always said to his friends about me, "She's got it," although he never did say that directly to me—not once. But I know that I owe him big-time for my ability to sing and perform.

My desire for some kind of closure with my father may well be what was behind the urge I was feeling to attempt to do my father's music. I had spent the first part of my career rebelling against it. Always in the back of my mind I was trying to stay as far away from it as possible. In July of 1986 I *had* sung "Unforgettable" at the Newport Jazz Festival, and it had been very well received. I had experimented also with the song even before that—back in the early 1980s when I was still with Kevin Hunter and in Las Vegas, starting to work with an orchestra. I sang the song live with a reel-to-reel tape of Dad's voice backstage. The reel-to-reel was piped through the speakers onstage and Dad's voice would come on. Then they'd push the mute button and the orchestra would start playing. We had a little click track so that the band would start at the same time the tape did. Dad's voice would come through the house, and then they'd mute his voice along with the track while the live orchestra kept playing. First Dad would sing "Unforgettable, that's what you are," and then I would sing "Unforgettable, though near or far." (It was rather crude, technologically, but it worked.) The audiences were so moved that I backed away from doing it more than a few times. Singing that song stopped the show. It completely changed the mood and left me with nowhere to go as a performer.

In May of 1983, I had done a television tribute to Dad in London for the BBC with Johnny Mathis. We repeated that tribute later on in the year in Boston with John Williams and the Boston Pops Orchestra for PBS. The BBC eventually released the music from the London show in an album overseas with the title *Unforgettable: A Musical Tribute to Nat King Cole*—never available in the United States— and it sold approximately 800,000 copies. I was just stunned when I heard this, and I think that planted a little seed as well. It got me thinking that maybe it wasn't such a bad idea to do an album of Dad's music. Then in 1987, I recorded an R&B version of one of his songs in the studio for the first time—"When I Fall in Love"—for the *Everlasting* album. Little by little, I was preparing myself to do what I had avoided throughout my entire career. I suppose the fact that I had heard a few other singers were thinking of doing it made me pay attention. George Benson (who eventually recorded a great version of "Nature Boy") and I had discussed doing Dad's music together. Al Jarreau was considering doing something, and I'd even heard that Barbra Streisand was thinking about it. I thought, "How unfortunate that would be if other singers paid tribute to Dad before I did."

One of the reasons I had resisted singing my father's music was because deep down I believed that it would totally change my life—

and there were no guarantees that it would be for the better. Now, I felt I had made great progress with myself personally, emotionally, and professionally—I had paid my dues, and had my own hit songs. Now I was ready. Another reason I had stayed away from doing my father's music was that I felt that it would hinder what I wanted to do artistically. Furthermore, the last thing I wanted to do was exploit my dad's name. As I was starting in my own career, some people put me down for not doing my father's songs and others criticized me the few times I did do them. I couldn't win. When I did sing them—before I ever even had a record—I would get so emotional that I thought I could never do that again.

Once I felt that I had found my niche with Capitol, I just stayed true to my *own* music. Actually, one of the reasons I had signed with Capitol is that they didn't mention my father's name, and that was ironic, because that was the label I least expected to go with—since that was the label my father had been with. I knew then that doing Dad's songs was going to be a long way off if I ever got to it. When I recorded "When I Fall in Love" for the *Everlasting* album, the approach was different and I didn't feel as emotional, because the song was done in R&B style.

When Dan and I sat down and talked about my desire to do an album of my father's music, he said, "You're established now, you can do that." We met with the people at EMI—Gerry Griffith, Sal Licotta, and Joe

Smith—and I told them my idea. They asked, "Why?" They saw it as a major, major career move. Basically, their thinking was: "Now Cole's going to do a jazz album—that's the end of her R&B and pop career." They told me that I should first do another pop album—another hit record. That way, if the album of my father's work didn't do well, I'd still have something to fall back on and it wouldn't be so bad. After the meeting I looked at Dan and said, "What if I *don't have* another hit record? Does that mean I have to wait till the next mil-lennium?" The folks at EMI just didn't get it. Actually, my last album with EMI, *Good to Be Back*, sold well, but it hadn't done half as well as *Everlasting*. Personally, I had not been happy with the choice of songs. I think that with *Everlasting*, the record company was worried that I was becoming too pop and that black radio had not heard enough from Natalie Cole on recent records. "Pink Cadillac" and "I Live for Your Love" had been pop hits—not R&B hits. And Dan was getting nervous that black radio was going to put me out to pasture because I was a black artist who wasn't delivering any black music to R&B radio. They supposedly were R&B; they just weren't good R&B. The Freddie Jackson duet on "I Do" was part of an attempt to pair me with someone who was very much R&B. Freddie and I were cool, but I didn't like the song. "Miss You Like Crazy" and "Gonna Make You Mine" were the big hits, and that was what sold that album. Then EMI tried to come back with the duet, "I Do." I had told them it was a big mistake and I was right and I was angry. I worried that I would lose a lot if I kept doing material like this in an effort to cater only to the R&B market, and my career would move backward.

EMI had been able to sell me with dance songs like "Pink Cadillac," but now all of a sudden they were having trouble marketing me. I was pop *and* I was R&B. They no longer knew what to do with me. I would go back and forth, and that was just the way it was. And now I wanted to do jazz? That's when Dan and I started talking about leaving. I was very unhappy, and I told Dan that I wanted out.

Ultimately, EMI let me out of my contract—not necessarily because they didn't want to do Dad's music—they were just ready to be relieved of the responsibility of trying to figure out how to market me. Once we were out of that contract, Dan and I went to see Bob Krasnow, the president and founder of Elektra Records, to see if he would be interested in signing me. Their roster was a mix of many different artists producing all kinds of different music. It was a very eclectic label and had the reputation of being run by folks who really knew what they were doing. Bob was a risk-taker. He spearheaded the company and the artists felt that if Bob was in charge, it was going to be okay, because he was behind you and was very much of a hands-on kind of guy. He was also a tyrant, but who cares? He knew where to go, he knew how to get the

interest, and he knew how to sell records.
He had a vision, and he was the next angel in
my life.

At the time that we visited Bob, he was in
the hospital. I remember him sitting up in his
hospital bed—he was recovering from hip
surgery—but he had agreed to meet with us.
I said, "I've got some songs in the works for
a pop record, and then after that I'd like to consider doing an album of my father's music."
I could never have predicted his response:
He said, "Screw the pop record, let's do this
record right now." I remember sitting there,
shocked that this man would want to do this.
I was just absolutely floored. So I said, "Huh?
Really?" and he said, "Absolutely, why not?"
I just didn't imagine that he would see that as
something to do now, especially given that my
last album hadn't done that well. I guess he
was taking me on faith.

Coming over to Elektra, my intention had
not been to do that album *right away*. I was
just glad to be on the label, so I figured I'd give
them a pop album, and then we'd do an album
of my father's music. I thought that maybe it
was right to wait until I had one more pop hit,
and that way if the Dad stuff didn't work, it
would be okay. We'd be doing it for pos-
terity. So, it was Bob Krasnow who really
had the vision to do my dad's album first. As
Dan and I left the hospital, I said, "Oh, my
God, this is going to be really nuts. This is going
to be crazy. How am I going to tell my family
that I'm actually going to do everything that

I have been running away from all these years?" When I finally did get up the guts to tell my mother, she said, "This is going to change your life when you do this." And she didn't necessarily mean positively. I think she felt it was going to put me in a place that I would not be able to get out of. And I just thought, "Well, if it doesn't work, basically my career is over—but, what the hell."

The basic concept was to do a tribute album of Dad's greatest hits. That's really all it was. Everyone wanted to call it *Unforgettable* from the beginning, and I wanted to add *With Love*. I wanted this album to be from me to my dad, a personal gift. I was thinking about it from the emotional place of a little girl who was getting a chance to do something for her father, as well as a chance to say, "I love you."

Bob Krasnow hooked us up with Tommy LiPuma, Elektra's senior vice president of A&R and a veteran producer. Tommy became the foundation of this project—the guy who would make the wheels turn—because Tommy knew this kind of music. He was the one who had all the history and all the knowledge. He'd been doing jazz for years and years, and had produced seventy-five albums for all kinds of people. He knew all the arrangers and all the musicians, so we made him executive producer.

Next step was to choose producers. We started having meetings at my house to hammer out the details. André was hinting and hoping to be involved. At the time, I really wanted to help give his career a boost. He had arranged and produced for Rufus and Chaka Khan, a little for Michael Franks and for Brenda Russell before doing a few songs for my last album, *Good to Be Back*. In 1990 he also had done a little producing, along with percussion, for Lalah Hathaway. I had to push quite a bit to get André on this record, even though Tommy had worked with him briefly several years before. Bob Krasnow was hesitant—but with some reluctance, he agreed.

It was suggested that we try out David Foster as one of the producers. David was totally a pop writer-producer at the time, and very successful. He had either written, produced, or played on close to 175 recordings and had won several Grammys by the time he got to us. I knew David through his wife, Linda. She and I had met in 1975 on *The Michael Douglas Show*, before she was married to David. At that time, she was an actress on the television show *Hee Haw*, and I was just coming out with my first single. David had been a fan of my dad's, and had seen him perform up in Edmonton, Alberta, not long before Dad died. He had also been following my career and had always loved my albums. This was our first opportunity to work together.

André, David, and I met for dinner at a restaurant called Splash in Santa Monica. It became quickly apparent that even with all the experience that Tommy and David brought to the project, we were treading on new ground. No one had done this kind of thing before and I don't know what we were thinking of. We had a formidable task in front of us. But Bob Krasnow had all the confidence in us and basically said, "Do what you've got to do."

First, we listened to my dad's catalogue of songs. Of course, everybody had a suggestion, from my mother and Aunt Bay and other family members, to all the musical friends of my father. The decisions were hard to make, because my father had so many beautiful songs, and there was no way they'd all fit onto one album. One lovely man who was very instrumental in helping us pick the material was Dick LaPalm, who Dan knew and who had known my father from before I was born. In fact, according to him, he kind of introduced my parents to each other. Because he was so close to my dad, Dick really put his heart and soul into this project for us. I couldn't even talk to him about Dad without his shedding tears. He just loved him so much. The songs for this album were right up Dick's alley, and he found some great stuff for us. We really went into this with everybody throwing in ideas. Every song had its own special quality and meaning for me.

I picked songs from my memory, including "Mona Lisa." I had always been fascinated by that song, and to me it always seemed wonderfully strange that Dad would be singing about a painting. It also seemed an essential song to include, given that it had won an Oscar for Best Song of the Year in the year that

I was born, 1950. It was that song that cata-pulted Dad into superstardom. Then there was "Straighten Up and Fly Right," which was Dad's own composition, based on a sermon that his father used to give about a buzzard who takes a monkey for a ride on his back. That was the first recording for Capitol of his own composition; the record sold more than half a million copies. (It's hard to believe that he sold the copyright to that song for $50.) "Route 66" was recorded in 1946, and "It's Only a Paper Moon" a few years previous. Dad had originally recorded that song in 1943, and then did eight different versions of it over the years. The list went on and on.

People had laughed, loved, and fallen in love to those songs. Elektra wanted us to include just ten or twelve, but our position was simple and unwavering: "This is a tribute to Nat King Cole, and we will probably never have the opportunity to do this again." We ended up with twenty-two songs, despite big argu-ments from Elektra that we were giving away the store. The company executives were tearing their hair out. Score one for the Cole family heritage: persistence.

With the songs selected and the record company sufficiently subdued, it was time to get started. Tommy LiPuma was not just the executive producer, but an active pro-ducer as well. He, André, and David sat down with me in a meeting and assigned them-selves songs they wanted to produce. We went down the list, and for most songs, one of them would jump on it—either it seemed right for their talents or they had always loved it. When we came to picking a producer for the song "Unforgettable"—which was down around fifteenth on the list—the three of them just looked at each other, and nobody responded right away. Later, André and I were at dinner with David and his wife, Linda, and I asked, "So who's going to produce 'Unforgettable'?" André just kind of shrugged his shoulders and neither of them seemed avid. Finally, David said, "Well, I love that song. I'd be glad to produce it." No big deal. Neither of them was that excited. In the end, Tommy did four songs, as well as supervising every aspect of the project as executive producer; André did a whopping eleven songs; and David did seven.

When it came to finding arrangers and musicians, Tommy knew who to call. He had good instincts for which person could contribute the most—which person was really right. We even checked on some of Dad's old recordings to see if there was anyone still around who had played on them. We did get a few musicians who had played on Dad's sessions. That they were still alive was fortunate; that they were still active was a miracle. In one instance, we were able to contact the same singers who had sung on Dad's "That Sunday, That Summer," from twenty-seven years before— it was John F. Kennedy's favorite song. I couldn't believe that we found them: Donna Davidson, Debbie Hall, Kerry Katz, Rick

Logan, Gene Merlino, Don Shelton, Sally Stevens, and Susan Stevens.

Now, it was up to Tommy to marry the right songs with the right arrangers—and I don't know how he did it. Most of these people I didn't even know. Some of the arrangers I knew by name only, but I'd never heard of the pianist and jazz arranger Clare Fischer, who was André's uncle. Clare had a big interest in Latin rhythms and by the time he joined up with us, he had thirty albums under his belt. He had also worked with artists like Prince, so he had done some contemporary work as well. The arrangement on "The Very Thought of You" came out beautifully.

Michel Legrand—the French composer, conductor, arranger, and pianist who had worked with Sarah Vaughan, John Coltrane, and Miles Davis—was nice enough to fit us into his busy schedule, right after he had recorded an album of Cole Porter's music. We also got Johnny Mandel to work with us. He had arranged for artists like Sinatra, Count Basie, and Artie Shaw. Although he was originally a trumpet and trombone player, he became a top composer. He was most famous for "Suicide Is Painless"—the theme song from both the movie and TV show M*A*S*H. I had at least a little knowledge of Johnny's work, but David Foster had not heard of him at all. That's how wet behind the ears we were.

I had actually worked with Ralph Burns years before. He has been around since the 1940s and had written, arranged, and performed with Ella Fitzgerald, Sarah Vaughan, Woody Herman, Bette Midler, Lena Horne, and even Aretha Franklin. Bass player Ray Brown came on board and also did some arranging. He had played with Dad, Dizzy Gillespie, Charlie Parker, and for fifteen years with Oscar Peterson. He had also been married to Ella Fitzgerald for a time. Marty Paich was another piano player-arranger; he'd been a fixture on the West Coast jazz scene when I was still in diapers, and had worked with Peggy Lee, Stan Kenton, and Mel Tormé. He also put out fourteen of his own albums. I hadn't known Bill Holman, but he was another great arranger who had worked with Count Basie and Stan Kenton. Alan Broadbent is yet another arranger and pianist, who continues to perform with me on some of my shows. Dad was one of his favorite singers, but he'd also worked with Woody Herman and Nelson Riddle and so many other great musicians.

This was an awesome group of talent, and for the first time in my life I was finally getting a chance to put some faces to names. A lot of these people had met me when I was a little girl and they were working with Dad. They remembered me, but I can't honestly say that I remembered everyone before we started working. It was extremely unusual to bring so many talented people together so quickly. Everyone involved made coming to work on that project a joy. From day to day, I didn't know what was going to happen. This was unlike anything I'd ever done, and it was certainly unlike anything that André or David Foster had ever done.

Before getting into the studio, I met with the arrangers. They had to have my keys before they could write the charts. They sat with me and we went through the songs a couple of times on the piano to make sure that everything was comfortable. From those sessions they made a musical sketch of me before getting out the oils and brushes to paint the picture.

I've always thought of music as creating a painting. You get an idea and you sketch it through, but once it goes onto the canvas, you can't change it. For this particular project, we weren't just dealing with one painting, but a whole houseful of them. Our job was to stay true to the character of the house, but to update things just a little. In a sense it was like remodeling. Although we kept the original "doors," and "walls," we changed the "furniture." We didn't change the outsides, but we did change some of the insides. We kept the character, but changed some of the colors. The arrangers came through brilliantly in absolutely amazing ways. It was incredible that they could do what they did, especially since some of them hadn't handled this kind of music in twenty or thirty years.

It was tricky trying to give these songs a fresh sound. We had quite a challenge on our hands—especially with twenty-two tunes. The songs "For Sentimental Reasons," "Tenderly," and "Autumn Leaves" were altered so we could put them together in a medley. That was Marty Paich's pride and joy. Other than that, he maybe used some different chords and changed the arrangements to fit a female voice, but Dad's arrangements were so pretty that we tried not to do too much. The results were classic.

When these folks came to work, they came ready. Johnny Mandel was really the star of the arranging team. For this album, he did the most gorgeous version of "Smile." He gave us mini-lessons in exactly what makes an arranger great versus good.

Not only did we have the best arrangers, we had incredible musicians. The rhythm section consisted of Harold Jones, who had been Count Basie's drummer, and Jim Hughart on bass. Jim had played with Sinatra and Sarah Vaughan for years and years; he'd also worked for and arranged for Ella Fitzgerald. Joe Sample, who had played on hundreds of albums with anybody and everybody—from Eric Clapton and Joe Cocker to Marvin Gaye and B. B. King—played piano. We had to work very hard to find the right person to accompany me on piano. In the end, the majority of the keyboard accompaniment was done by Monty Alexander. In developing his style, he had been heavily influenced by both my dad and Oscar Peterson. He was a sweetheart.

Brad Cole (not one of my many relatives) also played keyboards; he had played with a diverse mixture of people, from Ella Fitzgerald to Leonard Cohen. Then there was Mike Lang, who had played keyboards on a lot of movie soundtracks and had played with artists like José Feliciano and Barbra Streisand. Mike Melvoin, Aretha's pianist, who also had done a lot of movie scores, was there. He had done albums with Nina Simone, Frank Sinatra, and even the Monkees. These were all great guys. All in all there were about 225 musicians, arrangers, producers, vocalists, engineers, mixers, and copyists involved in *Unforgettable.* If you compare that to the ten or so people who worked on *Good to Be Back,* you get a picture of the magnitude of this project.

Most of the musicians hadn't played these kinds of arrangements in years. Except for movies and commercials, work for orchestras had been dwindling. The days of live orchestration had largely passed, and folks who hadn't worked in a very long time were called in for these sessions—like those singers from "That Sunday, That Summer." They were older, but they still sounded good. It was really cool. And this was the first time I had ever seen a lady contractor: Carol was André's manager's ex-wife. André's manager had to look at her every day, oops! She was very cool. It was like someone had put caffeine in people's drinks, it just gave them such a jolt. We began recording in Studio A at Capitol, the very same studio in which Dad had done "Unforgettable" forty years earlier. More amazingly, because of the way the scheduling worked out, Tommy first started to work on his songs on February 15, 1991—exactly twenty-six years after my father's passing. We recorded pretty much in sections. After Tommy, I worked with André, then David. I was there for almost every session. I had to put myself in Tommy's hands and more or less surrendered to the process. While it was my idea that had gotten things started and we had laid it out on paper, all of a sudden it actually was starting to happen. I knew I had something to do with it, but it was like a dream. I couldn't believe that it was finally coming together.

When I arrived, I was told, "Here's the stuff. Here's the arrangement. Let's go do the recording. Let's run through it a few times. How are you feeling today?" Everyone always wanted to make sure I was feeling good. The studio was almost always full, especially when we were working with an orchestra. And there were also all those different arrangers present, especially if we were doing two or three songs in one day. I must say that despite having three producers, nobody crossed over into anybody else's territory. The egos stayed in check and all three of them helped me. They had a wonderful sense of romance, a feeling for the integrity of these songs, and a deep sensitivity to me as the singer. It was clear that my father's memory was in good hands.

Even with all the extraordinarily competent help, I felt overwhelmed at times. I kept worrying, "How am I going to pull this off? How are we *ever* going to pull this off?" I started beating up on myself a little, thinking, "I could never sing these songs as well as Dad." I said that, yet I'd deliberately picked some of his most difficult songs—like "Lush Life." One of the first uptempos we did was "Paper Moon," and before we started I was scared to death. I'd walk into the studio, and there'd be this big orchestra and the arranger would be there at the podium. Then I'd go into my little booth, get in front of that microphone, and they would start playing. I would close my eyes and it would just happen. André said that it was almost as if something was guiding me. I'd run through a song a couple of times and then all of a sudden, it was right there. It's funny, but I never knew ahead of time if I was going to be able to do it. Recording these songs was a whole new ballgame. And with these songs, there was nowhere to hide. Every word was important and every note counted.

Deep down inside of me, I guess I knew these songs without ever having sung them. David pointed out that unlike many other pop singers who have tried doing standards, I was raised on this kind of music. As a child, I lived and breathed them. I didn't really have to learn them from scratch. I was amazed at what I might have absorbed while growing up with Dad. I was thrilled to discover that, as the daughter of Nat King Cole, I had inherited something quite special. I really didn't think I'd ever have the chance to find that out. This was so cool.

It had taken me fifteen years to feel ready to make this album and to carry my father's name in a gracious manner that reflected the stature he had achieved. I knew that there was a responsibility involved and that I could not fail.

There was something personal about the way Dad sang, and I think I just inherited it. I don't know how it happens, I just feel the music and it seems to come out that way. One thing he did was leave natural pauses in the music. You felt an intimacy in the way he sang a word, in his phrasing, or how he put a sentence together. Using the pauses is very effective— it's more conversational. It's called "caressing." Die-hard fans of my dad always loved not just his voice, but *the way* he sang. Something about my dad's style made you get to know him or want to know him. When people talk about Nat King Cole, they're not just talking about him as a singer. They speak of him as if they knew him or they felt like they did, and he brought an intimacy to his music that was uniquely his own. You felt that he was singing to only one person—you—and not to a roomful of people.

I've always felt that whenever I sing, I want it to be sincere. I ask myself, "If there were a blind man listening, what would his sense of me be?" Everything would have to be in the voice. That's how I started trying to work on how I sound. Do I sound sincere? Is there a smile *in* my voice? Is there a smile in that particular line that I'm singing? Or is there a sadness there? Can you feel it—not even can you hear it—but can you *feel* it? In the end, I focus on the feelings my voice expresses. That, to me, is where the heart is.

Although I really didn't have a great education in scat singing, I seem to know how to sing it. I don't know how I learned to scat. It is hard to explain. I was scatting back in the '70s. And it's absolutely a dying art, there's no question about it. But the scatting on "Mr. Melody" for my *Natalie* album back in 1976 pales compared to the scatting I ended up doing on this record—on "Paper Moon," for instance, which required a lot of legitimate scatting. Perhaps because I've always loved Ella Fitzgerald, I picked up some of those techniques by osmosis, just by listening to her, or to Nancy Wilson or Sarah Vaughan. This was the music that my parents played at home. Seeing my father at the Sands or at the Hollywood Bowl—I called up these memories to help me get in the mood.

When I got in front of the orchestra for this project, it was entirely different from when I had worked with orchestras before, early on in my career. There was no stress in my voice—everything sounded effortless. It is funny, because so often people referred to my dad as "The Man with the Velvet Voice" and many people have said my voice was like silk. I give all the credit to my voice trainer, Seth Riggs, who came to the studio and worked with me every day for an hour or so before the sessions. He is a wonderful, devoted, and brilliant person to work with. I now have many voices. It's almost like being a little schizophrenic at times. I like it, though, because I never get bored. I have to keep myself entertained, too, you know! When I knew that I was going to be doing some vocally challenging stuff, he would stay and help me through it if I needed it. He's such a doll. Thank you, Seth.

I have been known to make radical changes in the way my voice sounds—I can even sound raspy like Janis Joplin if I want to. For this album, I needed to change it again. It was a lighter approach. I had to have fun with it, without concentrating so hard—like with "Orange Colored Sky," which the Nat King Cole Trio and the Stan Kenton Orchestra had originally recorded in 1950, the year I was born.

I think Ella Fitzgerald also took little liberties, and even Sarah Vaughan had a tendency to sound very different on some of her songs. On some of the albums I have of her singing, she sounds different on almost every song. But there really wasn't *too* much liberty I could take with this kind of music. I had to be true to the essence and the notes—the melody was *very* important. It was actually hammered into my head early on when I first started recording—that you don't take off or get crazy until you've established the melody. Then, after that, you can kind of do what you want.

There is a compatibility between myself and music. I think of music as a living, breathing thing. It's like water to me. I step into it very carefully because I don't want to overstay my welcome. The song is my friend.

It is possible for the music to get away from you. I know sometimes halfway through a song, the listener can lose interest. To avoid that, the singer has to stay intense and involved, from the first note to the last. I learned very early that you've got to keep the audience's attention. That's one reason I don't like to make the instrumental part of a song too long. (Though in my humble opinion, I feel you should always include at least some kind of a brief, interesting interlude.) Some composers like Michael Masser and Burt Bacharach are not so big on instrumental sections at all—certainly not in my songs. They want to have me singing all over the place.

One characteristic of classic songs like those on the *Unforgettable* album was that back in the 1930s and 1940s almost every song had an instrumental break. If it is particularly long—oh, well—I just have to take a drink of water.

I loved these songs because they were so poetic. They are little stories, and if you take the lyrics away, the music can stand on its own, or if you take away the music, the lyrics have their own beauty, like a sonnet. A song like "Lush Life," for instance, has haunting and poignant lyrics. I was amazed when I discovered that Billy Strayhorn wrote that song when he was sixteen years old. I thought, "What?" I marveled at how Charlie Chaplin could write a melody titled "Smile," yet the words make you want to do just the opposite. It is touching when you find out about the people who created such beautiful songs and what was going on in their minds when they wrote something so sadly beautiful. It's that bittersweet quality to some of these love songs. You just want to cry. "The Very Thought of You," another lyrically poetic song, also had special meaning for Bob Krasnow. He called me on the phone and was almost in tears because he was so moved by the finished version of that song. He was so excited that it was going to be the very first song on the album.

The biggest challenge was how we were going to do the song "Unforgettable," since we were going to be blending my voice with Dad's old recording. It wasn't until David and I sat down to go over it that he discovered that this was supposed to be a duet. I had said to him, "Okay, so now I sing this part," and he said, "Well, who's singing the other part?" When I told him it was going to be my father, at first he looked shocked, and then he got really excited. He told me that it was at that moment that he knew we were going to be doing something great here—that we were going to be making history.

To locate Dad's original recording, David had to go out to some storage vaults in Glendale, where he had an experience that was right out of the movies. He walked in and there was the vaultkeeper, this old gnome who looked about eighty years old who told David to follow him. They walked down a long corridor with tapes lining the walls, and then he stopped and said, "Aha! There it is!" He pulled the master to "Unforgettable" down off the shelf, blew on it, and all this dust came off. Of course, he didn't give David the original. He made a copy of it and sent David on his way. We had no idea what shape it would be in, but when we played it, it was flawless. The vocal quality was incredible. Apparently, the tube microphones that they used back then were amazing. People now will pay $20,000 or $30,000 for one of them, even though they only cost something like $300 originally. Actually David had me singing into a tube mike on other songs of this album, as well.

In the duet, my father sings and then I sing—I answer him and then we sing together. At one point, David thought, "Wouldn't it be incredible if not only she answers her father but *he answers her*, as though he was right over her shoulder?" The next morning he went into the studio with Al Schmitt, engineer extraordinaire, and figured out the technical aspect of laying Dad's voice inside the new track. They sampled Dad's voice and took it out of the track and moved it. As it happened, the chords worked perfectly, so he could lay Dad's voice in later. It was as though Dad had come in and redone the vocals. David phoned me up and said, "Natalie, you're not going to believe what I have just done." Then he played it for me over the phone. I just screamed out loud when I heard it. It was a rare moment. He had actually changed the shape of the song.

When we started to record "Unforgettable," and I sang my part around Dad's vocals, everyone just stopped. The musicians could hardly play. They gasped when they heard Dad's voice come in and then heard me sing. By coincidence, my mother had decided to visit that day—she had no idea what song had been scheduled. It was an emotional moment for all of us.

I was really trying to keep it together—we all were. This album had exceeded all of our expectations, in every way. It was a love project. Everybody was in love—every day. All of a sudden my childhood came back, the life that I had growing up with my parents came back and was inside of this music. I went to many of my dad's shows, and I sat there listening to some of these great arrangements. I remember loving them even back then as a little girl. And, in essence, that's what these people were giving to me. They were giving me back a piece of my father. His spirit lived again in me and in these songs.

There was, indeed, a reverence in the way these songs were put together. Sometimes we talked in hushed tones, as if not to disturb the moment. I know it all sounds a bit dramatic, but it was as if we were witnessing an exhumation of treasures that had been buried and forgotten. When we were making this album, one thing for certain is that we didn't try to make it sound old. The presentation wasn't old and my whole attitude about it wasn't old. But the arrangements, which were just so lovely, still felt like we were back in the old days. I think that it was just meant to be.

At the end of the session, when the last song was finally mixed and after we had labored for two weeks over the order in which the songs would go, we invited the core team of people to listen to the album for the first time. All the arrangers came, the producers, of course, and myself, Dan, and a few others. It was at the Bill Schnee Studio in Burbank. We stood around that small, intimate room and listened to all twenty-two songs. No one said a word—not a word. People were breaking down. Grown men were just bawling their eyes out. For some, having had the opportunity to be around this music twenty-five or thirty years before and now sitting down to do this again was an event they could never have anticipated. (Come to think of it, other than my son, I was very possibly the youngest person in the studio on any given day.) I was overwhelmed with how perfectly it came out. The orchestra was amazing and I had never sounded so beautiful.

The entire process from start to finish took approximately eight weeks. My vocals probably took around four or five weeks; the rest was the mix. In the meantime I was taking pictures for the album cover with the famous photographer George Hurrell. He had been the photographer George Hurrell. He had been the Hollywood photographer who created the "glamour" portraits that became the trademark for the Hollywood stars of the 1930s and 1940s. He had literally helped shape the careers of stars like Joan Crawford, Jean Harlow, and Jane Russell. Someone in the art department at Elektra had recommended him to me, although the man had been retired for many years. Retired or not, when George was contacted for this project, he was getting ready to go off on a SCUBA diving trip. He was in his eighties and sharp as a whip. And he knew exactly what to do for the cover.

With the help of my stylist, Cecile Parker, I picked out a Pamela Dennis gown—very retro—which we found with the help of Fred Hayman's boutique in Beverly Hills. My hairdresser also knew exactly what to do, and the whole package just came together. Part of George's genius was his lighting. He did his own and his camera equipment was at least fifty years old. Particularly uncanny was his ability to take the photograph without needing a Polaroid to test the lighting (as almost every contemporary photographer does). The result was breathtaking. I had never seen myself look so...well...beautiful.

If I had planned every element of this project in advance, it could never have turned out so well. So what do you do after all this? You go home and you count your blessings and you say your prayers and you say, "Thank you, God." I've always believed—and I still do— any artist—whether singer or painter, writer or sculptor—we all wish to do just one thing special, something that is totally ours and no one can take it away from us. Once the record was turned over, I started to breathe a sigh of relief. As far as I was concerned, I had done the impossible. A major demon throughout my life was laid to rest. Being liked and being in the shadow as "the-daughter-of"...these afflictions and lesions now were starting to heal. Whatever the reaction finally would be to this project was now up to the Lord. As for me, I knew Dad was smiling—and that was worth it all.

CHAPTER 24

Unforgettable
Goes on the Road

The feelings of satisfaction and completion that washed over me when we finished recording *Unforgettable* were in many ways similar to the way I felt when I had finally given birth to Robbie after nine months of pregnancy. But as any parent would know, the birth of the infant is really just a beginning—and this child, which required more than 225 people to deliver, would be no different.

Things were not the same in the 1990s as they had been in my dad's era. A beautiful recording was no longer enough to satisfy audiences—now we needed a beautiful video, too. MTV and VH-1 and all those other music television stations around the world would have no choice but to ignore "Unforgettable" if we didn't have a video to offer. With David Foster's ingenuity and the help of some brilliant technicians, we had been able to marry Dad's sound recordings with my own to create that gorgeous duet. Now the challenge was to find moving pictures and photographs of my father from decades before, somehow cut them in with new footage of me, and make a video that worked—not only technically, but artistically and commercially, too. Such a video had to accomplish all of that *and* tell a compelling story, in exactly three minutes and twenty-eight seconds.

To take on this challenging task, we found Steve Barron, an English director who had directed *Teenage Mutant Ninja Turtles, Coneheads,* and music videos including Michael Jackson's *Billie Jean* and Dire Straits' *Money for Nothing*—experience that would be very helpful to our project. I understood the complications of the task at hand, and there were many. We had to take the old film footage of my dad and cut it alternately with new footage in a way that was not too jarring. We also had to find scenes of Dad specifically singing "Unforgettable." Once we found that, then we had to match up his lip movement from his performance footage to the words he recorded in a studio decades ago. This made lip-syncing look easy—the problem is that when we sing songs at different times, we don't always sing them at exactly the same tempo or phrasing. On top of that, a variety of other issues complicated the process, such as the fact that some of Dad's footage was in black and white and some was in color, or colorized.

While not technically complicated, it was the drama of trying to get clips of Dad that was the most unreal. Who would think that it would be so difficult for a daughter to obtain photos or film footage of her own father? I guess a lot of people want to own a little piece of him and just don't want to share it—not even with his own family. Begging and pleading for clips of my father was the most uncomfortable thing I had to go through for the video. The process of putting together the video was extremely long and burdensome, primarily for that reason. My sister Cookie, God bless her, was in charge of this piece of the "Unforgettable" project. But we were running out of time—I had a rigorous schedule of concert dates in place, so I was available for only a small window of time, and the release of the video needed to coincide with the release of the album.

To add to these difficulties, there was also the drama of getting the licensing to use the name "Unforgettable" for television use. I was told that the publisher, BeBe Borne, was very difficult to deal with, and every time we wanted to use "Unforgettable" for television purposes, it was a nightmare. In trying to get all this stuff together, one thing my family and I learned is how easy it is for outsiders to gain literal ownership of your family heritage.

We did, however, find a few great pieces right out of the blue. One of the film clips in the video shows Dad playing the piano while I am looking in at him in what looks like an old nickelodeon. It's a very old film, and it was the property of Mark Cantor, a fellow who had amassed a remarkable collection of Dad's stuff. Another thing that we managed to find was some footage of me with the family that came from the Edward R. Murrow show, *Person to Person*. Then there was some film of my dad picking me up when I was a baby and holding me up high in the air—with my mom standing by beaming. That was from some 8mm home movie footage that belonged to my godparents, Dr. David and Hannah Daniels, which their son Peter had saved.

Steve Barron was able to incorporate some of the stills that I presently use in my stage performances. He then shot a lot of footage of me singing "Unforgettable." This video was originally done on film, and then transferred to tape. Although more expensive, film provides much better quality than videotape. It was really interesting the way he dissolved from the modern-day video of me to the old footage or photographs of Dad. There's one part where Dad is at a microphone and he turns; the camera pans to me at a microphone, and Dad's microphone transforms into mine.

Before that he fashioned an image that went from being a silhouette of a sax player into a row of silhouettes that turned in unison— sort of the Rockettes. They used my cousin Eddie as the sax player, and that portion of the visuals occurred during the sax instrumental, which worked out really cool.

Of course, the whole time we were shooting, I couldn't tell how it would turn out. When you are doing everything in sections, it's all chopped up and it's difficult to get a feel for what it will look like in a finished video. Steve used some very clever and innovative editing techniques. Making the video turned out to be extremely complicated, and no one had ever been able to make something like this look quite so real before. Steve Barron proved himself to be a genius, and he rightly received a lot of accolades for this piece.

Once all the filming was done, it took a month or so of editing before it was ready. Finally we went to Steve's studio in London to see it. Dan came with me, as did my friend and personal assistant, Benita Hill. When we sat down to watch, it was another one of those heart-stopping moments. Steve did a beautiful job of putting me and my dad together "with love." What was so amazing was that he was able to take the present and the past and fuse it so seamlessly. When people saw it, they filled up with emotion, even if they didn't know who Nat King Cole was. Once the video played on VH-1 and it passed over to MTV, young people responded to it, and they had no clue who Nat King Cole was. They knew this singer called Natalie Cole, whose dad had been a singer, too. When they saw the video, it told a sweet story about a daughter and her dad that you could understand, even if you never knew anything about either one. Out of that three-minute video came all this emotion. I received lots of letters from people who had lost their fathers. Many of them were from women who had lost their dads, or who still had their fathers, and wanted to do their own videos.

For me, one of the greatest challenges in making the video was that I had no human element to work off of. There was no one for me to interact with, because Steve used blue screen technology, or what they call matting. I did my parts in a void, yet I had to look like I was interacting, not only with an environment, but with my father. It took a very long time—we worked around the clock—and for atmosphere they used a lot of smoke. The smoke really got to me, and I ended up sick as a dog. We taped on Mother's Day, May 12, 1991. Robbie was there at the studio with me—he even slept there. I'll never forget lying there in a daze on a cot and someone coming in to get him. I remember him going out, and when he came back in, he had a Mother's Day card for me. That was so cute.

By the time I got home, I was too sick to do anything. I was supposed to go directly afterward to Columbus, Ohio, where I was going to do my first *Unforgettable* performance.

That's where we were going to get our feet wet,
but I couldn't fly, and I couldn't sing. We had
to postpone the date, and everyone was very
disappointed.

Throughout the process of recording *Unforgettable* and making the video, I continued to
go out onto the road periodically to perform
my R&B show. My last R&B concert, just
before the release of *Unforgettable*, was May
17 and 18 at the Casino Estoril in Estoril, Por-
tugal. Having been immersed in the recording
project for four months, I had been away
from my R&B material so long that I almost
had to relearn it. When I started *Unforgettable*,
I'd been doing R&B for fifteen years. I had not
sung jazz on a regular basis ever before. For
Unforgettable, I needed to develop another
kind of voice, a smoother voice. I needed different chops. R&B, pop, and jazz are three different head spaces, and they place three
different demands on the voice, physically. You
can get really hoarse doing pop music or
R&B, because they require a lot of emotional
projection, with hollering or little punctuations
that you don't have in singing jazz standards.
The voice behaves like a muscle. It's developed for a certain kind of work, and when you
don't use it for that kind of work anymore, it
loses its tone, and it loses some of its capabilities.

Unforgettable was released on May 28, 1991,
just in time for Father's Day. One week later
on June 5, I was performing the *Unforgettable*
concert for the first time—at Chastain Park
in Atlanta, Georgia, with the Atlanta Symphony

Orchestra. I don't think I've ever seen so many nervous grown men—even Dan was a wreck. I was trying to keep calm, but it was every man/woman for him/herself. We pulled it off, but I don't remember a thing.

After Atlanta, I was off to play concerts scheduled all over the world. While I was out there singing my heart out, Bob Krasnow and his vice president of marketing, David Bither, were busy back at the ranch. They put together an unconventional advertising campaign for the album with a carefully devised marketing strategy, including orchestration of Father's Day media stories. Usually record companies focus their marketing on radio stations, knowing that if they can get the recording on the air, then people will find out about it. But this time, they decided to market to the public directly instead. Yes, we *were* going to sit on a couple of doorsteps of some radio people to see if they'd play it, but we didn't expect a lot of airplay on pop stations. We knew it would get played on jazz stations, and maybe a few adult contemporary stations, but pop? No. R&B? No.

Bob came up with a totally different strategy—take it to the street. He took out ads in magazines; I'd never had ads before in *Time, Newsweek, Vogue, Ladies' Home Journal, Cosmopolitan,* or *Life* magazine—or in newspapers—even the business section. I hadn't had that kind of coverage in my R&B and pop career, ever. Pictures of the album were appearing all over the world—from Japan to

Brazil. The beautiful cover photograph done by George Hurrell gave them something really nice to work with. Elektra's planning for the release of *Unforgettable* had been based on the assumption that between the end of May and the Christmas season, we'd be gradually infiltrating the public's consciousness.

When the record first came out, there were actually some negative responses that were morbid and hurtful. *Saturday Night Live* did a spoof on it that was disturbing, and then someone put a cartoon in the *Gavin Report*, which is a weekly radio survey of what's being played. The cartoon was a caricature of me at the microphone in a recording studio with a skeleton hanging behind me. I could hardly look at it. Some people felt that what I had done was in poor taste—not the album, but the single. I remember someone telling me that when they first heard it on the radio, they had to pull their car over because it was just so weird to them. Up until then, no one had really perfected that kind of sound, or at least it hadn't gotten a lot of notice—the ability to put the voice of a living human together with the voice of someone who is dead, and to have them sound like they were singing together. Nevertheless, it's one of the best recordings ever of two people singing a duet—dead or alive. Dad's voice and my voice were somehow very compatible, even with a thirty-year time difference.

I personally loved performing "Unforgettable," and I loved the album, but I thought it was just me, and truly considered the album a nice "aside." I knew that there were a lot of hard-core fans of my dad who would love it, but I really didn't know what the general reaction would be. As it turned out, the immediate response exceeded all of Elektra's expectations and the planning to gradually infiltrate the public's consciousness went right out the window. When the album was released, the record company was so flooded with orders that they ran out of albums, and it was moving quickly up the charts. Although Elektra had been enthusiastic, nobody in their wildest dreams thought it would have such an impact on the industry. People in the music business were stunned. And radio programmers were pulling their hair out. They were getting requests to put the music on their playlists—and it was a crazy decision to make because their rosters had nothing to do with this kind of music. These were Top 40 stations playing music by groups like Metallica.

One newspaper report said, "For some reason in the midst of heavy metal, rap, and dance-pop hegemony, Natalie Cole's *Unforgettable* stands out like a single rose in a patch of weeds and the public and the industry have responded in unprecedented ways." Another writer stated that *Unforgettable* was the "best album of remakes ever made," and yet another described the album and the tour as "popular both with her father's fans and baby boomers who are eager for the comforts of nostalgia." Record stores were reporting that people who hadn't been in a record store in twenty years were coming in and buying this record. I think this made a very clear statement to the music industry, saying: "You've forgotten a whole generation of people out there."

Over the first several months of touring, I had the honor of performing with some great symphony orchestras in this country—the Boston Symphony, the San Francisco Symphony, the Pittsburgh Symphony, the St. Louis Symphony, and the Washington Symphony Orchestra, to name a few. There was so much I had learned while working with a live orchestra in the recording sessions, and it had been such an important experience for me to be able to walk into a room or onto a stage and have the acknowledgment, support, and even respect of those musicians. I carried my own jazz quartet, who knew the music well. That's because I was lucky enough to have some of the musicians who had played on the album. We had Alan Broadbent on piano, Jim Hughart on bass, Harold Jones on drums, and John Chiodini, a wonderful guitarist who had played a lot with Peggy Lee over the years. They were all jazz greats, and I was so fortunate to have such great musicians backing me up. They taught me in their inimitable way, and I was back in school again—Jazz 101.

When I switched over from R&B to *Unforgettable,* most of the members of my band could not make the transition. Some of them had been with me for ten years, so letting them go was really hard. But this was a whole new ballgame. The only band member who did stay with me was Charles Floyd. He was able to make the transition to jazz, and ended up becoming my conductor. Although Charles had started off with me as a piano player playing R&B, his background was more classically based. Whenever he didn't know how to do something, he'd just sit down and figure it out. We had a beautiful relationship, like brother and sister. He was meticulous, just like me, and funny, and an artist himself. Working with these symphonies was something that he never dreamed could be a part of his life, but getting the respect of the symphonies he would be standing in front of would not be a simple task.

Over the next eighteen months we performed 256 shows. A lot of the summer concerts were outdoor dates with symphonies. They were beautiful. People were fainting from the sheer joy of hearing this music done live. The extra little sparkle was that something about it really wasn't old, and I think it was because it was a young woman sitting up there singing it, and the fact that she was Nat King Cole's daughter just made it that much more magical. Oh my God, how cool could this be? Over those months I worked my tail off. For the first nine months of the tour, we played the continental United States, Canada, and Hawaii. We performed in maybe fifty-five different cities, crisscrossing North America from Chattanooga, Tennessee, and Miami,

Florida, to Whistler Mountain in British Columbia, Canada—and from San Diego and San Francisco to Toronto. It was demanding, exhausting, and exhilarating, all at the same time.

Since the concert tour started out in the summer, Robbie was out of school and able to come with me. Robbie was a teenager now, and would watch the show from the wings, just like I watched my dad when I was young. I also hired Benita Hill to work with me. She had done some baby-sitting for Robbie as a baby, and we had been friends ever since I met her in Japan with Chaka Khan in 1976. I really needed an assistant and a traveling companion, and someone to help get Robbie where he needed to go. He wasn't a baby anymore; at the age of fourteen, the chauffeuring duty gets demanding. Benita came on the road with me at a very crucial time. André and I grabbed moments together whenever we could. With the success of *Unforgettable*, he was in huge demand as a producer and had his own career to tend to—not to mention his two children.

By July of 1991, the album had hit number one on the *Billboard* chart, moving up past what one journalist referred to as "the assaultive gangster rap of NWA and the screeching hard-rock of Skid Row." The album had "seized the country by quiet storm." And with sales of 1.2 million at that point, we had gone beyond the platinum mark. I was looking at printouts of sales from across the nation, and there was *Unforgettable*—right at the top next to the likes of Extreme, EMF, and Color Me Badd. I thought it was hysterical.

Even Bob Krasnow was taken by surprise. This was a very commercial time for music, and jazz was considered "old-timey"—cool, but not worthy of big sales like pop or rap. People in the music business were stunned. It raised a lot of eyebrows. They were beginning to realize that it had been totally ignored—so when something like this came along, it went through the roof. Not one but two generations of record buyers were buying this album. I'll never forget the day I stopped at a red light and looked over to witness a bunch of rappers blasting "Unforgettable" on their car radio and singin' away. This album had taken me to another level. It had altered everything by opening up a whole new realm of possibilities. Part of that involved educating some of my younger audience with this "new" material. Despite the fact that it was considered a rough period in the concert market, the tour had become a huge draw. Concert halls were selling out all over the place.

We toured all summer long, and by late August, we were back in familiar territory—Caesars Palace in Las Vegas. The response there was just as wonderful. Dan Cleary said afterward that he had never seen a Vegas audience that quiet in his life. The room was hushed. One of the things that I always marveled at about my dad was how he could control a room like that. I used to sit in the audience while my father was onstage, and I would get the biggest kick out of watching people. They would have this funny look on their faces. I thought it was so neat. Back when I had been singing in bars and lounges, I had yearned for the day that I could be in a room where people would actually want to listen. And they were listening now.

My very next concert was at the Universal Amphitheatre—right in my own hometown—and it was a real highlight for me. The setting was gorgeous—the whole look was incredible. The curtains opened to a vision right out of another time. There were six towering Doric columns, all scalloped with chiffon, and they formed a kind of backdrop. Fresh-cut roses lined the stage and the floor was black and white—the whole set was black and white. And there sat a thirty-five-piece orchestra dressed in white jackets and bow ties, sitting behind elegant white music stands with my monogram—NC—on them. It was reminiscent of big bands from the swing era of the 1930s and 1940s. The set was so incredible that people started clapping just at the sight of it. We opened the show just like the album, with "The Very Thought of You." Charles Floyd raised his baton and the strings started to play. I started singing from backstage. On this night, I wore a spectacular black and white dress that was right out of an old Lana Turner movie—big chiffon and tulle with black beading—it had a little flamenco flair to it and it was stunning. When I walked out onstage, the audience jumped to its feet and everyone started clapping again. The place went into a five-minute ovation. We had to stop, and I just couldn't believe it. I tried to maintain my composure. I wanted to cry, and in fact, I did. Sometimes you wonder if people get it, you know? And when they do and you're all on the same page, right at that same moment, it's the most wonderful experience. Yes, it's positively orgasmic. I couldn't breathe I was so happy.

"God, can you just freeze-frame for a minute?" I thought to myself. I knew this wouldn't ever happen again. This was my moment, the pinnacle of my musical achievements. Right here. Right now. Everything that I've worked for, thought about, fantasized about—is right now. And Charles Floyd just stood there with his little baton and his arms crossed over in front of him, looking at me with this little admiring smile on his face. And his look said to me, "Get it, girl! Just take it all in, suck it up. This is all for you." It was awesome, and the whole concert was just like that. Those are the moments you wish you could capture forever. Shame on us for not thinking of videotaping this show. I got through the rest of the night, and I don't remember how. I was home.

On every tour, there are not only highlights but catastrophes or near-catastrophes that are simply a part of the business. You breathe a sigh of relief once you get on the stage, because once we're onstage, we're pretty much safe till the end of the show, unless something breaks down, like the projection screen, which malfunctioned more than I care to recall. We always held our breath until that thing came down.

Sometimes things go wrong before the show. One night we were in Cincinnati to perform with the symphony there. We flew in the day of the concert and United Airlines decided that the mail was more important than our equipment. Our equipment got bumped, and the majority of that equipment was cases full of music, which hadn't arrived by showtime. On that occasion, Alan Broadbent was the conductor. This was the first catastrophe for our copyist, Yvonne, who was usually very cool and very together. But this night, she was backstage taking Mylanta, on a minute-by-minute basis. My gowns were in the missing cases as well, so I had nothing to wear.

At 8:10 P.M. the curtain opened and it's just me in my street clothes—jeans and a T-shirt—with the quartet, and about sixty empty chairs where the orchestra should have been. I told the audience what had happened and said, "Don't blame this on us. Just consider it a gift from the Friendly Skies of United Airlines." Fortunately, the audience was awfully good-natured about it, and it was nice to see how resilient an audience can be. The quartet and I spent the first half of the show basically winging it.

The next flight came in and our music came with it. We passed it out furiously. The orchestra had not seen these charts, so they had to go on cold without any kind of rehearsal. After intermission, the curtains opened up again and this huge orchestra was sitting in the chairs wearing their white jackets and bow ties, and I walked out newly clothed in a gorgeous gown. Ta-da! In a way, the effect was even more profound, given what had happened in the first half of the show. The orchestra was just brilliant that night, and the audience could not stop clapping. The whole incident had a kind of cliff-hanging drama to it—and we all developed little nervous tics in various forms for the next several weeks.

September was a quieter month for me. While the record company had me hopping with one thing or another, at least I could stay home for a bit and see Robbie back into school and spend some time with André. By October, however, we were going nuts again. We did fifteen sold-out shows that month— once we did two in one day. It was pretty hectic. We worked, went onstage, did our job, came offstage, got on the bus or got on the plane and went on to the next place. There wasn't a lot of partying going on, and not because we were dedicated—we were dead tired. There wasn't time for much in between.

Sometimes I felt as though I was caught up in that Charlie Chaplin movie *Modern Times*, in which the Little Tramp is swept along by the mechanized waves of progress. I just worked like crazy, and Dan kept saying,

"We've got to ride the momentum,"—and ride it I did. The truth is that many artists have to do the same thing when they have a big tour. You have to go with it, although you have to be really careful because you can get very sick. I was lucky that I didn't come down with anything. I don't remember getting sick, or canceling a single show, and I didn't lose my voice or get hoarse, either.

My vocal coach, Seth Riggs, monitored me and kept in touch with me as I moved from city to city. In many respects this music was more challenging than anything else I'd performed. As I've said before, you can't cheat or fake with this music. It's some of the most honest music I've ever done. But once I got into the rhythm of doing it, it was easier on my vocal cords. R&B had been much more of a strain—not only on my voice, but on my whole body. These new songs came so easily to me that I wasn't even sweating when I came offstage. In fact, sometimes I came offstage feeling like I had not really worked. It was just as smooth. I needed between six to eight hours of sleep so that my voice could be in pristine shape to sing these songs and make them soar. On this part of the tour there were no background singers—the music was all on me.

Despite the long hours and the intense pace, I was caught off guard by how much I loved every minute of this tour. I truly enjoyed the people in the audience, and received energy from their emotions every night. It was not about power, but about a great sense of sharing. There was yet again a bitter-sweetness to it all, with Dad up there on that screen, but also there was a sense of celebration, and a lot of love and joy. When the tears flowed, they were tears of joy and tears of gratitude. I was beginning to see another side of the world that I had never seen before—and another side of life as well. It was like I had begun a second career. I had spent the first fifteen years doing R&B and pop music, and now I was having a new career with jazz. The places I traveled to or the people I met along the way I never would have seen, had it not been for doing my dad's music. How ironic—that after running away from it—and him—for so long, it ended up helping me grow. It was yet another gift, this time not only from God, but from Dad.

This happy personal discovery was a concept not overlooked by the press. One journalist observed, "It wasn't until she did this album that she overcame the self-doubts that had been haunting her most of her life as a result of growing up in the shadow of a legend." Another wrote, "That she should have a mammoth hit covering the songs of the person whose success fed her insecurity is an irony that doesn't escape her. She has finally grown into the legend." I was also described as "standing toe-to-toe and mike-to-mike with the father who never even knew she wanted to sing." And another writer pointed out, "Singing with her father seems to have eased the burden of the inevitable comparisons that have plagued Cole since the beginning of her career."

I remember one night back in the day, when I had finished a show at the Copacabana in New York. A man came up to me and said, "You will never be as good as your father." That hurt, not because I ever expected to be as good as him, but because I was being recognized only in comparison to him. I was just "the-daughter-of Nat King Cole," and not Natalie Cole. There is no question that it had been hard getting out of Dad's shadow. Thank God I was born a girl, because if I had been born a boy, it would have been twice as difficult. One thing is for sure, though, I had gotten more of an education in the months since the *Unforgettable* project began than I had gotten in the entire previous ten years. I deeply respected the musicians who played this music. I developed even more respect for my dad. People didn't know I could sing like this. Hey—I didn't know I could sing like this. This album opened doors to a whole new career and a whole new world.

CHAPTER 25

The Grammy Bonanza

It was my hope that in some way I could offer my father's memory something in return for the many gifts he had given me. That had been my original intention with *Unforgettable*. So it was with great joy that I began to see articles in newspapers and magazines expressing ideas such as, "Natalie Cole's *Unforgettable* has brought renewed focus to her father's often overlooked legacy. Capitol Records would soon afterward release a boxed set featuring 100 songs and a 60-page book on Nat King Cole." And even my mother had to admit to reporters, "A whole new generation is going to hear my husband now." Consider that only fourteen albums of my father's work had been available in the twenty-five years between his death and the making of *Unforgettable*, and that in the ten years following the making of *Unforgettable*, over one hundred Nat King Cole albums have been published. I have to say that I accomplished much of what I set out to do. You go, girl.

By October of 1991, the album had reached the number one position on both the pop and jazz charts, and sales had gone over the two million mark. It was a remarkable moment in pop music history, really a phenomenon.

Perhaps one newspaper was right when they said, "It is as if one has drifted off into a time capsule and relived an era when love and romance were inseparable, and the concept of family was still sacred—these are values that record buyers are turning to in droves."

On November 1 and 2, we hit New York City—Radio City Music Hall—for two sold-out shows in this prestigious hall. I was pet-rified. It was a big deal, and I was so glad that I had a big beautiful gown on because I was so nervous that my knees were knocking underneath it. Big venues like that are numbing, overwhelming, anxiety-ridden events. As wonderful and joyous as they are, you can't help being scared to death. Despite the gigantic roar that went up at the beginning of the show, I was not soothed. I was so afraid of one horrific thing—that I would forget the words. That's what I always fear the most. When I think of artists like Barbra Streisand, who has such fear of being onstage—I don't know if it's her fear of being in front of an audience or if she's afraid she's going to forget the words—I understand that fear and I still have it. But I remember what my father used to say about being onstage: "If you're nervous, that's good." It's when you're not nervous that you're maybe a little overconfident and your performance becomes a little too glossy, a little too pat. I have never been able to shake my nervousness. I suppose some of it is energy and adrenaline, but whatever it is, according to my dad, it's good to have. In this case, it definitely worked in my favor. The reviews were great—one reviewer gave me a "ten" and declared that I "must be considered a Superstar." Now that's the kind of praise that'll put a big smile on anyone's face.

A few days after New York, we went to Boston, performing with the Boston Symphony Orchestra. One of the really nice things that would eventually come out of that performance was that my conductor, Charles Floyd, would end up getting work later with the Boston Pops. On his own merit, Charles impressed John Williams, the conductor of the Pops, who invited him to be a guest conductor. For a young black man, conducting orchestras of this stature was really a significant experience. Even in 1991, a lot of these symphonies had never seen a black conductor. Charles had to work very hard and be very diligent and very focused, because the superbly trained musicians with symphonies can be difficult. But Charles earned their respect, and I was so proud of him.

Throughout November until December 11, we continued the breakneck pace, giving twenty-seven more concerts before breaking for Christmas. Not long before that, Elektra had decided I should do a Christmas single— my dad's "Christmas Song"—sometimes known as "Chestnuts Roasting on an Open Fire." The song was originally written and performed by Mel Tormé, but Dad's version had become the standard. Elektra wanted to do a boxed set for Christmas, which would include the album, this single, and the video.

Thus, in one of my short visits home, we all went back into the studio to produce yet one more song. With the success of *Unforgettable*, the atmosphere was more electric than ever. I had developed a bit of a cold when it came time to do the recording, so I was sniffling and sneezing and wheezing between takes. Strangely enough, when I opened my mouth to sing, it sounded perfectly fine. I sure got all weepy singing that one. A friend of mine gave me this neat pin to wear while I was recording. It was a clear plastic box with a picture of Dad's smiling face in it, set against a pen-and-ink drawing of a snowy landscape and a tiny Santa Claus affixed to the bottom.

I was not expecting "The Christmas Song" to be an even more emotional experience than recording *Unforgettable*. I miss my dad all the time and, since his death, hearing "Chestnuts Roasting on an Open Fire" had often been very painful for me because it reminded me that he was gone. This year there would be another version—with my voice.

This holiday was actually a wonderful one for me. Although my mother and brother and sisters were now scattered and it was difficult for us all to be together, I had my own family now with Robbie and André and his two children. The news that *Unforgettable* was still topping the charts and that sales had now reached the almost four million mark certainly didn't dampen our spirits any. Nor did the fact that the media was citing *Unforgettable* as one of the best albums of 1991. It was almost impossible to conceive that at exactly this time seven years earlier, I had been sitting at Hazelden, alone and broken.

While the Christmas season provided something of a break, January brought a whole new round of excitement. The biggest thrill came on January 8, when the National Academy of Recording Arts and Sciences (NARAS) announced that we had been nominated for a total of nine Grammy Awards for *Unforgettable*. We couldn't believe it. We just couldn't believe it. It wasn't that I hadn't won a Grammy before—I had won three of them over the years. It's just that it seemed incomprehensible to me that anyone who had put themselves through what I put myself through over the last decade could possibly make this kind of comeback. It was unheard of.

On one hand we were thinking "Yes!"—and on the other hand I just didn't believe that *Unforgettable* had a chance. There was all kind of speculation flying around in the press about who was going to win—they dubbed our specific nominations the "Granny" nominations, and charged that "Unforgettable" couldn't possibly win, given that the song was forty years old. In one of the four categories I was nominated in, I was up against Harry Connick Jr., Johnny Mathis, Diane Schuur, and Barbra Streisand—incredibly formidable peers. And in some of the other categories, I was up against Bonnie Raitt, who had four Grammys under her belt already, Amy

Grant, who had five, the popular R.E.M., who were newcomers to the Grammy Awards, Bryan Adams, who received a total of six nominations this year, and Paul Simon, who had a grand total of twelve Grammys to his credit. These were all great talents and contenders to take seriously. Unfortunately, these nominations were announced seven weeks before the February 25 award ceremonies, which gave us seven weeks to walk around on pins and needles.

To add to the excitement, just a few days later I had the honor of receiving three NAACP Image Awards—for Outstanding Female Artist, Outstanding Jazz Artist, and Outstanding Music Video. The NAACP had established these awards to recognize films, television programs, and entertainers who reflect positive images of blacks. Wow—from one extreme to the other. I knew that there had been a time when I wouldn't have deserved this award. Other winners that night included Whoopi Goldberg, Oprah Winfrey, Patti LaBelle, Janet Jackson, Arsenio Hall, and Magic Johnson. I felt as if I had been placed among a rarefied group and I thought to myself, "Girl, you better enjoy this now, because it may never happen again."

The Australians had become great *Unforgettable* fans, and I had some of the highest album sales per capita there in the world. Everybody had been trying to get us to Australia, and finally a friend of Dan's made it happen. I did four concerts in total—in

Sydney, Melbourne, Perth, and Brisbane—and their reaction was good evidence of what we already knew—*Unforgettable* had been number one on their charts for the last six weeks. It was a quickie tour, and we had to be back in Los Angeles by January 27 for the nineteenth annual American Music Awards. Unlike the Grammys, where votes are determined by people in the music industry, these awards are voted upon by a national sampling of citizens who are a fair representation of the general public. I thought it was too good to be true when I heard that I had been nominated, but I was afraid to even entertain the notion that I might win. So I was astonished to be awarded two American Music Awards—one for Best Contemporary Album, and the other for Favorite Adult Contemporary Artist. I was starting to believe that maybe, just maybe, I had a chance at another Grammy.

The end of the month was marked by the taping of the *Unforgettable* concert for the PBS show *Great Performances*. They had picked the beautiful Pasadena Civic Auditorium, and we taped it in front of a live audience. It was also a fund-raiser for the Permanent Charities Fund for Hunger and Homelessness, and out of it came the Natalie Cole Scholarship Award to help in the training and education of teachers who work with homeless children. I was proud to be a part of it.

The first part of February provided some downtime for me and my family. It is interesting to note that in the seven years that the

Grammy Awards existed before Dad's death, he had received seven nominations, two of them for Album of the Year, but he never won. And Dad was a founding member of NARAS and had been instrumental in creating the Grammys. Actually, this year he was to be inducted into the Grammy Hall of Fame. That was nice for our family and for his legacy—but in my opinion, it was about thirty years too late. One thing I knew was that if I did win a Grammy for *Unforgettable*, I would be winning it not only for myself and for all those who had worked on it, but ultimately I would be winning it for Dad.

A few nights before the Grammy Awards, I was already in New York. I was early for a couple of reasons. The first was to go to Clive Davis's Arista Records party. Until 2000, Clive Davis had headed up Arista for years, and he remains one of the grand ole men of the music business—a suit with soul. He had also become sort of the Swifty Lazar of the Grammys—Clive's do was *the* party. That year it was at the Plaza Hotel, and as Dan, his wife, and I were walking up the stairs to the gala, who do we see coming down the stairs but Gerry Griffith! Since his no-show in Cleveland, Gerry had gone from working for Bruce Lundvall at EMI to working for Clive at Arista. He was gracious enough to congratulate us on our nominations for *Unforgettable*, but for himself, he had to have been thinking about what might have been.

The other reason I was in New York early

was to help raise money to save the legendary Apollo Theater in Harlem. The night before the Grammy telecast is the traditional night for the Arista Records party, but in 1992, it was a day early so we could do the Apollo benefit. The seventy-nine-year-old Apollo had always been linked to great black performers like Cab Calloway, Duke Ellington, Count Basie, Billie Holiday, Josephine Baker, Sammy Davis, Jr., Stevie Wonder, Aretha Franklin, Mary Wells, Smokey Robinson, and of course, Dad, who had performed there some forty years before. If you wanted to know if you had really made it, the Apollo was the ultimate testing ground. (I had played there early on in my career, so I guess I passed the test!) The audience could love you or ruin you, and they had a great reputation for being brutally honest. Back in the days of segregation, the Apollo was one of the only places where black talent could showcase their acts. And if you wanted to see some of the greats, you had to go to Harlem. It is kind of ironic that desegregation actually weakened the Apollo. Great black performers could go downtown to other venues, where it was easier for an audience to get to them and visits to Harlem were no longer as necessary. For years the Apollo had been struggling, and now they were considering closing their doors.

I was very pleased to be able to donate a full-blown *Unforgettable* concert—with orchestra and a choir from the La Guardia School of Performing Arts, who sang "Our Love" with me.

They were awesome! Elektra helped to under-write it, and they sold tickets from $25 a seat to the $1,000 Golden Circle tickets that included a party and dinner at Sylvia's Soul Food Restaurant, which was right in Harlem. The turnout was tremendous. John F. Kennedy Jr. was there with a mystery date, and so was Mayor David Dinkins. I was really pleased that the theater managed to reach the $100,000 goal they had hoped for. On that same day, February 21, 1992, the city of New York had declared Nat King Cole Day and the mayor presented me with a plaque—well, actually a street sign—that read "Nat King Cole Walk." It was going to be hung on 125th Street between Seventh and Eighth avenues—the block where the Apollo Theater is located.

On the heels of that big day came a big MusiCares fund-raising event at the Waldorf-Astoria—a $1,000-per-plate black-tie gala. I shared the spotlight with Bonnie Raitt, another Grammy nominee, so it was less like work and more like play for me. MusiCares is another organization I like to support, because its goal is to help down-and-out musicians get back on their feet. Anyone who knows the music world, knows how many down-and-out musicians there are out there. So many gifted and even famous musicians have died broke and sick and forgotten—unable to provide for themselves. Not very many musicians were born with the advantages my father had given me, and they are in need of help and support.

With so many events and activities going on during Grammy week, I had no time to think. I still did not really believe that I could win. I had little chills going through me just trying *not* to think about it! It was an exciting, exhilarating time. New York City had put on its finery and was catering to the event big-time. They filled the subways with street musicians and changed street signs from Sixth Avenue, where Radio City Music Hall was located, to Grammy Plaza. Then they painted signs on the streets that said, "New York City Loves the Grammys." In Times Square, just a few blocks away, they were all set up for a live videocast on a giant television screen.

This, the thirty-fourth annual Grammy Awards ceremony, was to be the biggest in history. It was going to be beamed live to two billion viewers around the world, in something like ninety countries. And for the very first time, people in the fifteen former republics of the Soviet Union would receive it via satellite. There were some three hundred performers and presenters scheduled, 220 stage hands and, apparently, three thousand miles of television cable—all orchestrated by my friend, producer Pierre Cossette. Although the Grammys involved seventy-eight categories in twenty-eight fields, not all of them were televised. It would have taken a week.

There were going to be only sixteen Grammy Award presentations actually made on camera. Whoopi Goldberg was to host the show, and she would be the first woman ever to do so.

There would be performances by musicians like Michael Bolton, Seal, Bonnie Raitt, Mariah Carey, Johnny Mathis, Luther Vandross, my "new best friends."—Metallica—and me. I was slotted for the very last performance that night, right before the announcement of the grandest award—Album of the Year—was made. It wasn't hard to figure out what song I was going to sing.

The place was absolutely sold out, but despite this, there was a waiting list of four thousand people who hadn't been able to get in. For the day of the event, February 25, 1992, 350 police officers had been assigned to Radio City and drivers were instructed to completely avoid the areas around there. It was gridlock. The side streets near the stage doors were lined with trailers for producers and technicians to use. The weather was gloomy, but the freezing cold drizzle didn't seem to dampen anybody's spirits. The day was finally here and thousands of fans lined up around Radio City. They had been there for hours, holding their place in line, so they could get to see their favorite musicians and stars up close and in the flesh. They were hooting and hollering and photographers were everywhere.

So much of that evening is a big blur. But, as has been so well documented, *Unforgettable* won seven Grammys. I was shocked. We were all shocked. "Unforgettable" won the first award of the evening, Song of the Year, and after that it just kept on winning. It was wonderful. Then, it was incredible. Then, outrageous.It even was absolutely embarrassing—albeit an embarrassment of riches.

I was saying to myself, "I don't deserve this. I don't deserve this." Well, honey, by the end of that night I was grinning from ear to ear and telling myself, I *do* deserve this. Damn, I'm good!

CHAPTER 26

Tick-Tick-Boom

The shot of me in that black and white dress holding the armload of Grammys is another piece of my life that follows me everywhere. The *Unforgettable* sweep, a career highlight few artists experience, was in fact an 8.0-on-the-Richter-scale matrimonial earthquake. From the moment I walked off the stage, my marriage started crashing down around me.

André had wanted desperately to be named Producer of the Year, and when that went to David Foster, he was—for lack of a better word—pissed. We had won Album of the Year as a group, and when all of us were interviewed by the media backstage, André behaved like a petulant four-year-old. He monopolized the press conference, and just ran his mouth in the first person—I-I-I-me-

me-me—until the reporters simply put down their pens and stared at him. Neither David Foster, nor Tommy LiPuma, nor I got a chance to say much of anything.

It was no surprise that André despised David for winning the Grammy for Producer of the Year. André had produced half the songs on the album, but they don't pick Grammy winners by majority rule. Numbers didn't matter—whoever had done the song "Unforgettable" would have been the winner— David would have won the Grammy even if he'd produced nothing else on the album but "Unforgettable." André's relationship with David Foster was one casualty that night—our marriage was another.

Not that things weren't already bad between André and me. As the *Unforgettable* juggernaut gathered momentum in the summer and fall of 1991, he had more and more trouble dealing with it. He felt that he wasn't being suffi- ciently acknowledged for his contribution to its success, and resented the fact that the publicity was centered on me. What they used to call the green-eyed monster—jeal- ousy—was eating him alive.

The morning after the Grammys, I had to get on a plane for Italy, and André was headed back to Los Angeles. Parting was not exactly sweet sorrow—he was horrible, extremely spiteful and nasty. This was exactly how he'd promised *not* to behave. Before we married, André had convinced me that he was okay with being the sideshow in the media circus and not the main event, and he had assured me that it wouldn't bother him. But André couldn't deal with being "the-husband-of"—he hated it when anyone called him "Mr. Cole," even by accident. After we got married, the only time I could be "Natalie Cole" was onstage. I had to change my driver's license and even change my stationery letterhead. When some poor hotel clerk asked me, "How are you doing today, Ms. Cole?" André considered it an insult, and snapped: "Mrs. *Fischer.*"

When Marvin and I were married, I'd seldom been called "Mrs. Yancy." Of course, unlike Marvin, André was a very insecure and very angry man. He, too, was a recovering addict, but because he had to keep earning a living, he didn't have the luxury of getting help at a place like Hazelden. He had to do it on his own, as do a lot of people. That made him bitter, along with other baggage that he carried through his life.

When we were first married, I noticed that he didn't have a lot of friends. After a while it was a drag. When you're first in love and a man is giving you all of his attention, you take it as total flattery. You relish the fact that he just wants to be with you and no one else. But when he tells you, "You don't need anybody else in your life, you've got me"—that's a bad sign. After a while you start asking—don't you have anybody else you can hang out with? I watched him destroy a couple of friendships—fifteen- to twenty-year relationships. Both in his business and his personal life, he imagined slights and snubs where there were none—or certainly where none were intended—and lashed out accordingly.

Sometimes he lashed out verbally, and sometimes it was physical, and it got more and more difficult to hide the cracks in our marriage. The first time he abused me physically, he pushed me, naked, clear through a wall—yes, through plaster and all. You could see daylight on the other side. Then, less than two months after the Grammy Awards ceremonies, just as André and I were moving into our new house in Tarzana, there was another physical altercation. It was bad, and I ended up with a busted lip and a black eye.

My cousin Pam, Bay's daughter, arrived shortly after it happened.

"Did you hit him back?" Pam, God bless her, always got right to the point. She knew I didn't walk into no door. "How'd it happen?" I was starting to cry, and I pointed to the Bible on the table.

"No way. He heaved the Holy Bible into your face?" Pam was in disbelief.

I nodded because it hurt too much to speak—inside and out. The Bible is not something we would use in our family as an instrument of pain. It was bad enough that he'd hit me, but knowing how much my faith means to me, how could he have hit me with the Bible? The terrible irony was that this was the same Bible I had fasted and prayed over, and in which I had put the letter begging for God to send me André.

I knew Aunt Bay would be on her knees praying as soon as she heard about it, but the truth was that it didn't take long for *everybody* to hear the story—Aunt Bay could have read it on the front page of the *National Enquirer*. As a result of the fight, André and I separated, and news of the separation hit the papers. The press was hounding me again—this time at my home. They were hanging around the gate of my house, waiting to ambush me at the airport, trying like crazy to get a glimpse—and a photo—of my face. I was still paparazzi bait when I left for a long European tour a couple of days later. For the first ten days of the trip, we had to do all kinds of stuff with makeup and hats and sunglasses to camouflage the bruise, and I spent a lot of time in interviews fending off questions about my marriage.

I had seen signs of André's abusive personality, and this was not the first time he had put his hands on me—but I had chosen to ignore the incidents. I was determined to fix him. Ideally, I believed that I could change him. What I really needed to do was fix and change *me*. I had still not learned how to be more discerning in my choices in men, and I was still paying the price for bad judgment because I wanted so much to have a man in my life. I wasn't just naive. I was dumb and I was hardheaded. I'm still working on the latter, but I got over being dumb—just not fast enough.

On the fifteenth of June, I filed for divorce. But by September, we had "reconciled."

Actually, that's a lie. In truth the only person doing any reconciling was me—I basically begged André to come home. While I was doing *Unforgettable* in Europe, I started getting weepy and whiny and weak, and I decided I didn't want the divorce after all. This is the textbook syndrome of the woman with low self-esteem, and every battered woman has the same MO. It's the worst manifestation of the I'm-nothin'-without-a-man blues. You figure that somehow this is your fault, that you've done everything wrong and maybe if you could just do a little better, everything will be okay. And besides, you really believe that you love this man.

André really didn't want to come back to me. But I kept pleading until he did. We went on a cruise, a sort of second honeymoon, to try to put our marriage back together. We even renewed our vows on the ship. It would have been better for both of us to cut our losses then and there, but I couldn't let go. I could not face yet another failed marriage.

Around Thanksgiving, I was back at Caesars in Las Vegas and got a visit from the writers of the TV series *I'll Fly Away*. I loved that program, and I'd been looking for a way to explore acting. Actually, I had met with Carroll O'Connor, one of the producers of the show, earlier that year to ask if they could create a role for me that was nonmusical. It took a year for them to get back and they thought they had the perfect role for me, but first they wanted me to do a screen test.

This opportunity to stretch my acting wings came at a surprising time, but I was eager to pursue it. I had not really done any acting since Northfield, when I played the part of Lutiebelle Gussie Mae Jenkins in *Purlie Victorious* by Ossie Davis. (Lutiebelle was played by his wife, Ruby Dee, in the original Broadway cast; a musical version, *Purlie*, had the marvelous Melba Moore in this role.) I had really liked acting in high school, but I had no idea how to really act. The fact that I loved to perform was the best thing I had going for me. There was a scene where I had to cry, just kneel at the lip of the stage and boohoo. At first, I had no idea how I was going to manage this— once, maybe, but the play ran for two weeks! I shocked myself on opening night. I really cried, and the audience was boohooing right along with me! I guess I had a lot to cry about, even then.

The story for my *I'll Fly Away* segment was based on the life of a real young woman who got involved in the civil rights movement and ended up going to prison. My character was the girl's mother, who, after much hardship and emotional turmoil, establishes a school for black students that teaches nonviolence and race relations as part of its curriculum. Once I had read about the character, I felt that I could play her. She was a mother who was very emotionally involved in the life of her child and I understood that very well.

They sent my videotaped audition to Georgia, where the series was filmed, and word got back that I'd gotten the part. I packed up my bags and headed for Atlanta. On the set, I was introduced to Sam Waterston and Regina Taylor, the stars of the show, and to the young woman playing my daughter, a budding young actress named N'Bushe Wright.

Everyone was great to me; the only thing I didn't especially like about the experience was the hours. I'm basically a night owl—and, honey, you cannot survive in the music business if you go to bed with the chickens. But acting is early to bed, early to rise. I was in bed by half past nine every night. I had to get up at four-thirty in the morning and then we were driven for about an hour to the set. I wasn't wild about the long technical delays every time the camera had to be moved, either. Hurry up and wait is truly the name of the business. Acting is hard—at least it was for me, because I've been spoiled. I get up onstage, sing some songs, and everybody loves me, and I get instant gratification. With acting, you get up; you do your thing over and over until you get it right; and you have to wait for your gratification until the premiere and hope that your work has not ended up on the cutting room floor. But I did enjoy the experience. By comparison, singing is a breeze. That first day on the set, I couldn't figure out what to do with my hands, because I was used to holding a microphone. Although I was pretty much at ease in front of the camera, gesture is an important part of singing, and I didn't know if I was going to be able to express myself in character without using my hands.

I must have done well enough, because at the end of the week, the director came up to me and said, "You know, if you ever decide to go into acting, the world would lose a great singer, but we would gain a great actress." The fact that he went out of his way to say that gave me so much confidence and so much encouragement, and believe me, I needed it, because things were going to hell at home.

Everybody was in therapy. I was in counseling; André was in counseling; Robbie was in counseling. We were a mess. There were red flags popping up all over the place, but I was in big fat denial. I couldn't believe I'd made a mistake—I mean, wasn't this the very man that God had sent me, after my Bible request?

These personal problems burbled beneath a happy family-successful career facade. In 1993 I sang at the Oscars for the second year in a row. The year before I'd sung Linda Ronstadt's part in her duet with James England from *American Tail*. (I took my mother to the show.) For the '93 show, Whitney was supposed to sing "I Have Nothing" and "Run to You" from *The Bodyguard*, both of which had been nominated for Best Song, but she'd just had a baby and couldn't be there, and she asked me if I'd do it for her. Of course I said I would.

Oh, my Lord, I was so nervous. Everything at the Oscars is timed right down to the second—it runs like a Swiss watch, or it's supposed to. I was wearing this fabulous Ed Johnson red dress—it was one of those things where I didn't have to do anything, just stand there and sing. I looked to die for, but there was this one teensy little problem—I forgot some of the lyrics to one of the songs. I was so embarrassed I would have run off the stage when I was done, but the dress was too tight. Linda and David Foster (who had co-written the song) were in the audience, and Whitney was watching it on television, and they swear they were the only three who knew. I think they were just trying to be nice.

When I called Whitney to apologize, she was laughing the whole time. She said, "That's all right, girl, you did me proud. Don't worry about it."

"By the way," she added, "how's Tick-Tick-Boom?" That was her own name for André, and her way of reminding me that I was sitting on a keg of dynamite.

My next project was good, but was released at the wrong time. *Unforgettable* could have kept selling for three years, but instead we came out with another album, *Take a Look*, in June of 1993, which was about a year too soon. The audience was expecting *Unforgettable II*, and instead I gave them something with much more pop and jazz. People weren't ready for it, and it's too bad, because there were some great arrangements on it, such as "I Wish You Love," "Let There Be Love," and "I'm Beginning to See the Light," to name a few. André produced eleven of the eighteen tracks on *Take a Look*. As long as we were talking about music, we were fine.

Robbie also had a chance to be involved—he played the drums on a song called "Calypso Blues," which was the only song of my father's on the album. It was Robbie's debut, and I was very proud of him. The little drummer who had come onstage with me when he was four was now accomplished enough to play on an album people would pay money to hear.

That November I was part of an AIDS Project L.A. fund-raiser concert at the Universal Amphitheatre in Los Angeles. Everyone did something from *West Side Story*. We had a bitch of a time getting the rights to do the songs, but when we finally took the stage, it was tremendous. Elton John sang "I Feel Pretty" (Ha!), Barbra Streisand and Johnny Mathis did "Somewhere." Patti LaBelle, Sheila E., and I teamed up on "America," and it was one of our finest hours as entertainers.

My brother, Kelly, was in the audience that night. Our relationship had been spotty through the years, but now I felt extremely close to him. He had just told me that he had been diagnosed with HIV, so our time together felt precious. Kelly had told me that he was gay when he was nineteen years old, and although he felt comfortable sharing that with us, I never had a long conversation with him about it until much later. As an adult, he'd become rather distant, because his lifestyle was so different. Kelly was one of those complex unfinished human beings. Both fascinating and

maddening, he was brilliant, funny, and creative, but he was lazy as all get-out. He was
a wonderful writer, but he could never bring
anything to fruition. Kelly could be a very thor-
ough researcher, at least about subjects he
wanted to know about—like Sophie Tucker
and Josephine Baker. He was never content
with learning just a little bit; he wanted to learn
everything. But all of his great undertakings
were abandoned before they were completed,
because he was on to the next new thing.

I don't think Kelly ever made more than a
few grand off anything he did by his own
effort, but he sure had a ball squandering his
inheritance. He became a real man about
town. He was into all kinds of sports—skiing,
swimming, horseback riding, and polo. He
worked out like a maniac, and because he
was born gorgeous, he did a little modeling.
He lived a self-indulgent lifestyle, with fine
clothes, lots of parties, luxury trips, and a series
of affairs. It seemed like he had a guy in every
port; when I started traveling extensively,
there wasn't hardly a city where people didn't
know my brother.

Even though he was adopted, he knew more
about Dad than anybody, and he took it upon
himself to become the family historian. He knew
all about every song Dad had recorded,
including some that I'd never heard of before,
like "The Frim Fram Sauce." He had started
writing a history of Dad's life that was quite
good, but like most of his projects, he never
finished it. He had a unique perspective on the

relationship between my mother and my father that, although not unkind, was certainly unorthodox. That autumn night when we were all onstage singing *West Side Story*, he was still quite well enough to sit in the audience, but his illness would eventually take his life.

Nineteen ninety-four started out on a strange note. I sang at Bill Gates's wedding reception; my house took a major hit from the January 17 earthquake; and I had to leave for Atlanta while it was still a mess in order to sing the national anthem at the Super Bowl. At about the same time, "Take a Look," the title track on the last album, was nominated for a Grammy as Best Jazz Vocal, and I performed "It's Sand Man"—a high-spirited Count Basie song that had been lyrically reinvented by a vocal group from the 1950s called Lambert, Hendricks, and Ross—at the Grammy Awards on the first of March. The Grammys were in New York again that year, and I had the best time! Clive Davis's Arista bash was a blast. At the end of the night, a bunch of us got up to serenade Aretha Franklin, and when Whitney Houston, her mom Cissy, Bobby Brown, Gladys Knight, BeBe Winans, and I got into "Respect," it was a scream.

Dressing room space for the Grammys was at a premium that year. I shared with three powerhouse divas—Lena Horne, Dolly Parton, and Gloria Estefan. Let me tell you, honey, it was girls' night out! The four of us in there howled and laughed the entire time we were getting dressed. We were all so in awe of

Miss Lena (whose regal bearing has a certain resemblance to my mother's)—it was just a sim-patico evening. I won in the Best Jazz Vocal category for "Take a Look." You could have knocked me over with a feather.

In the summer of 1994, I got a call from director Delbert Mann, asking me to discuss the possibility of playing the lead in a made-for-television movie, *Lily in Winter.* I was totally awed by the prospect of meeting him. Here was a man who had directed Sophia Loren, Grace Kelly, Jack Lemmon, Paul Newman, Frank Sinatra, Henry Fonda, Humphrey Bogart, Lauren Bacall, and Lau-rence Olivier, to name just a few. Dan Cleary and I went to his office, and his mantelpiece was covered with Oscars and Directors Guild Awards. That was pretty intimidating. I felt like a schoolgirl, saying to myself, "Oh my God, oh my God. I'm talking to *the* Delbert Mann."

Delbert immediately put me at ease. He really is one of the most gentle, classy men that I've ever met, and he knew exactly what he wanted. The movie that Delbert had in mind for me was set in 1957 during the Christmas holiday season. It was based on a true incident in the life of a woman named Lily Covington. Delbert wanted me to play the lead role of Lily, and it was more than I could have hoped for. In preparation for the part, I started working with Nina Foch, a notable drama coach who was a fine actress in her own right. What I wanted from her was not only instruction but honesty—I needed to know whether I was wasting my time or anyone else's time trying to act. Nina could not have been more supportive—tough, but encouraging. We worked at her house, and every day we dove into the script. Nina was theatrical and colorful and bright. She kept reassuring me that I could do this, and then gave me the tools. One of the things I learned was how to dredge up pieces of my own life and use them to enrich my character.

In one scene, my character mourns her father at his grave site in Alabama. I could very well have been talking to my own father in that scene, and it was quite emotional for me. Thank goodness, Delbert only made me do that scene twice. It's a credit to the magic of the movies that Disney Ranch in Valencia, California, in August passed for rural Alabama in December. We shot six days a week for five weeks, so I basically didn't have a life during that time. I became someone else—Lily Covington.

Although I was learning how to carry parts of my own experience into my acting, it was also a way to get away from myself. I spent a lot of time being Lily Covington and for me that was a good thing. At that moment I would have swapped identities with almost anyone, because being Natalie Cole *Fischer* had become no fun at all.

CHAPTER 27

Lord, What a Family

At the end of 1994, it seems that my face was all over the place, busily infusing everyone with the Christmas spirit. *Lily in Winter* aired on USA Network on the eighth of December, and the premiere was the first time I'd ever seen myself acting on the big screen. It was also the first time that I watched *Lily in Winter* as one continuous story, and I was pretty pleased with the result. The process was still very new to me, and I couldn't wait to do it again. *Lily in Winter* ended up doing very well, and has aired on USA Network practically every holiday season since it was made.

I'd also taped a PBS *Great Performances* Christmas special concert in the winter wonderland atmosphere of SUNY Purchase, and my guests included the New York Restoration Choir and Elmo from *Sesame Street*. In some cities, including Los Angeles, *Natalie Cole's Untraditional Traditional Christmas* aired opposite *Lily in Winter*—I was competing with myself on cable TV.

My Christmas album, *Holly & Ivy*, came out that season, too. Alan Broadbent, who'd worked on *Unforgettable*, did the arranging. Because I cherished the idea that Dad's version of "The Christmas Song" had become such a holiday tradition for so many families, I recorded it again on this album, with an arrangement by Johnny Mandel. I even survived another dose of Michael Masser and recorded a song he wrote called "No More Blue Christmas," which was also released as a single. The guy still drove me crazy. God love him.

During this period, Dan had called and asked how I felt about going to Japan with Frank Sinatra for a pre-Christmas concert. With the promise that I'd be home for Christmas, I quickly agreed. The show was held at the Fukuoka Dome in Tokyo on the nineteenth and twentieth of December. I've had some wonderful opportunities to stand on the same stage with legends like Barbra Streisand, Tony Bennett, and Ella Fitzgerald. But sharing a performance with Frank Sinatra, the Chairman of the Board, has to be near the top of the list of anyone's peak experiences.

I met Frank Sinatra in my adult life in 1977, when he invited me to appear on a television special with him—this was the time I found out I was pregnant with Robbie. He was then, and had always been, very kind to me. I worked with him another time at Carnegie Hall, where he headlined a show dedicated to the music of George and Ira Gershwin. When I went to his dressing room to say hello, he had a roomful of people, but stopped what he was doing to walk over and give me a big hug. Very cool.

By the time we were to perform in Japan, I

had become fairly friendly with both Frank and his wife, Barbara—a great lady. I had been to parties at their home in Beverly Hills and I had been their guest at their compound in the desert. Before the performance at the Fukuoka Dome, Mr. S. invited me to dinner in his hotel suite, along with some members of his entourage. (Frank never traveled without an entourage.) He sat at the head of this long table, and I sat right next to him and he talked a little about my father. "Your dad was just cool," I remember him saying. "He was a man and *and* a gentleman." Frank talked about how much he admired him, how much fun they'd had together—and how much mischief they'd gotten into. He even told me about how when Dad was dying, he and Sammy Davis had sprung him briefly from St. John's to take him down the street for a drink. What made it special for me wasn't even so much what he said, or the details he recalled. It was the gentleness and the reverence that he held in his voice that I remember most of all.

It was a nostalgic ride down memory lane for the Chairman of the Board, and I treasure that time he spent reminiscing with me. Because he'd been so eloquent over dinner, it was a shock when I saw Frank falter onstage. It was all he could do to get through "My Way," and I couldn't believe that he was losing the lyrics to signature songs like "The Lady Is a Tramp" and "New York, New York." He had a TelePrompTer that was as big as a giant TV screen, but it was as if he didn't know how to read it. I could tell that it was really tough on him—it seemed to me that he knew what was going on, but couldn't do anything to help himself. He just stood there blankly while the music kept going. Finally he turned his back to the audience and glowered at Frank Junior, who was conducting, like it was *his* fault.

As I watched the TV monitors in the dressing room I wondered, "What the hell...?" Later on, it was reported that Frank Sinatra had Alzheimer's. I'd never known anyone with this disease, but I did know that one characteristic is that you can recall things that happened years before, but you can't remember what happened three minutes ago. Maybe that was why he could recall so much about my dad, but so little of what he was supposed to do onstage.

In 1993 I had recorded with Frank "They Can't Take That Away from Me" on his *Duets* album, but he wasn't actually in the recording studio with me. As is often the case with recorded duets, Frank put down his track, and then I did mine separately. Frank's voice was still in pretty good form; he didn't have to be digitally enhanced. When Sinatra sang, he didn't need anything, and he was quick— just a couple of takes at most. The great Phil Ramone produced that album, and the trick for me was to curl my voice around Frank's to make it sound like we were singing side by side. Whatever problems he was having then were hidden from me, because we didn't actually work together.

Over dinner before the concert, Frank had invited me to fly home with him and his entourage on his private jet. There were nine of us onboard altogether: Frank, his man-ager, his travel agent, his doctor, his house-keeper, a stewardess, a steward, his valet, and me.

We'd hightailed it direct from the arena, as was Frank's custom. For years after a gig, he'd gone straight from the stage to the car to the airport as soon as he finished the last number—he was an Elvis-has-left-the-building kind of guy. In no time the bags were loaded onboard and we were taxiing for takeoff. In addition to Frank, I knew Elliott, his manager, and he and I were making small talk in the lounge area of this custom-configured Boeing 727. Frank was sitting off by himself unwinding, feet up, tie off, but still in his tux. Even before the wheels left the runway, however, he was knocking back the Jack Daniel's one after the next like there was no tomorrow.

We had been in the air about an hour or so when Frank suddenly looked around at all of us in the cabin and bellowed, "Who the hell are all these people?"

I thought that must be the Jack Daniel's talking, and because Frank always was a kidder, my first reaction was to laugh—until I realized that no one else was even smiling. At that point, Frank stood and started going around the room, confronting everyone in turn, getting close up in each face and demanding to know, "Who the hell are you?"

It was a belligerent challenge, issued nose-to-nose at the top of his voice. He started with his housekeeper, who'd been with him some fifty years. His personal valet was next. "Uh-oh," I thought to myself. "It's just a matter of seconds before he gets to me."

The love that he transferred to me because of my father was something that I really appreciated and was always in awe of. Now I was just one more face in a sea of "strangers." As soon as Elliott realized what was happening, he quickly crossed over to where I was sitting. "Natalie, why don't you go in the back and take a nap? I don't want you to have to go through this." I ducked out and slept until we landed in Honolulu to refuel. At that point Frank suddenly had a moment of clarity. He was lucid, but he had no idea why he was on the plane. I'm sure he must have been terrified. For that instant, at least, he knew there was something wrong.

As far as I know, Frank made one more singing appearance at a golf tournament in the desert in February of '95, and that was it. I think I must have been one of the last performers to work a paid gig with him. (Although incidents of Frank's erratic and forgetful behavior continued to increase, it was never acknowledged that there was anything wrong with him neurologically, and Frank Sinatra died in May of 1998 after a series of hospitalizations.)

Once we landed back in Los Angeles, I had my own dilemma to deal with. Christmas was only a few days away, and I was far from being in a Christmas mood because my marriage was getting worse. Those merry and bright holidays of my childhood were in stark contrast to the cloud of holiday gloom that now hung over me. I knew all kinds of people who got depressed at Christmas, but I never thought I'd be one of them. The worst of it was that I felt like a hypocrite. Christmas is a celebration of love and family, but December can be a brutal time of year if your love life and your family are falling apart. Whatever Christmas spirit I was generating for other people with *Lily in Winter*, *Holly & Ivy*, and *Natalie Cole's Untraditional Traditional Christmas* was more than offset by the misery I was generating for myself in my relationship with André. I was all elf on the outside and all Grinch on the inside. I was miserable, but I was immobilized. I didn't know what to do about what was happening at home.

There are certain kinds of men who need to pick on people who are weaker than they are. They need to blame someone for the way they are feeling. They need to vent. They must be in control in order to feel important. I don't know who I felt sorrier for: André or myself. When people asked me what I wanted most for Christmas, I didn't dare tell them. The number one item on my Christmas list was a way out of my marriage. The way I looked at it, this wasn't quite the same thing as a divorce. Since I'd prayed and fasted and written the letter to God asking for a husband, I thought that by complaining so much, God would see me as rejecting the gift that He had given me. So considering divorce for real was the furthest thing from my mind.

André and I were not the only sad family news. My brother, Kelly, was getting sicker. He was no longer merely HIV positive; he was beginning to fall prey to all of the opportunistic infections and diseases of full-blown AIDS. Suffering from pneumonia, he'd already been in the emergency room at Cedars under the name "John Casey." Shortly thereafter he called me with a surprising announcement. He had become a Catholic.

Kelly had been brought up in the same proper, socially upstanding Episcopalian faith as the rest of us, but he had never been exactly devout. As he started trying to come to grips with what was happening to him, he began going to classes at St. Victor's, which was the Catholic church down the street from his house. Kelly struck up a friendship with the parish priest, and their discussions helped him put his lifestyle into perspective. He began to face his mortality and the extreme change that was about to take place—not just the transition from life to death, but what he could do to make his life meaningful in the time he had left. I was touched when he asked me, "How do I explain to my friends that I can no longer live the lifestyle I've been living? How do I tell them that I'm a changed man? How do I say that now I see I was not doing what God wanted me to do?"

I never wanted to judge my brother, just as
he had never judged me in my crisis. I just
thanked God for helping him come to a new
self-realization. I really wanted that for him,
because as brilliant as he was, as passionate
as he was, as funny as he was, and as good as
he was, he'd been desperately unhappy. For
a long time his tongue was so sharp it would
make you bleed. Through his pain and suffering,
Kelly found the strength and the faith to walk
bravely toward the end of his life.

Kelly came to stay with me for about ten days
in the spring. He was not entirely bedridden
yet. My mother also came to town. Although
she did not stay with me, she visited Kelly every
day. It's very telling to think that if he had not
been there, she would very probably not have
stepped foot in my home. Nevertheless, we managed to have a fun time. For a moment we were
able to put aside our conflict and grow a little
close to each other.

About three weeks later, I got a call from my
attorney, Jeff Ingber. Along with my siblings,
I had been named as a defendant in a lawsuit.
The plaintiff was Maria Cole, and she was suing
Capitol Records and all her children. As our
brother lay closer and closer to death's door,
our mother was preparing to take us to court.
They say the Lord doesn't give you more
than you can handle, but I was starting to
wonder. Lord, what a family...

CHAPTER 28

My Mother, Maria

I have prayed long and hard over this chapter...and given the dynamics of the relationship between myself and my mother, I find that I'm facing a difficult challenge of portraying a true but loving picture of this woman who gave birth to me, fed me, clothed and raised me—and yes, even loved me.

It's no secret that my mother and I have had a strained, sometimes estranged relationship for at least a decade or more. It has been public knowledge, and private pain. And rarely have we been able to get past the hurts.

I don't believe I know anyone quite as complicated as my mother. And as I sit here, I realize that there are still so many things that I do *not* know about her. It would be very easy to use this as an opportunity to vent all my frustrations, anxieties, and every other resentment that I felt toward this woman since I was born. Could not most of us fill up volumes of pages with wrongs—real or imagined—that we believe were done to us in the past? And isn't it easier to blame than to forgive?

Certainly it is. As I said before: To forgive is not human—it is divine.

Rather than go through a litany of all the stuff old hurts are made of, I choose first to give my the Palmer Memorial Institute, a rigidly run Sedalia, North Carolina, where they attended Brown, who took her and her sister Baba to my Great-Aunt Lala, Charlotte Hawkins she was little. She was also partially raised by sachusetts. My grandmother had died when who was a postman in Cambridge, Mas- her dad—my grandfather Mingo Hawkins— her own life. I know that she very much loved My mother never talked very much about bottle. It's called Youth Dew by Estée Lauder. nostalgic and melancholy, I'll purchase another I left college. Sometimes, when I am feeling became my favorite for years and years up until a waist to die for. She wore a perfume that until my own hair grew long like hers. She is not tall, but not short, either, small-boned with that grazed her shoulders. I couldn't wait back then in the 1950s she wore it in a style is very light-skinned with jet black hair, and she was always impeccably put together. She seen. On occasions when we went out together, one of the most beautiful women I had ever When I was growing up, I thought she was stylish clothes.

work ethic, my manners, and my eye for in me a respect for education, and gave me my giving me my love for reading. She instilled tered my love for music, and I credit her with sion on my life. Along with my father, she fos-

My mother has left an indelible impres- write your own book!)
you who think I'm trying to play it safe, go and mother nothing but praise. (And to those of

prep school for young black women. That says a lot right there.

I didn't know my grandfather very well. By the time I met him, he was very old. I don't remember spending much time with him. It wasn't until about twelve years ago, at my sister Casey's wedding, that she revealed that our grandmother was from the Bahamas. I've kind of had to ask other people about my mother's life. And this is what I've been told:

Before she married my father, my mom was married to Spurgeon Ellington, a fighter pilot who was killed on a routine training flight just after World War II. My father, too, had been married previously. In fact, he had been married to his first wife, Nadine, when he met my mother. And as I've said, my father was the son of a Baptist minister. Small wonder that his parents were not too happy when she arrived on the scene and turned his head around. So initially this did not make for great family relationships.

Although my mother speaks rather fondly of Dad's father, I was told there was some friction in the family when she became his wife. My dad's oldest brother, Eddie, supposedly never stopped seeing her as the woman who broke up the first marriage, which may be the reason her reaction was so reserved when the mortuary showed me his corpse. I could never get her to talk about these kinds of things, and early on I didn't feel that I could confide in her or that she would ever confide in me. You know, the kind of mother-daughter things that are taken for granted; late-night talks about boyfriends or dishing the dirt about so-and-so did such-and-such. She just didn't seem to look at us (my older sister Cookie and me) as being on any kind of equal ground with her.

I got the distinct impression that there was not a lot of nurturing in her family, and this was reflected in how she raised us. Her own nurturing skills were definitely lacking, so she hired nannies and maids that could provide for us what she seemingly could not. And there were some wonderful women who did the best they could in that department, but of course, it's not the same as the real thing.

Each of my siblings has a very different kind of relationship with my mom, but I can't say exactly when mine became so markedly different from that of the others. Maybe it was because I was so hardheaded, and had a bit of a mouth on me. I was stubborn and had a rebellious streak that she constantly had to put in check. I am certain that my mother wanted the best for me—for all of us—it's just the way she went about it that left much to be desired. One had to agree with her on everything, and when it came to having an opinion or having a debate? That was not an option.

Yet there is a part of my memory that recalls Mom as being a fun, high-energy person, lively and laughing. She loved to go to parties, throw parties—she loved having a good time. When my father died, there is no question in my mind that a large part of her died, too.

And she changed. Little by little. I believe that her life began when she met my father, and she was not ready to let it go in any way. For her, this was her identity and for the next thirty years she wore it like a shroud. In fact, even when she remarried, she still would use the name "Mrs. Nat Cole" to her advantage. Even now, she has returned yet again to "Maria Cole." This is her comfort, and this is where she lives.

When my mother and father met, she was singing with the Duke Ellington band and her aspirations to be a singer never died, so she later attempted to revive the career she had given up. It was a brave but brief attempt, and in retrospect I, for one, wish that she had pulled it off, but it was not meant to be. Now, you can imagine that when one of her daughters attempted the same thing—and hits big—well, it's just possible that she might have experienced at best a bittersweet reaction and at worst downright envy. Hence, the encouragement that I received from her came in spurts. As much as it seemed there were times when she really was genuinely proud of me, I rarely felt that she was really happy for me. It is unfortunate, in terms of our relationship, that I'm having the career she never had.

Strangely enough, I would have to say that the women who are role models for me—all of whom are singers—remind me of my mom. Women such as Dorothy Dandridge, Lena Horne, Barbara McNair, and Nancy Wilson. They were her friends, and I was introduced to them as a child. But they all have little personality traits that relate to her, too. I learned a lot from each of them, and when I think of them, I think of her. I don't think I ever told her. I have always wished that she had been more of a role model for me, and maybe, through them, she was.

It would not be fair to exclude the fact that my mother made it possible for me to get treatment for my drug addiction. It was she who found both the first rehab center in California and Hazelden. The fact that the first time was ineffective was not her fault.

When she took over my affairs in the conservatorship, I did not resist. Even in my drug haze, I knew she was doing the right thing—I believe she was trying to protect me and I trusted her. But as I've said, when it came to being a part of my therapy—now that was something she could not do. My mother is a fiercely proud woman, not the kind who readily admits to making mistakes; I suppose for her the idea of sitting in therapy with me meant drudging up not only my faults but hers, too.

But how do I understand why she chose not to pay for my son's care while I was away? This is a hard one for me to overlook. Hard as I try, I could never rationalize it away. Believe me, I wish I could. From her perspective, I had somehow rejected her when the decision was made to leave Robbie with his Nana. And I am certain that she was deeply hurt by my deci-sion to keep my marriage to Marvin a secret from her for six months, and saw that as a public snub in reaction to our private issues. These hurts undoubtedly were as difficult for her as they were for me.

But money was to be the catalyst for the biggest conflict with my mother yet. After I came back home from rehab and began to work again, my brother, Kelly, was visiting at my condo and somehow noticed that I had written a check to my mother. He asked what it was for, and I explained that when I came out of rehab, I was broke with a lot of bills to pay and Mom had been kind enough to loan me $70,000 at a low rate of interest. Kelly blew his stack. I don't recall ever seeing him so angry. "Sweetie, that's *your* money your mother is loaning to you at interest! Don't pay her another cent. Go ask her yourself." Of course, I did. When I called on the telephone and told her what Kelly had said, her response was unruffled, "Well, if that's the way you feel, dear, you don't have to repay me anymore." Shortly thereafter, seemingly out of the blue, she made gifts of $20,000 to each of my sisters.

Kelly was the catalyst who brought to our attention that something in the family finances just wasn't quite right. All five of the children gathered together one day to talk about money issues, and Kelly encouraged us to investigate Dad's will.

This was actually the second time I had tried to see Dad's will. When I first got started in the music business, I was having a talk with my manager, Kevin Hunter, and told him that I had always felt sad that my father had not remembered me in his will. We were all told that Dad didn't leave us anything, that he left everything to my mother, and that after her death, we would basically get everything that was left. The assumption was that a mother would care for her young children. Kevin asked me if I had ever seen the will, and when I told him I had not, he suggested that I should ask to see it. (Remember, he and my mother didn't like each other anyway.)

When I called my mother's business office to ask if there was a copy of the will I could see, I was told by my mother's business manager that to look into this matter would jeopardize my relationship to my mother. Of course, he was working for her. My own attorney at that time tried as well, and although he was quite a bulldog, they managed to stonewall even him. Once I backed off, he had to back off, too.

I don't remember why Kelly said that something wasn't right and we needed to look into this, but in 1984 we were shut down almost immediately. I mean, we just couldn't get anywhere. It was like a brick wall. We hired a lawyer to investigate, and he went digging through files but couldn't get access to the will. For whatever reasons, we couldn't get to the inner workings of my father's estate through public records, and it took nearly a decade before we found out exactly what was happening. We were all over twenty-one, and Mother was still rationing out a few thousand here and a few thousand there to Timolin and Casey. By then I was into my career and I never needed the money. But that wasn't the point. The point was how we kids felt when people asked us, "Did your dad remember you in his will?" We always had to answer, "I guess he didn't." I didn't want to make my dad look bad, and I wasn't angry thinking that he didn't mention us, but I just kind of felt sad about it.

As we got older, my mother was adamant in her statements to all of us that "Your father didn't leave you anything." This issue would come up every couple of years and in the meantime, she was living very well. We had never had to sign a piece of paper for anything at all, ever. And she never involved us in her business or in Dad's business. And why should we have been? We were told we had no inheritance.

Then, one day in June of 1990, we all received telephone calls requesting that Nat King Cole's children attend a meeting in a law office in Century City. Once we arrived at that attorney's office, all of us, Kelly included, the story began to unfold. The office belonged to Sidney Machtinger of Machtinger, Klamen and Fields, tax attorneys. The reason we were asked to attend this meeting was to sign off on papers to authorize tax payments for a trust fund. The money was coming through a branch of the Royal Bank of Scotland in the English Channel Islands. All my father's royalties from a lifetime of recording, more than

25 million records for Capitol, had been flowing through this bank. Machtinger, the attorney, was under the impression that my mother, Maria Cole, was the only beneficiary of the estate. For the first time, however, I was allowed to see my father's last will and testament. He had prepared this document in 1960. There, in no uncertain terms, he had made loving provision for two trusts: one designated for my mother, and one designated for all of his children. It turned out my dad had remembered us after all, and had always wanted us to know that he loved us. I was overcome with emotion as I read that document. It had been such a burden, such a sadness to believe that my father had forgotten us. Now, at last, we had proof that he cared and reached out to us. I was elated, as were my sisters and my brother.

The business side of this meeting was not nearly so happy. Apparently, immediately after Dad died his large group of attorneys and advisors had managed to commingle the two trusts so that all the money flowed into one corporate entity through the trustee, the Royal Bank of Scotland. My mother was the owner of the corporation and held the title of president for many years. And she was the recipient of all the money. You can't commingle trust moneys without the help of an attorney. It's not like she did it on her own. Since the lawyers had been in charge of my father's business affairs, and they had drawn up my father's will, they knew where the loopholes were. One of the lawyers had been named guardian of the children's trust until the children reached their majorities. Another, who was the tax attorney for my parents, continued to represent my mother after my father died.

So the lawyers managed to commingle the trusts. For a long, long time.

Those lawyers avoided indictments or even censure at the time. But we all must come to a more important reckoning in the end, and they will have to answer for this shameful disservice to my father and everything that he worked for. I could care less about the money. I make money, money doesn't make me.

A remarkable irony is that the lawyers might have pulled it off. They might have persuaded us to sign the papers that afternoon and go home ignorant. But my mother had taught her children too well. She was very rigid about certain proprieties and smart business procedures for her children. Mom instilled these ideas in us as we were growing up. She gave me my work ethic. She taught me how to be disciplined, and, beginning when I was fifteen years old, she taught me how to go out and get a job. She taught me how to be domestic, how to clean a house and how to keep a house clean. She also taught by example, because she has always kept a lovely home.

The one piece of advice she drummed into us as we grew older was ironic in light of our current situation. She told us over and over: "If anyone ever puts a piece of paper in front of you to sign, make sure you get an attorney before you sign it. Don't ever sign anything without an attorney." When we got a call to come down to Mom's tax attorney's office to sign a piece of paper, we did what we'd been taught by our mother to do. We brought an attorney with us.

My mother hit the ceiling when she saw our lawyer. To this day she still is furious at Kyle Lapesarde, the wonderful woman who represented us. Kyle did a hell of a good job. I mean, she got to know this family very well and got to the bottom of this case. My mother was upset, and when we reminded her that she was the one who gave us the advice to have a lawyer when you signed anything, she bristled, and said, "I meant that advice for dealing with everybody else, but not with me."

When we walked into that situation, we had no idea what was going on. The whole mess simply unfolded before our eyes. The ones who took it the hardest were my brother and my twin sisters. They were closest to her. They thought she had been generous to them. It was hard enough to have lived all of their lives believing that our father never mentioned us in his will. For them, it was crushing to learn that their own mother had concealed the truth from them.

The financial finagling that had been done with Dad's estate came to light. It had all begun around 1960, when the attorneys convinced Mom and Dad to get into some off-shore tax avoidance schemes with extremely complicated structures. It was an unfocused arrangement that affected the estate plan and the tax situation. In all fairness, there was some logic to establishing international banking relationships, because my father's income was coming from sources all around the world. However, the financial tomfoolery revealed in these papers went far beyond legitimate banking needs. Just one little question could unlock a whole vast array of information that we really, truly didn't want to deal with.

Once this started, I remember sitting at my sister Casey's house for one of the frequent meetings I was having with my brother and sisters at this time. We were all sitting around eating catfish and talking, surrounded by a mass of papers that our attorney had just picked up from Mom's attorneys. Piles, just piles and piles of stuff, you know. Many dealt with complicated, corporate tax shelters—things that weren't really real but seemed real on paper. Basically, ways of hiding money. And we were just dumbfounded.

For a short time, the twins got their own lawyer, Peter Gilhuly of Latham and Watkins, because they started out trying to believe Mom's version of events. She attempted to portray Carole and myself as ungrateful troublemakers. There was some friction among us for a while, but as the story continued to be revealed, they gave up having a separate attorney. Eventually, in 1992, we were all represented by Jay Cooper of Cooper, Epstein and Hurowitz, and Kyle continued as a consultant counsel.

Yet another strange turn in this legal maze with my mother appeared in 1994 when her now divorced ex-husband, Gary Devore, sued Mom and all of her children for payment of a tax bill that had been presented to him by the Internal Revenue Service. Apparently, they had filed joint returns as a married couple, but had forgotten to mail in a check. The IRS, with their customary jolly sense of humor, calculated that the taxes, late fees, interest, and penalties added up to about $2 million. This matter was really a legal dis-agreement between Gary and my mother, but he tried to drag the kids into the problem on the assumption that collectively we might have more access to money than my mother. His assumption may have been right, but his suit was found to be without legal foundation a few years later. It is an interesting legal footnote that he was basically claiming to be the "innocent spouse" to the IRS, although that defense had not yet been recognized in courts. He appealed the decision and lost the appeal, too.

Perhaps it is not too surprising to disclose that in the middle of all this, all five of us children agreed to go into psychological counseling sessions together. That was a trip. The four sisters went. Kelly even went briefly, until he got too ill. The whole lawsuit thing had all of us upset. The therapeutic sessions helped us to deal with why this was happening, how this was happening, how we could prepare ourselves for what would happen next, and how to work on ourselves emotionally. We were trying to separate out the financial issues, the legal issues, and the emotional issues. All kinds of stuff started coming out, because the twins began to understand that our mother had not been entirely honest with them. She had painted a picture of Carole and myself that was very negative. For a moment, Mom convinced them that it was just our attorney, Kyle, who was trying to make her look bad.

Finally in 1995, after five years of investigation and legal wrangling, the trustees of my father's estate announced a settlement, in which the corporation, KCP, Inc., that controlled the assets from the Nat King Cole estate was turned over to the five children. We had just stopped to breathe a collective sigh of relief and were happy to put all this behind us, when my mother sued all five of her children, Capitol Records, and the Royal Bank of Scotland. Somebody's got to explain this to me. I don't understand how you can spend five years working on an agreement and then drag everybody back into court because you don't like the way the agreement came out. One of these days, God's gonna explain it to me, because no one else has been able to.

Essentially, my mother announced that she didn't care what the will said, she didn't care what the trustees said—everything in the Nat King Cole estate belonged to her because she was the wife. Once the trustees had determined that the children should control the corporation that received the income from the estate, she sued, saying that the money did not belong to us. After that it was up to us to show that it did, which we did. In a separate suit against Capitol Records and her children, my mother claimed that Capitol was improperly diverting royalties to the trust controlled by the Royal Bank of Scotland and that she was owed 100 percent of the royalties. In 1998, after three more years of public embarrassment, this matter was settled, and I am legally prohibited from disclosing the terms of that settlement.

My mother's biggest concern since the revelations of the meeting in June of 1990 has been that she's afraid it makes her look bad. Mom has always placed a great value on being well regarded, and she's worried that people might think that she was trying to take something away from us. That's really what's bothering her. That view implies all kinds of things about her, and I don't think such a judgment accurately reflects what happened. I believe that the lawyers and accountants who represented her talked her into a lot of things, and I know that she's not the kind of person who listens closely. She went along with the deal as long as she got what she wanted, which in this case was money—and the lifestyle that went with it. I believe that they talked her into signing a lot of documents by telling her that if she signed them, she'd be okay. She didn't question them, and it turned into a big problem years later. But up until then, while she was living the good life, what reason was there for her to stir up the pot?

The last thing that you would wish on the history of the family of Nat King Cole is an ugly legal brawl like this. I don't think that my mother is able to understand that as the Cole family, we sink or swim in the public eye together. It does her own reputation no good whatsoever to try to make her children appear grabby and ungrateful. It really is an unpleasant, unfortunate situation. My mother did not have to sue. But that's what she chose to do. She's a strong-willed woman who doesn't have to do what lawyers tell her. It would be nice if she could say, "I made a mistake." Or "I'm sorry." Or "Forgive me." I think the real tragedy here is that she doesn't believe that she made a mistake, doesn't seem to be sorry, and therefore does not feel she needs for-giveness—especially from her children.

In one sense, this lawsuit was just the icing on the cake. Our family was pretty fragmented already. But the public spectacle of Mrs. Nat King Cole suing her children was too delicious for the press to ignore. The newspapers and some TV news programs jumped on it with glee. I was the most visible person out there when this mess became public, so it was interpreted quickly as a fight between me and my mother. Everybody else in the family kind of went on their merry way, and I've been the one who's had to deal with it, handle it, squelch it, or what-ever. But the battle over my father's estate has repeatedly reared its ugly head because my mother refused to stick to the settlement. Regardless of how much love I have for her, I have to tell the truth.

Although she clearly had issues with all of her children at this time, the focus was on me. The story for public consumption was that my mother and I were not getting along. I started to have a hard time answering the simple question: "How's your mom?" What am I supposed to say? Sometimes I would call my sister Casey and tell her, "I ran into someone who said to tell Mom hello." That way it doesn't come from me, and I ask her to relay the message and I've done my part. But other than that, I wished people wouldn't ask me, because it was just so hard. What answer could I come up with? Sometimes I kind of gritted my teeth and said she was fine because I didn't want to discuss it.

Today I'm able to look at it more objectively than I could have even five years ago. I don't hold bitterness, but I do want accountability. That's something my brother was able to do, as he was dying in the fall of 1995. He found that being accountable and recognizing the truth as the truth and embracing it really *does* set you free. Oh my goodness. You don't have to be afraid of anything. You don't have to be afraid that it's going to come back and haunt you, because it's truth. I think he was great about confronting himself, his life, and his family— he knew this about this family. We would laugh about it because you can't choose your family. You can choose your friends and you can choose your spouse and you can choose where you want to go on vacation, but you can't choose your family. God just gives you what you're supposed to have.

Nothing would please me more than to say that our problems have been resolved, but they have not. One of the hardest emotional issues for most people to understand is a distance or a coldness between a child and a parent. I have tried to explain this to friends, but unless they have the same kind of issue with their mom or dad, they just can't grasp it. Friends tell me that there must be some way I can resolve this, that I have to try harder. Bless their hearts, they really want to make it happen, but there's only so much one person can do in a relationship with another person.

One of the people who has tried very hard to bridge this gap between my mother and me is my friend and manager, Dan Cleary. When the Rock 'n' Roll Hall of Fame Foundation wanted to induct my father in 2000, they called Dan and asked if I would accept a plaque on behalf of the family. Without even telling me, Dan's immediate response to them was that Nat King Cole's widow was the appropriate person to represent the family in this situation, and when he told me what he said, I agreed completely. My mom apparently was pleased to be asked, said she would come to accept the plaque, and agreed to provide a piece of Nat King Cole memorabilia from her personal collection for the Rock 'n' Roll Museum.

Everything was fine, until the foundation people called Dan back and candidly admitted that because of my visibility in the music business, it would be important to have me at the ceremonies. They asked if I would please come sit in the audience while my mother accepted the plaque. I understood their need to promote the event and agreed to be there, but only in the audience. When my mother was informed that I would be attending, she can-celed, and suddenly she couldn't find a piece of Nat King Cole memorabilia for the museum, either. My twin sisters, Timolin and Casey, and I accepted the plaque on behalf of the family, my father was smiling down on us, and my mother was at home, *tsk-tsh-*ing at the television set. And Dan, who tried to do the right thing? My mother is no longer speaking to him.

What am I supposed to make of that? What am I supposed to understand about how my mother feels about me from the fact that I invited her to share in the celebration of my fiftieth birthday and she declined, even though she'd come to Los Angeles from her home in Florida and was staying in town with my sister that entire week?

This is not a situation that anyone gets any pleasure out of at all, because it shows that this family is still falling apart. It was always dys-functional—like everybody else's family. That we can deal with, but once I ended up singing, it pretty much fell on me to carry the Cole family flag. I was the one who was supposed to keep

Dad's name blameless and spotless. When I didn't do a very good job of that at the beginning, I had my own guilt and humiliation to deal with.

The truth is that my mother has not carried my father's torch, much as she might like to think that she has. She had endowed a room in the cancer wing at UCLA, but that was about when he was dying, not about when he was living, not about his music. For many younger people, his music had been reduced to "The Christmas Song"—or "Those Lazy-Hazy-Crazy Days of Summer." Only when we did *Unforgettable* did people rediscover the rest of his musical legacy.

When that album came out, Ella Fitzgerald came up to me and told me, "Sweetie, I am so proud what you have done for your father, I cannot tell you." It was lovely to hear that from her. I just wish my mother said anything like it, but she didn't.

My whole approach to my mom in the years following the lawsuit is that there are boundaries, even between children and parents. When you get to the age I've gotten to, with a life that has been incredibly full and rich, I can still look on it, smile, and say to myself, "I've been through some tough stuff, but I'm so much better for it. Even the conflicts between my mother and myself have made me a better woman." As painful as it is, as confusing as it still is, remarkably, I look at her now with love, respect, and understanding.

This is a woman who has lost a lot. She's lost

three husbands. She gave up a career to be a wife and mother. And she has alienated her children. My mother is still a woman who is living in the past, basically. That's what a lot of this is about. She has so much to be proud of, and so much stuff to get rid of that is in the way. My whole way of dealing with my mom is with compassion, but at the same time, I will not be disrespected. I will not be made to look bad in front of my friends and family. If I've done something wrong in my life—and I have done plenty—I'm totally account-able. That's been something I've learned to deal with. But I cannot be emotionally pushed and pulled by my mom for the rest of my life. I can no longer be responsible for the way she feels. I have to set some boundaries, and that's what I've done. I have done every-thing, short of prostrating myself buck naked in front of this woman's front door, to end this conflict. We're both at a point where we should let the past go and be at peace with each other.

When I was in treatment at Hazelden, I learned about getting comfortable with the neg-ative stuff in your life, and I learned about get-ting rid of old habits. I learned how you can be your own best friend or your own worst enemy—and it's taken me a long time to become my own best friend. I also learned how to get rid of guilt. In fact, the last thing I got rid of was guilt, and that was a real biggie. You don't realize how much you can be moti-vated by guilt until you live without it hanging over you. I don't feel guilt about my mom. I feel love and compassion.

I really do. There's so much she missed out on. She's never had a close relationship with Robbie. I've always tried to be honest with Robbie—I have told him that there were things that she did with me when I was growing up that I didn't want to do with him. I also told him that she didn't have a lot of love when she was young, and that it affected the way she raised her kids. And even with Timolin and Casey, although she has communication with them, the relationship she has with them is really strange. She did raise them, and they do have that connection with her, unlike Cookie and myself.

The twins never knew our dad. He's a part of their lives that will always be a mystery. I hope that they read about him and listen to his music and get to know more about the man who was their father. He wasn't just an average guy. He was a special, special man. He gave all of us so many reasons to be thankful.

I don't have any illusions anymore about the need to protect my mom. My mother doesn't need protecting; my father needs protecting. It's his memory that I have worked hard to protect and to nurture. It will continue no matter what I do, but I've managed to contribute by singing some of his music, being a part of his living legacy. Who he was and what he accomplished as a person and as a singer is precious to me. Of course, I have a special debt, because everything I have, in the way of musical gift, is from him.

When things started going downhill between my mother and me, I worried that my father's memory would be affected, that somehow our conflict was going to stain everything he worked for. I really don't want that to happen, but I'm afraid people will say, "Oh yeah, Nat King Cole was such a great man. It's so sad that his daughter and his widow can't get along." To me that's downright tragic, all the more so because I can't fix it. We've made attempts at reconciliation on a number of occasions, and whenever she's called, I've been there for her. But then she pulls back again and it's painful. It's emotionally exhausting to have someone reach out to you, and then when you reach back, they pull their hand away. My mother and I will either move forward together, or we'll move forward apart. She has her hurts, and I have mine. And now, looking back on it all, I know I have no choice but to find a way to forgive, to understand, to heal myself, and to try to be an instrument of healing. For life must go on for us both, together or apart.

CHAPTER 29

Heartbreak

In 1995 I was having a terrible time dealing with my marriage. I was in counseling with a Christian therapist that Benita found, Dr. Minnie Claybourne. I had a problem contemplating divorce, because I was still so certain that André was the man that God had sent to me. Whatever the problems were in our marriage, I felt that God had intended me to be with André.

I was also in counseling with my sisters about the relationship with our mother. It seemed like I was spending as much money on psychotherapy as I used to spend on cocaine back in the bad old days. Despite everything, however, André and I just weren't getting along. He decided it was best if we separated, at least temporarily. All of this came on the heels of another physical confrontation—this time, witnessed by my housekeeper. André had ripped my clothes and hurled me against the car in our garage. Afterward, I remember he cried like a baby and said he was sorry.

While André was moving out the first weekend in October, I was opening for the Pope in New York. Pope John Paul II was to celebrate mass on the Great Lawn in Central

Park, and Roberta Flack, Jon Secada, and I, among others, were going to sing starting at seven o'clock in the morning before mass began. I had Robbie come in from L.A. to join me in Manhattan, not to hear me sing, or even to see the Pope. I just didn't want him to have to deal with watching his stepdad move all his stuff out of the house.

Robbie and I came home to empty drawers and closets and gaps in the bookshelves. Though God knows it was overdue, the house felt very strange without André. Almost immediately, I got a call from a casting director named Reuben Cannon, who was a friend of mine. He wanted to know if I'd appear in an episode of *Touched by an Angel.* "I've got a part for you, Nat. It's just perfect," he told me. "You gotta take it. Can you be in Salt Lake City in forty-eight hours?"

"Reuben, I think I'll do it—I really need to get out of the house—but I have to check with somebody first." The role was of a woman dying of AIDS, and before I was going to take it, I wanted to talk with my brother, Kelly. He didn't have much time left, and I thought it was painfully ironic that this opportunity would present itself at such a horribly difficult time.

My character was a woman named Megan Brooks, who had returned to her hometown and met up with her old high school sweetheart when she discovered she was dying. The powerful message of the episode was that her boyfriend, who loved her when they were in their teens, loved her still—her disease didn't change how he felt about her.

I hadn't met Roma Downey before, but Della Reese had known me since I was a kid in Hancock Park. Because the show is so successful, there may be a whole bunch of people who only know her as an actress and don't realize that she's also a great singer—that's Della on the show's theme song. Della has a very strong maternal energy about her, which was just what I needed then. Every morning at five I'd be struggling to wake up and she would come in all happy—her enthusiasm was contagious and it helped get me moving. She's also a strong Christian woman with her own church who has been *Touched by an Angel* for sure.

In addition to Della Reese and Roma Downey, the guest cast included Michael Beach as my boyfriend, and Maya Angelou as my mother's best friend. Maya is such a magnificent lady, and very special. We had a grand time, and she's really very funny.

Maya and I had some nice discussions between takes. We sat around and talked about life. One night she read some of her poetry, and although I had had the privilege of hearing her before, I was transported by the majesty of her voice and the impact of her words. What a brilliant and incredibly intuitive woman she is! She's also very grand, and her whole demeanor is reminiscent of some of the women that I met when I was growing up. They wore their blackness and their womanhood like empresses. They were proud, with marvelously erect postures that com-manded respect.

Doing that episode was a true blessing, and I'm grateful that those two strong and nur-turing ladies were there for me when I needed them. With André newly gone from the house, and Kelly very close to death, it seemed like my life was falling apart again—in fine form. But the episode came out well, and I was proud of my participation in it.

My brother never lived to see it air. On the twenty-fourth of October, in Rochester, New York, I got the call that Kelly had died. I took the first flight home. Kelly had asked me to help him with his will. He bequeathed me a few pieces of jewelry and gave Robbie a number of sets of cuff links of my dad's. He divided the rest of his estate among Mom, Cookie, Casey, Timolin, and Robbie.

Just before the funeral, André called, asking whether he could come to the service at St. Vic-tor's. I was stunned, because my brother could not stand André, and I'm sure the feeling was mutual. André sat with me at the memorial ser-vice, and it was apparent that he was trying to make it look like we were still together. At this point no one knew we'd separated, and I cer-tainly wasn't broadcasting the fact that we'd split up, especially since I was hopeful that it was temporary. When I looked at his hands dur-ing the funeral, I noticed that he was wearing his wedding band—check that: He was wearing what *appeared* to be his wedding band. On closer inspection it was a signet ring that he'd turned around so that it looked like a wedding ring. It disgusted me that he'd do something so incredibly tacky, but it didn't keep me from asking when he was coming home. "I don't know," was all he could tell me.

Things were still up in the air when I left for New York in early November to do a benefit for the Children's Defense Fund. It was an in-costume concert performance of all the classic songs from *The Wizard of Oz* performed at Avery Fisher Hall in Lincoln Center, and taped for TV broadcast later that month. Jackson Browne was the Scarecrow, Roger Daltrey was the Tin Man, Joel Grey was the Wizard, Jewel was Dorothy, and Nathan Lane was the Cowardly Lion. I played Glinda, the Good Witch of the North.

When I got home, there was a call waiting for me from Jeff Ingber, my attorney, saying that André's lawyer had contacted him indicating that André wanted a divorce. In the Marquis of Queensberry rules that seem to apply in such matters, it's considered proper etiquette to allow the wife to file the papers. André's lawyer, however, asked Jeff to hold off for a while, because we were starting to work on my next album, which André was supposed to produce. It must have been pure arrogance that made this man think that I would want to continue to work with him.

I thought that holding off on the proceedings until we were finished with our business dealings together was considerate—until I got a call from Cookie.

"Sweetie," she said, "sit down. I think André's been messing around."

"Excuse me?"

"André has a girlfriend."

"How do *you* know?"

"A friend of mine's been asking me over and over how your marriage is. I finally asked her why she wanted to know, and she told me that another friend of hers has been bragging about how her daughter was going out with your husband."

I certainly didn't give the Other Woman much credit in the IQ department. Seems to me that it would take a pretty dim bulb to tell your mother, "I'm going out with André Fischer, Natalie Cole's husband." Actually, it must run in the family—what kind of mother would boast about that to a friend of hers? I mean, how the hell do you drop that kind of bomb into a friendly conversation?

I felt bad for Cookie—it must have been so hard to break this kind of news to me—and I thanked her for her courage in coming forth with this information. Later, she told me that she had gone to the counselor we had been seeing to ask his advice on the best way to tell me.

Cookie's information may have come through the back door, but it wasn't wrong. About a month before he moved out, André had asked me to loan him some money, ostensibly for business. I later found out that he used it to put a down payment on a house that he moved his lady into. In fact, André knew he was leaving at least three weeks beforehand; I hired a private investigator who discovered that the house was occupied by her by then.

The first thing that betrayal does is knock you to your knees. The humiliation is overwhelming and you feel like a fool. The oldest cliché in any divorce is "the wife is the last to know." It was classic—the woman was André's secretary, who worked in our home for several months. On the twenty-first of November, I filed for divorce, citing the ever-popular "irreconcilable differences."

I made plans to move out of the house in Tarzana. Just being there made my skin crawl, and I was once again fair game for the tabloids.

NATALIE COLE BEGS JUDGE: KEEP MY HUSBAND AWAY FROM ME!

NATALIE COLE'S DIVORCE SECRET—I WAS A BATTERED WOMAN

I don't think you ever get used to having your laundry aired in public. Being a celebrity means that both your triumphs and your failures are out there for all to see—and judge. Even though we celebrities develop a tough skin on the outside, we're mush on the inside. We hurt and we bleed like everybody else. It's painful to have your life spread out in front of people who don't even know you; then they get to decide who you are by what someone else has written.

I remember that the movers were putting the last pieces of my life into boxes and getting it into the moving van when Robbie and I took a final look around. We sat together on the front steps of the house that had been home and was no longer. "Well, Mom," he said. "I guess it's just you and me"—and that was fine with me. For the next week, we lived the life of Riley at the Beverly Hills Hotel.

About a week later I took him with me to Vienna. I was due to tape a PBS television special called *A Celebration of Christmas* with Placido Domingo and José Carreras—Luciano Pavarotti had to cancel, and I was tapped to replace him. Before I left Los Angeles, the production company had sent me a whole packet of music. It was huge, and it was complex, and it read like the instruction pamphlet for a new waffle iron. There were lyrics in English, German, Spanish, and Italian. I couldn't figure out how I was going to learn it all by heart before rehearsals. I pride myself on being professional and being prepared, but there was just so much to cover.

When I walked into the first rehearsal session I was informed, "You get to keep your music." The tradition in opera is that you rehearse with everything in front of you, at least at the beginning. I ended up helping José and Placido with their English pronunciation, and dusted off what was left of my UMass German. They gave me a hand with the Spanish and the Italian. What warm and charming men they are! Benita and I giggled and blushed every day at rehearsals. They had charm coming out of their pores like butter. We would go out for dinner after rehearsal and have a ball. We developed a bit of a mutual admiration society, which was something I didn't expect—there's a big difference between R&B and opera. It was yet one more gift of *Unforgettable* and my father's music. If I hadn't grown musically since "Pink Cadillac," it's very unlikely that I would have been onstage in Vienna with two thirds of the Three Tenors.

After a few days of intensive rehearsal, we taped the show. We worked with the Vienna Symphony and the Vienna Children's Choir, and it was awesome. The time José, Placido, and I had spent together in the off hours contributed a lot to our rapport onstage. I was amazed to be there. "Look at you, this little black girl," I thought to myself, "up here between the two tenors, and you're holding your own. You go, girl!" I was having the time of my life! The second day I fell sick with the flu, and the night of the show, I was radiant and glowing, but that wasn't performance; that was because I had a fever of 104.

Christmas back in Los Angeles would have been far too depressing, so Robbie, a friend of his named Miguel, and I went to spend the holidays in New York and stayed in Brooklyn with friends. I was over the fever, but I was sick at heart. The you-go-girl singer who had held her own in Vienna with two titans of the opera world was nowhere to be found. On Christmas morning I was on my knees, sobbing, wailing, keening, and hysterical. No one had ever seen me like that before, including me. I was mourning the death of my marriage. Worse yet, I blamed myself. Even though I knew what he was, I was still upset that André didn't want me. I started to beat myself up—it's an emotional sleight of hand that women in abusive relationships are adept at pulling off. In the therapy biz it's known as the Stockholm Syndrome—you develop an affection for the person who's keeping you in prison. There must be something terribly wrong with me, I told myself, for him to walk out on me like that. If I had been more thoughtful, more loving, more whatever—he wouldn't have left me.

I remembered all too well that I had prayed for a way out of my marriage. A rational woman would maybe have figured out that the departure of her husband was in one way the answer to that prayer. I'd never come to terms with not wanting to be alone, or with my belief that I was somehow incomplete without a husband, which was why I was so devastated when it was over. It just wasn't supposed to happen this way. I was supposed to be the one to leave. Of course, the pathetic truth is that I couldn't.

There was no way I could lose myself in my work. I might have been all right if I had been performing a show that was nothing but Billie Holiday or Janis Joplin "my-man-done-me-wrong" songs, but my act at the time featured a lot of the *Unforgettable* repertoire. It was very painful to get those love songs out, especially since my soon-to-be-ex had been so much a part of putting that album together. And it wasn't like I could stand onstage and mope. I didn't have that luxury. Songs like "Smile" would kill me when I sang the lines:

Smile though your heart is aching
Smile even though it's breaking...

Many nights I felt like a martyr going out there—"Courage, Camille..." Benita, God bless her, practically had to wind me up and propel me out onto the stage. The audience had no idea what an effort it took for me just to present myself in front of them. It was a strange feeling to look out at all those expectant shining faces. They were waiting for me to give them this wonderful present, a magical romantic evening—and all I was waiting for was the final note so I could get the hell off that stage.

I walked through a lot of those performances. And I believed for the first time that I couldn't care less if I ever sang again—which, hands down, is one of the dumber thoughts I've ever had.

My poor band. Every so often I'd turn

around to get a glass of water, and I'd catch their faces looking at me and feeling sorry for me. They'd try to play their best, just to keep me going. For them it was like secondhand suffering. It was all they could do to keep from looking for what's-his-name and kicking his behind. If they thought they could have gotten away with it, they would have gladly stuffed him in a body bag.

Amidst the misery, I still had decisions to make. The first was what to do with my house, and fortunately I didn't have to split up the furniture or anything. Thank God for prenuptial agreements—which my lawyer had insisted upon. California is a community property state, so André might have been able to install the future Mrs. Fischer (the fifth) in *my* house. I may have been depressed, but I'm not stupid. Honey, I sold that house in three weeks, furniture and all. Didn't think twice about it. My home had been in *Architectural Digest* in September of 1993, but I didn't care. I parted with the eighteenth-century Gustavian commode in a heartbeat. Nineteenth-century Spanish mirror? Gone. I didn't want the four-poster bed with the Scalamandre fabric, either.

Come to think of it, I *especially* didn't want the bed, considering who I suspected had been sleeping in it while I was gone. (And it wasn't Goldilocks, depend on it.) In some ways, it was like being in a fire—what do you choose to save? I took the photos, the heirlooms, and I took what had been my bed from my marriage to Marvin. Once you've had to end a marriage, it's easy to let go of everything else. No matter how nice it is, it's just stuff. And when I closed the door behind me, I never looked back.

Amidst all this personal turmoil, there were problems in the studio as well. André was to have been the executive producer of my next album, and he'd tried like hell to hold on to that role, which was why he'd asked me to defer filing for divorce. Before we separated, we'd already cut a couple of pop tracks, including a beautiful Kate Bush song, "A Man with a Child in His Eyes." Whatever our problems were at home, we'd always worked well in the studio together. In hindsight, I realized I should have just hired him, and never married him. At this point, my self-esteem was so far in the toilet that I'd convinced myself I couldn't make an album without André Fischer. But the album had to be made.

Small wonder that I felt really vulnerable when André took a swing at me—verbally— in *USA Today,* saying that I'd falsified abuse allegations and that I only asked for a restraining order as a publicity stunt. It didn't stop there. He spoke badly of me to his children, Liz and Kyle, who were so precious to me. He badmouthed me all over town. To hear him tell it—and honey, lots of people did—he'd taught me how to walk, talk, dress, sing, and screw. According to him, I was so bad at all those skills it was nothin' less than a miracle that I got as far as I did.

You know those little questionnaire stress tests they have, the ones that measure how much anxiety you're under? Between the emotional and financial issues concerning the divorce, Kelly's death, my mother's lawsuit, the pressures of going back on the road, and the obligation to put out this album, I was off the chart.

After this kind of verbal beating, I had all the self-esteem of a squashed grape. Once more I was carried along by the strength of other people around me who believed in me more than I did. The angels in my life at this point were: my sisters and, for a moment, even my mother, who was ready to put a contract on somebody, and I was grateful. Close friends like Benita, Whitney Houston, Patti LaBelle, the Pointer Sisters, Chaka, David and Linda Foster, to name a few, put me back together when I was falling apart, and people like Phil Ramone and George Duke rode to my rescue in the studio.

David and Phil, along with George Duke, another veteran producer, helped me rethink the concept of the next album. At this point it was more than I could do to go looking for original songs, but I knew that there was still this huge repertoire of classic songs that I could do with my eyes closed. I decided to call the album *Stardust*, and chose songs with the least resistance—the standards.

I didn't want my producing team to feel that I would never return to my R&B roots, but *Star-dust* was something I could do musically, and given the upheaval in my personal life, it was the safer and the wiser choice at the time. The fact that the album turned out to be quite lovely was nothing short of a miracle. David, Phil, and George produced the songs on the album, and I served as executive producer, and got involved on the nitty-gritty level from beginning to end. This time, I was able to immerse myself in my work, and it helped me tremendously. I chose the colors and the artwork for the cover, selected the photographer and set up the shots. It was a lot of work, but the result was—and is—very satisfying.

David made another trip to Glendale to see the gnome in the Capitol vault, and returned with a copy of "When I Fall in Love," so I could do another duet with my dad. There was one song on the album with lyrics I could definitely relate to during this time:

Dust yourself off,
And start all over again.

I still had no idea how hard it was going to be to do that. In September of '96, when the album was released, I did a guest spot on *The Oprah Winfrey Show.* (I'd first met Oprah in 1990, when I was hosting a syndicated talent show called *The Big Break.*) We talked about my divorce, the legal issues of our family, and my history of drug use. She even dug up that ancient footage of stoned-out me, lying about the joys of sobriety to David Hartman on *Good Morning America.* I watched

the Oprah piece when it aired and I was pretty
fragile, but I was better than the basket case
I'd been at Christmastime. Self-esteem that
is lost, like sobriety, doesn't come back all at
once. It comes back piece by piece.

When André and I split up, there was a
tidal wave of people who were anxious to tell
me how happy they were that I was rid of
him. I think people who knew me felt deceived
by the person they thought my ex was, compared to the person he really is. It became of
great concern to a lot of people, but I didn't
really get it until afterward, because people
didn't want to say anything negative. I probably wouldn't have believed them anyway.

Dan confessed that his biggest concern
when my marriage ruptured and I fell apart
was that I'd go back to drugs. But that never
even occurred to me. By then, I'd been sober
long enough that whatever happened to me,
going back on drugs was no longer an option.
A few of my friends and family did speak up—
they had made no bones about how they felt
about André from the very beginning. There
had been Kelly, of course. Whitney, too, had
never liked André from the first time she laid
eyes on him, and never stopped calling him
Tick-Tick-Boom. My cousin Pam Harris was
relentless. Since the days in Chicago in Aunt
Bay's apartment, she's been more like a sister
to me than a cousin; she also has a special relationship with Robbie that goes back to the time
when I was smoking so much crack I couldn't
take care of him. Pam was on me about André

from the start. "I know a rat's ass when I see one," she told me. Once, when things got bad, I'd met her at a deli to talk and she pretty much let me have it. "You've married a man who has no relationship to your child," she said. "I talk to Robbie every day, and you can't tell me a day that he's spent with André that he hasn't come home frightened, uncomfortable, or unhappy. I can't believe you're letting this go on."

Robbie himself was very torn about all of this. As much as he wanted to have a dad, and as well as things started out between them, he could tell that something about this man was not right. It wasn't until after André left, however, that I discovered that Robbie, too, had been the recipient of André's lashing out. He told me that once André had punched him in the stomach and another time he knocked his head against the car window.

I was stunned. I'd seen André yell at Robbie—hell, he yelled at everybody—but obviously I would have gotten out of the relationship much sooner if I'd known my son was being harmed. "Robbie," I asked, "why didn't you say something?"

"Well, there was this one time when André came into my bedroom in the middle of the night and asked, 'Are you afraid of me?' Of course, I told him I wasn't, but after that, I sure was."

Holding on to my marriage as long as I did had been a big mistake. Not only did I suffer, but I had allowed my son to suffer as well. And by not paying attention, I am sure I painted a very confusing picture to him. I did not protect him like I could have. Robbie was virtually ignored because I was too consumed with trying to fix the wrong thing.

In February of 1997, the Grammys were held in Madison Square Garden, in New York City. They say success is the best revenge, and that night "When I Fall in Love" from the *Star-dust* album won a Grammy. Thank you, God. I certainly needed that affirmation that I could do quality work without André Fischer. My divorce papers arrived the next day. Life went on without André. I performed in concerts around the country and abroad. I got a chance to act again, once with Laurence Fishburne in a gritty TV drama entitled *Always Outnumbered*, and a year later in *Freak City*, a Showtime original movie in which I played a car crash victim who is committed to a mental institution with aphasia. In June of 1998, I went to Italy and sang with Pavarotti—the only one of the Three Tenors I'd missed in Vienna. In October of that year, *The Magic of Christmas*, an album of holiday music I recorded with the London Symphony Orchestra, was released. In 1999, I went to work on another album, *Snowfall on the Sahara*, which was produced by Phil Ramone. The songs I chose prove that my musical tastes haven't narrowed down much, if at all. There's a little bit of everything there, from Judy Collins's "Since You Asked," to "His Eyes, Her Eyes" by Michel Legrand and Alan and Marilyn Bergman, to Bob

Dylan's gospel anthem, "Gotta Serve Somebody." When Phil asked him to write some new lyrics for it, just for me, he faxed them to us in just a couple of days, and they were terrific.

Meanwhile, my mother sold the huge estate in Tyringham and moved from Massachusetts to Florida. Robbie graduated from high school and went away to college—studying music, of course, at the Berklee School of Music in Boston. Not that I sat around the house with time on my hands—I developed a new show to celebrate my twenty-fifth anniversary as a musical performer, and hit the road!

I wish I could say that with all these positive changes in my life, my taste in men immediately improved, but I seemed destined to make the same mistake one more time. I was still radiating the vibe of being a giver, so I attracted another taker, another abuser. Guys like these have radar for girls like me. The relationship didn't start off bad, but then, they never do. But it's the same pattern: incredibly charming, incredibly good-looking,...incredibly manipulative, and finally, incredibly toxic. Same old song.

It took some sound advice from an unlikely source—my own son, twenty-plus years my junior—to break the pattern. One day he said, "Mom, why don't you take a break from dating for a while?" What a concept. I got the message: I heard him loud and clear, and it was the best advice my angel could ever give me.

CHAPTER 30

Natalie Cole:
A Work in Progress

I've been given a lot of advice in my day, and I've ignored more of it than I care to admit. But when the advice came from my own child, I thought maybe I needed to listen. For the longest time, I didn't think it was possible to feel good about myself without being in a relationship. I was still a victim of that myth about how a woman needs a man to feel complete. And there are a whole lot of stories just like mine out there.

Okay, so it took me until I was almost fifty to get it. My life is now filled with friends, love, and laughter—but the best friendship I have is with me. When I started going to events by myself, people would ask, "Who are you coming with?" Well, I'm coming with me, myself, and I. And that's just going to have to be enough.

You may think these discoveries are no big thing, but for someone like me, it's a whole new kind of life—a new attitude, if you will. I even look better, because it is a gift that I give to myself—every day. I walked into a party one night, and a woman said to me, "Oooh, you look good. You must have a new man in your life." Think again... I've stopped looking at myself as 50 percent of two and now I'm very content to be 100 percent of one. Now watch: If somehow this philosophy should hit the tabloids, don't be surprised if the headline reads:

WHY NATALIE COLE IS TURNED OFF BY ALL MEN!

You just can't win.

I've spent these last few years trying to strengthen my relationship with God. What a surprise to see how I have gotten closer to who I am and who He wants me to be. I am quite happy seeing myself through God's eyes.

We all come to self-knowledge in different ways and at different times. Sure I wish I could have been smarter when I was younger, and then again, I know women my age and older who still haven't figured this out. Can they be judged or criticized? No more than anybody else. I may be the last person who can give any advice about anything, but I am willing to share the little that I've learned, and it's an ongoing process.

Sometimes it's about choices. You can choose how *you* will use the world around you. But the trick is also how you let the world use *you*.

Where am I now in my life? Well, I know that

I can snap back. But the key is not to let my life and see that I am like a rubber band. flexible than we dare realize. I look back on

Women are so much stronger and more about?

to a guy, so he can feel bigger. What is that many times I tried to make myself smaller next breadwinner. I am ashamed to admit how has put such pressure on the man to be the It is supposed to be getting better, but society feel emasculated in this kind of relationship. it. His ego cannot handle it, and many men drance—even if he benefits financially from or girlfriend's money as a psychological hin-

Compare this to the man who sees his wife's *happy* about it.

friends that make more money, and they are are, however, some men who have wives or girl- other has created problems for them. There making more money than their significant celebrities or not, who complain about how know too many women, whether they are help the man who comes into your life. I woman who is financially independent, heaven and all the mess it can create. If you are a

And don't even get me started about money Lord, I'm not what I used to be. may not be what I ought to be, but thank the doing everything right. Far from it. I still blessing!" This is not to say that now I'm and into God's word...and don't block your is a saying that goes, "Get out of God's way could. But I have to stop fighting him. There God knows best what I need—better than I ever myself get stretched to the breaking point for anyone. Easier said than done, but when I consider the alternative, I definitely don't want to go back there again.

My life is a journey that has covered a lot of ground. If your own life is filled with hills, valleys, and deserts, count it as *joy*. All you have to do is keep on livin' to know that eventually life will kick your behind and knock you down. It's your job to get back up and kick back. Character is born when you're tested, so when you *are* tested, know that Someone is trying to tell you something.

It's tempting to put your tail between your legs and run for the hills. Or you can always hide your head in the sand with your backside sticking out. Or you can change your name to "It-Wasn't-Me-I-Didn't-Do-It-Leave-Me-Alone." The choices are many. You can choose to live a life that is bitter, or better.

When I was in rehab, I learned how easy it is to become comfortable with negativity. Consequently, we spend the rest of our lives—or a good part of them—stuck in pessimism and cynicism, and we give the best "pity parties" that you've ever seen. This is a prescription for disaster. You will either find solace in the medicine cabinet, the neighborhood bar, or some other mood-altering substance. A negative outlook eventually takes its toll on your relationships, your health, and everything else you hold dear.

I know the story well. I was consumed by guilt, which I am convinced is the most nonproductive feeling ever born out of the human psyche.

I had guilt over not being black enough, I had guilt from having too much, I had guilt over being my father's daughter. I wanted to be liked and I felt that being "the-daughter-of Nat King Cole" sometimes worked against me—then, to make matters worse, I felt bad if it worked *for me*. There is also the guilt I felt for the shame, the pain, and the embarrassment that I put my family through when I was in my altered state, and the guilt I had for the kind of mother I was *not*, because I was hell-bent on the road to self-destruction...and the list goes on.

But I had to put an end to it because I want my life to be a *blessing* to others and not a burden anymore.

As I reach this part of my life, I am more than amazed that I have come this far. I am also extremely proud of what I have been able to accomplish in my career. However, once I went through all the hell, I gradually began to realize that this thing called success is rel-ative. As long as I am working on keeping my insides together, my better self will show on the outside sooner or later. Indeed, I am still a work in progress—we all are.

I guess what I am trying to pass on to you, dear reader, is this: Don't give up... God ain't through with you yet.

There's a scripture in the Bible that reads: "To whom much is given, much is required."

If you only focus on what you don't have,

you are missing out on so much. If you're too consumed with what others may have, be careful. You don't know what goes on behind closed doors. They may only seem to have it all together, but they also may be going through hell when nobody is looking. And don't discount someone who seems to not have very much at all; that same person might be the one who saves your life.

Do I have regrets? I think it's a bad question, but I would say yes—and no. I could never have become the woman I am today without each and every experience I've gone through. There were times I put myself in the fire, and there were times that God put me in the fire. Both times, He brought me through it. For every negative, there was a positive. For every dark passage, I was ultimately led to the light. I appreciate the pleasure, because I've had the pain. That's the way it is. There is no victory without the battle.

It is up to us to take the pieces that are left over, and reinvent ourselves. You'd be surprised to discover just how precious and valuable those leftovers can be.

I want to tell you one final little story. Recently, I was staying at the Peninsula Hotel in New York. Across the street was a church and a young homeless man sat there day after day, on the ground near the cornerstone of the building. And every day, he never spoke or asked for money or anything. One day, I couldn't take it anymore. I went over to him, knelt down beside him, and asked him, "May I pray for you?"

He just looked at me and I started to pray. I don't know what I said, and as a matter of fact, I don't remember if I gave him any money. But after I was finished, he whispered to me, "No one has ever done that for me before."

I looked for that young man the next day, and the next, and the next. I never saw him again. Some will say, deeply embedded in their cynicism, that he just found another corner to hang out on. I believe that this time, I was *his* angel, and God went on to do the rest...

That day filled me with so much joy... I want more like those. How could something so small mean so much! My life may sound nothing like yours. My trials, as well as my triumphs, may be far removed from your own. Nevertheless, I would hope that there is maybe one thing, one feeling, one moment that appeared in these pages that has made you think, "Yeah, I know that one," or "Hey, I never thought of that before," or even, "Wow, that's pretty cool." If one of those crossed your mind, writing this book was well worth the effort.

Oh, and another thing. As you walk your own journey, keep your eyes open, listen well, and if you look real hard, you just might find an angel on *your* shoulder, too. I sure hope so.

With love,

NATALIE COLE DISCOGRAPHY

COMPILED AND ANNOTATED BY KEVIN E. TAYLOR

*Indicates a recording on which Natalie sings, but is not the featured artist

"I'm Good Will, Your Christmas Spirit" (1956) (single) Capitol, with Beth Norman

Natalie's first recording at age six is a sweet musical accompaniment to Beth Norman's spoken narration of a Christmas tale. Natalie is backed by the Billy May Orchestra, and Nat appears with Natalie in the jacket photograph for this single, although he is not credited with singing or playing.

"Ain't She Sweet" (1961) (single) Capitol, with Carole Cole and Nat King Cole

This rollicking version of the jazz classic was recorded with Nat at the piano and his two daughters singing at the top of their lungs. You certainly can't miss Natalie, better known in those days as Sweetie, singing that last note: "Sweeeeeeeeeeeeeet."

Inseparable (1975) Capitol (gold), Chuck Jackson and Marvin Yancy, producers

Natalie's impressive debut album features two number one hits, "This Will Be (An Everlasting Love)" and the title track. Also included is the rousing, gospel-tinged "I Can't Say No." Natalie won Grammys for Best R&B Female Vocal Performance for "This Will Be" and Best New Artist—the first African-American to be so honored.

Natalie (1976) Capitol (gold), Chuck Jackson, Marvin Yancy, Gene Barge, Richard Evans, producers

This second album, recorded at Curtom Studios in Chicago, featured "Sophisticated Lady (She's a Different Lady)," which Natalie co-penned, and "Mr. Melody," her first foray into her jazzier roots. This album also features her rendition of the Billie Holiday classic "Good Morning Heartache." The stark and poignant "No Plans for the Future" is also on the album, featuring Natalie at her sinewy best vocally. Natalie won her third Grammy for "Sophisticated Lady" and the song would become her third number one single.

Unpredictable (February 1977) Capitol (platinum), Chuck Jackson, Marvin Yancy, Gene Barge, producers

"I've Got Love on My Mind," Natalie's fourth number one single, is featured on this third album, recorded in Chicago. Her sound becomes richer and more mature on this project, with such chestnuts as "Peaceful Living" and "Still in Love." Additionally, another scorcher was born with "I'm Catching Hell," Natalie's foray into the popular "my-man-is-gone" songs of the day. Listen for Natalie wailing *Somebody turn up my microphone!"* as the song fades.

Thankful (November 1977) Capitol (platinum), Chuck Jackson, Marvin Yancy, Gene Barge, producers

Natalie released her second platinum album later in the same year, which established a record for a female recording artist. This project, her first recorded in Los Angeles, features "Our Love" (her fifth number one single), which remains among Natalie's personal favorites and often still closes her show. Natalie's strength as a writer is heard on such songs as the tale of a young runaway—"Annie Mae"—and "La Costa" (later recorded as an instrumental by jazz great, pianist Ahmad Jamal), which are among the best songs she has ever written. Oddly, although never released as a single, this album's "I Just Can't Stay Away" has been covered by both En Vogue (on their multiplatinum debut in 1990) and Alicia Myers (on an earlier release).

Natalie...Live! (1978) Capitol (gold), Chuck Jackson, Marvin Yancy, Gene Barge, producers

Adding such material as "Lucy in the Sky with Diamonds," the only commercial single from the two-record set, and "Something's Got a Hold on Me" to a lineup of her hits, Natalie is a powerhouse live. Among the highlights are her version of "I Can't Say No," which leads into "Something" and becomes a gospel, church-inspired anthem. Listen to her departure from the stage and the crowd's chant for her return at the end of "Thankful!" and the rousing "Party Lights." The album was recorded at two separate concerts, one at the Universal Amphitheatre in Los Angeles in August 1977, just prior to her maternity leave, and the other at the Latin Casino in Cherry Hill, New Jersey, in March of 1978.

*"'What Love Can Do'" (1978) ABC Records, with Stephen Bishop, on *Bish*.

Natalie joins Art Garfunkel, Michael McDonald, and Chaka Khan to give Stephen Bishop some all-star vocal backup on "What Love Can Do." The two met when he appeared on her April 1978 CBS special and she returned the favor by appearing on this project, which was the follow-up to his highly successful *Careless* debut album.

I Love You So (1979) Capitol (gold), Chuck Jackson, Marvin Yancy, Gene Barge, producers

Such songs as "Oh, Daddy" and "Sorry"—both somber in tone—expand Natalie's range as a singer. "Stand by Me" is the album's hit single, and "Your Lonely Heart" gave Natalie airtime on country music stations. Natalie expresses her love in the liner notes for: Aretha Franklin, Diana Ross, Donna Summer, Smokey and Claudette Robinson, Dionne Warwick, Ben Vereen, and Thelma Houston, whose "Don't Leave Me This Way" won the Grammy over "I've Got Love on My Mind." This album was nominated for a Grammy, Natalie's sixth nod.

We're the Best of Friends (1979) Capitol, with Peabo Bryson, Marvin Yancy, Peabo Bryson, Mark Davis, Johnny Pate, producers

Having toured together and being label mates, it was inevitable that Natalie and soul balladeer Peabo Bryson would record a duet album. "Gimme Some Time" would be a Top 20 smash and on "What You Won't Do for Love," the Bobby Caldwell tune, they would weave their rich voices together beautifully. Natalie's self-penned "Your Lonely Heart" was re-recorded for this album and she displays even more musical diversity as she yodels on this track! These are especially fine performances

by both singers on "Love Will Find You"
and "Let's Fall in Love/You Send Me," a
clever duet out of two separate songs.

*"Thank You" (1979) (single) AMI, recorded
with the Fountain of Life Choir, Kevin Yancy,
producer

The Reverend Marvin Yancy served as senior
pastor at the Fountain of Life and was in the
studio recording the choir for his church. As
the story goes, Mrs. Yancy, as Natalie was at
the time, stopped by the studio to hear her husband at work. They were doing the vocals
with the choir for "Thank You" and Natalie
thought that something was missing. She
stepped into the vocal booth and laid down
her soulful riffs and ad libs and the rest is gospel
music history. The song was nominated for a
Grammy and can be found on the 1995 release
The Best of Rev. Marvin Yancy.

Don't Look Back (1980) Capitol, Marvin
Yancy, Gene Barge, Michael Masser ("Someone
That I Used to Love"), producers

The first single, "Someone That I Used to
Love," was featured on a special edition of the
popular *Merv Griffin Show*, as Natalie's sound
became more adult contemporary. The album
features "Stairway to the Stars," which is
dedicated to Maria Cole, and ""Beautiful"

Dreamer," a Natalie-penned track on which she plays piano. It is apparent that Natalie is trying to broaden her sound, with such tracks as "Cole-Blooded," which has a rock edge to it, while holding on to her R&B base with the soulful "Don't Look Back" and the exquisite "Hold On."

Happy Love (1981) Capitol, George Tobin and Mike Piccirillo, arrangers and producers

In an attempt to solidify the broadening of the Natalie Cole sound, a new producer, George Tobin, was brought in to work with Natalie. The result is this middle-of-the-road set of such tunes as "Nothing but a Fool," which is Natalie at her storytelling best, and "These Eyes," a remake of the classic Guess Who song. Additionally, Natalie continues to feel more comfortable with unveiling her own compositions, such as "The Joke Is on You," "Love and Kisses," and "Across the Nation."

I'm Ready (1983) Epic, Chuck Jackson, Marvin Yancy, Stanley Clarke, Chuck Bynum, producers

The project was originally titled *Movin' On,* which would have been a more accurate indication of where Natalie's head and heart were at during this time. "Too Much Mister" was the sole single and would generate some radio

duction duties.

would include Stanley Clarke on extensive pro-
format would unearth five additional songs that
career. Later release of the project on CD
play, but not enough to revitalize her stalling

***Unforgettable: A Musical Tribute to Nat
King Cole*** (Recorded live May 1983, released
September 1983) Columbia, with Johnny
Mathis, no producers listed

Natalie joins personal friend and paternal
peer Johnny Mathis on this homage to her legendary dad. With Natalie featured as Johnny's
special guest, she does a medley of her father's
songs and later joins Johnny for a pair of
duets. The pair would later take their live
version of the show to PBS and in the audience would be Maria Cole, Natalie's mom, and
the gathering of all four of Natalie's siblings,
which had not happened in some time. Natalie
would be lauded for her eloquent vocal styling
of her father's material on such jewels as
"Straighten Up and Fly Right," "Love (L-O-
V-E)," and "Ballerina."

Dangerous (1985) Modern, Gary P. Skardina
and Marti Sharon, Harold Beatty, Eddie and
Natalie Cole, producers

Natalie's return after her bout with drugs and
divorce was met with a mild response. The title

track (and first single) sounded too much like the Pointer Sisters' recent hit "Jump," written at about the same time, and had to contend with Aretha's huge hit "Freeway of Love." The album did feature some stellar songs, including "A Little Bit of Heaven," which would be the only other single, with its reggae-flavored soul. Also included was "The Gift," a song so personal in the telling of the Natalie Cole story that it would be the only song ever to follow "Our Love" at the close of her live show.

Everlasting (1987) EMI/Manhattan (gold), Burt Bacharach and Carole Bayer Sager, Reggie and Vincent Calloway, Jerry Knight and Aaron Zigman, Dennis Lambert, Marcus Miller, producers

Natalie returned to her successful days of the 1970s, and back to the top of the charts. Producers Reggie and Vincent Calloway, who had guided Midnight Star to success, have Natalie "Jumpstart (My Heart)," a rousing funky dance ditty that would broaden her audience. "Split Decision" and "In My Reality" were written and produced by Burt Bacharach and Carol Bayor Sager especially for Natalie. And "I Live for Your Love," written by Pam Reswick, Steve Werfel, and Allan Rich, would solidify that she was back. Cool and soulful in her performance, Natalie would later win *Soul Train* and NAACP awards for her much applauded return. The big success of this album, however, is Bruce Springsteen's "Pink Cadillac." In Natalie's voice, the song comes alive in a new way, and when remixed by David Cole and Robert Clivilles, the pop hit would become a number five dance anthem. Another highlight from the project is "More Than the Stars," the singer's pairing with Latin great José Feliciano.

*"Over You" (1987) Geffen/MCA, a duet with Ray Parker Jr. on *After Dark*, Burt Bacharach and Carole Bayer Sager, producers

Though not much of a fan of duets—"sometimes the voices just don't sound genuine together; it has to be right."—Natalie rounded out 1987 by recording "Over You" with Ray Parker Jr. This Burt Bacharach-Carole Bayer Sager song, which marked Ray's Arista Records debut after a great deal of R&B success, would become a Top 10 smash.

* "The Christmas Song" (1988) A&M, on *Scrooged* soundtrack, Jimmy Iovine, producer

Natalie records "The Christmas Song" for the first time. She would do her version for Bill Murray as Scrooge in this holiday film. Featured in the closing credits and receiving a great deal of radio play, it was quite apparent that the world was hungry to hear Natalie Cole's voice wrapped around her father's material.

Good to Be Back (1989) EMI/Manhattan (platinum), Ric Wake, Lee Curreri, Dennis Lambert, André Fischer, Michael Masser, Eddie Cole, producers

"Miss You Like Crazy," produced by hit meister Michael Masser, launched this album and would become Natalie's first number one single in a decade (her sixth). The song would be followed by "I Do," a duet with Freddie Jackson that would go to number five and set up *Good to Be Back* for platinum success. The album took a turn for the middle of the road and "As a Matter of Fact" was released in an attempt to capitalize on Natalie's pop success. Such songs as "Don't Mention My Heartache," "I Can't Cry," and the jazz classic "Someone's Rocking My Dreamboat" were overlooked on this album, while "Rest of the Night" and "Starting Over Again" would be released as singles, to marginal success.

"Caretaker" (1989) Gospel Capital Records, from *The Yancy Family Album...From One Christian Family to Another*, Kevin Yancy and Michael Wade, producers

Natalie pays tribute to her late husband, the Reverend Marvin Yancy, by joining his family for this recording. While long divorced, the two had shared a great bond and strong family connection. "Caretaker" spotlights Natalie at her best, rousing and spontaneous, controlled and passionate. Featured as the lead vocalist this time (as opposed to her supporting vocals on Yancy's "Thank You") Natalie is crystal clear in her delivery, and the lyrics "He's taking good care of me" seem to resonate and you can almost hear her smiling and waving her hands while she's singing.

*"Wild Women Do" (1990) EMI, on *Pretty Woman* soundtrack, André Fischer, producer

This hard-edge rock-tinged single would feature the sexy singer in a different light. Sporting a Cleopatra-like bob in the music video, Natalie rocked out! Her vocal perfor-mance is fiery and soulful at the same time, and she would perform the song before Nelson and Winnie Mandela in London upon his release from prison.

*"Heaven's Hands" (1990) Columbia, on *Nancy Wilson: The Lady with a Song*

Natalie joined a remarkable lineup of R&B/soul/pop talent—including Chaka Khan, Howard Hewett, and Teena Marie—that would assemble to provide choral background vocals to jazz/R&B great Nancy Wilson's *The Lady with a Song* album, on the song "Heaven's Hands." The song would be a return to

Nancy's more R&B style material and continues to be a live chestnut.

★"Grown-Up Christmas List" (1990) Atlantic, on *River of Love*, David Foster, producer

Natalie is the featured vocalist on the only track that got heavy radio play from Foster's jewel. Natalie and David Foster had a long-standing relationship throughout the 1990s and it was born with this recording, which was later included on *A Foster Christmas Album* (1993). Natalie's delivery is innocent yet powerful, subtle and sincere. The song is the story of an adult who makes a wish for a better world to an unexpected source: Santa Claus.

★"Long 'Round Midnight" (1991) GRP, *Am I Cool...Or What?* (*Garfield* soundtrack), André Fischer, producer

Natalie recorded "Long 'Round Midnight," a sexy jazz tune, for the popular cartoon's soundtrack. Her vocal styling on the track is Ms. Cole in her finest voice, seductive and sophisticated, while measured and oh so cool.

Unforgettable...With Love (1991) Elektra (multiplatinum), Tommy LiPuma, David Foster, André Fischer, producers

With the production savvy of Tommy LiPuma, David Foster, and then-husband André Fischer, Natalie recorded the project of her lifetime. This collection of twenty-two masterpiece Nat King Cole songs would prove phenomenal. The first single—"Unforgettable,"—was released on Father's Day 1991 and music lovers flocked to it instantly. The project would debut at number twenty-five on the *Billboard* charts and leap from number eleven to number two to number one in a matter of a few weeks. Eventually, sales grew to more than 14 million units and would win the project—eloquent, exquisite, and brilliant in its musicality and sentiment—seven Grammy Awards of its nine nominations. In one case, Natalie was nominated against herself—including Song, Record, and Album of the Year. This album was re-released in 1992 for the holiday season with a special edition of "The Christmas Song."

Take a Look (1993) Elektra (gold), Tommy LiPuma and André Fischer, producers

"Take a Look," the first single from the album, was discovered on an early Aretha Franklin album of the same title. Natalie composed additional lyrics for the ending of this powerful song. Such jewels as "It's Sand Man," "Fiesta in Blue," and a new rendition of her own "Lovers," from her *Thankful* (1977) album, spotlighted her voice at its most dazzling. The project won Natalie a Grammy for Best Jazz Vocal Performance.

*"They Can't Take That Away from Me" (1993) Capitol, on *Duets*, Frank Sinatra, André Fischer, song producers

Natalie joined a lineup of musical greats who paired with the Chairman of the Board for a variety of duets. "They Can't Take That Away from Me," with Natalie sounding almost giddy in her delivery, was recorded separately, but her practice with her dad's recordings clearly prepared Natalie for the task.

Nursery Raps With Mama Goose (1993) MCA/Golden Books, Casey Cole, producer

Natalie provides special narration and an introduction to this updated version of the Mother Goose Rhymes. Her sister Casey produced the Golden Book video with "Humpty Dumpty," "Jack and Jill," "Peter Piper," and many other rap music renditions of these classic children's poems.

*"Since I Fell for You" (1994) MCA, with Reba McEntire, on *Rhythm, Country and Blues*, Tony Brown, producer

The pairing of soul and country stars for

songs from both genres might seem foolish to the musically uneducated, but anyone with an ear for music would realize the infinite pos-sibilities of such a coupling. Natalie was paired with country great Reba McEntire for the classic "Since I Fell for You," which they had to record separately because of their hectic schedules. The singers would meet and perform the song during a one-night-only gathering of all of the talents—including Gladys Knight, Patti LaBelle, Travis Tritt, and Conway Twitty—live onstage!

*"Did You See Jackie Robinson Hit That Ball?" (1994) Elektra, on *Baseball: The American Epic* soundtrack, Tommy LiPuma, pro-ducer

The Ken Burns-produced documentary for PBS would have a strong soundtrack, with Natalie handling the only released single. "Did You See Jackie Robinson Hit That Ball?" was Natalie's contribution to history, with this pow-erful but skillful song about pioneering the sport with dignity and grace.

Holly & Ivy (1994) Elektra, David Foster, André Fischer, Tommy LiPuma, producers

Featuring everything from a sexy, jazz-filled version of "Jingle Bells" to a blues opus, "Merry Christmas, Baby," which she performs like a true veteran, to a rousing gospel stomp on "Joy to the World" with the Restoration Choir, Natalie displays all sides of her musical talents on this holiday gem. Other highlights include "Silent Night" and the classic title track. The project would also be released as a PBS special, *Natalie Cole's Untraditional Traditional Christmas.* "Jingle Bells" would also be featured on the *Miracle on 34th Street* soundtrack.

★"Both Sides Now" (1996) Kid Rhino Records, on *For Our Children, Too*, David Foster, song producer

This recording benefits the Pediatric AIDS Foundation, and Natalie offers "Both Sides Now" for the Children's AIDS Project, with a lilting rendition of the Joni Mitchell classic.

★*The Wizard of Oz...In Concert* (1996, live) Rhino, no producers listed

Her one-night-only performance in the role of Glinda the Good Witch demonstrates Natalie's diversity. She takes the stage in the live offering of the original *Oz*, which was performed as a benefit for the Children's Defense Fund, with all of the music restored for this production. Natalie's "Out of the Woods" is so stirring and so soulful that Jackson Browne, onstage as the Scarecrow, cites it as the "finest moment of the night."

*Cats Don't Dance (1996) Polygram, sound-track

Natalie offers the singing voice (actress Jasmine Guy, the speaking voice) for Sawyer, a feline chanteuse, for this animated romp around the barn. She had worked on the project for a short while with her vocals, although the animation process would take a few years to complete. She swings on "Tell Me Lies," offering a jazzy, soulful ballad style and finesse, while jumping with co-stars Scott Bakula and Kathy Nijimy on "Nothing's Gonna Stop Us Now."

*"America" (1996) RCA, with Patti LaBelle and Sheila E., on The Songs of West Side Story, David Pack, producer

Imagine, if you will, a one-time-only live offering of the songs of West Side Story. Imagine further still Elton John performing "I Feel Pretty" and Kenny Loggins and Wynonna taking the stage to do ""Tonight." Already a near musical fantasy, imagine soul songstresses Natalie Cole and Patti LaBelle, seductively commanding the stage on either side, with drumming great Sheila E. dead center, roaring through their version of

"America." That moment is captured forever on this project, a night of performances to benefit the AIDS Project Los Angeles on the night of their "Commitment to Life" award ceremonies, where David Geffen was honored for his philanthropic efforts for AIDS.

A Celebration of Christmas (1996) Erato in Europe/Elektra Entertainment for U.S. release, with Placido Domingo and José Carreras, Lalo Schfrin, arranger/adapter (available on video)

Natalie joins opera legends Domingo and Carreras, two thirds of the Three Tenors, for a holiday gathering in Austria that was recorded for a PBS special. She sings in three different languages, and lends her sweet soprano to a number of pairings. Her duet with Placido of "Amazing Grace" is so magnificent and chilling that, coupled with the full orchestra and his rich tenor, you are sure to be in tears.

★"A Smile Like Yours" (1996) Elektra, on *A Smile Like Yours* soundtrack, Walter Afanasieff, producer

Natalie's return to her R&B/pop ballad roots is clearly foreshadowed on this sweet and melodic offering to the Greg Kinnear/Lauren Holly film. Natalie's song would be the only new composition for the soundtrack of classic pop and R&B classics.

***Stardust** (1997) Elektra, David Foster, Phil Ramone, George Duke, producers

Natalie continued along the path that had proven so successful for her in the 1990s. With this project, she offers more classic and newly unearthed material from America's finest days of song. She also opts to join her father on another duet, as a final tribute to the 1990s. Natalie and Nat perform "When I Fall in Love," which Natalie had sung previously on *Ever-lasting* (1987) with a more soulful arrange-ment. Here, true to the original in its tone, Natalie and Nat won yet another Grammy for their vocal union. Celine Dion would later pair with Frank Sinatra and Lauryn Hill with Bob Marley to perform classic "departed duets."

*"Tonight" with Luciano Pavarotti and "Let's Face the Music" (1998, live) Poly Records, on *For the Children of Liberia*, no producer listed

Natalie has her opportunity to perform with the one tenor missing from her 1996 *A Cele-bration of Christmas* project, the opera great Luciano Pavarotti. The two perform a stirring rendition of "Tonight" from *West Side Story* and, later, Natalie, adorned in a red dress so fitting and a smile so glowing that she looks like a woman half her age, tears the house down on "Let's Face the Music."

Christmas With You (1998) Hallmark, Fred Salem, producer

This "special event" Christmas album, created exclusively for Hallmark and marketed only through Hallmark stores, sold an astonishing two million copies. Elektra was duly impressed and re-released this album to the consumer market the following year under the name *The Magic of Christmas*.

Snowfall on the Sahara (1999) Elektra, David Foster, Phil Ramone, Natalie Cole, Peter Wolf, producers

This album is Natalie's attempt to meld all of the musical parts of her twenty-five-year career, including R&B, jazz, soul, and pop material. Natalie co-penned the title track (with Peter Wolf, with whom she also co-produced the song) several years prior to recording it. She would offer such R&B classics as "Say You Love Me" and "Reverend Lee," while tearing the roof off with the Bette Midler as *The Rose* torch song "Stay with Me." Natalie would receive the Lena Horne Career Achievement Award from *Soul Train* this same year.

The Magic of Christmas (1999) Elektra, Fred Salem, producer

This glorious album recorded at Abbey Road Studios in London with the London Symphony Orchestra allowed Natalie to close out the millennium in elegant style. The project would be a collaborative effort with Hall-mark, and the CD would include her versions of "Mary, Did You Know?," which she had performed live with Wynonna, and "Sweet Little Jesus Boy," featuring a poignantly sweet and poetic performance.

Greatest Hits, Volume One (2000) Elektra

A retrospective of her career, created to complement her autobiography, this album mixes many of her classic performances such as "Unforgettable" and "Miss You Like Crazy" with new material. Two new songs are included: "Angel on My Shoulder" (cowritten with Richard Marx) and "Livin' for Love" (cowritten with Garriano Lorenzo)."